THE AD▽PTERS

THE ADAPTERS

How the Travel, Tourism and Hospitality industry
is adapting and innovating to connect the world!

SEÁN WORKER
AND GLENN HAUSSMAN

gatekeeper press™

Columbus, Ohio

The Adapters: How the Travel, Tourism and Hospitality industry is adapting and innovating to connect the world!

Published by Gatekeeper Press
2167 Stringtown Rd, Suite 109
Columbus, OH 43123-2989
www.GatekeeperPress.com

Library of Congress Control Number: 2020948099

ISBN (paperback): 9781662905407
eISBN: 9781662905414

Visit www.theadapters.net to learn more about our services
Contact: sean@t5strategies with comments or requests
Comment online: http://www.t5strategies.com/
Comment on YouTube at - https://www.youtube.com/channel/UC3Scg66hFpXOOCD_Z48DuEg

The Adapters is a business book for curious founders, entrepreneurs, academics, and the entire Travel, Tourism & Hospitality industry. Learn from 22+ business leaders how to think about running a business, Investment Banking, Data Analytics, and People Management for the New Reality, as they are adapting and innovating during the COVID storm. The Authors' case study and storytelling style will grab your attention and give you dozens of ideas to help your business thrive. Click to watch and listen to all the interviews, and follow the QR codes and links to up-to-the-minute reference materials and resources.

Click or Scan here with your phone to access content and interviews.

Acknowledgments

This is a series that is about and for all the hardworking and smart people in Travel, Hospitality, Tourism, airlines, cruises, restaurants, bars, associations, and professional bodies, as well as food truckers, educators, and all the suppliers that make it possible for us all to travel for business and fun.

Big thanks to our publisher, Gatekeeper Press President Rob Price, editors Jason Perry, Margarita Martinez, and editor and contributor Andrea Worker, and all the leaders who shared their Gutsy Genius Thinking with us.

This book is for you.

Thanks for picking it up off the shelf or downloading the sample from your digital content provider. *The Adapters* is a business book with a heart and a few smiles. Produced as a series, it's about and for all the hardworking and smart people in the Travel, Tourism and Hospitality (TT&H) universe: hotels, alternative accommodations, tour operators, airlines, cruises, restaurants, bars, associations, and professional bodies, as well as food truckers, educators, and all the suppliers that make it possible for us all to travel for business and fun. It's also for anyone in the services business that wants a *LOOK OVER THE FENCE* at how other industries think about their problems and how they adapt or innovate to solve them.

If you think this doesn't apply to you and you're considering moving on, wait just a minute!

As you'll discover in these pages, TT&H is a pretty large piece of the full economic puzzle, and what we talk about here is important to understanding the interconnected world of all business. Our **Formula for Success** can be applied to any industry and to any position or level of authority, to any moment on a reader's progression along his or her career ladder, from still looking for that ladder, to nearing the top.

What's in it for you?

The Adapters has blended traditional writing with today's technology to allow you more access to where our information, interpretations, and extrapolations come from. Because we link the written word to digital meetings with industry leaders and to an extensive "library" of resource materials and insights from still other thought leaders— both in and outside the TT&H domain—you are getting a package of data and knowledge in *one easily accessible container.*

What else?

Unlike a lot of prosy business books, we don't just tell you stuff! Nor do we leave our readers hanging, wondering what's next, how do you use what you've just read? Along with their actual words and video conversations with what we call our Gusty Genius Thinkers (GGTs), so *you* can see and hear how they put these ideas and principles into practice, we offer you *Scribble Zones* to capture thoughts and promote your own notions. We also include a healthy portion of Tips and Takes, Traps to Avoid, and ways to help determine if you're on the right path to where you want to go.

And one more thing.

The content of *The Adapters* is applicable, no matter where we are in the scheme of world events, but, of course, we can't ignore today's headlines. We will put our work here in the context of today's unprecedented events, and offer thoughts on how to move forward—and we'll even give you the opportunity to see how our GGTs' initial responses to the COVID crisis turned out, as they provide frank and straightforward updates to the interviews they conducted with our team.

So, what do you think? Are you in?

Dedicated to all the fun, positive, and hardworking people in the Travel, Tourism, and Hospitality industry that keep a smile going to help others enjoy life!

Contents

Preface xv

Introduction – Hi There! xxv

The Path We Will be Taking xxxii

Chapter 1   Today's World – Adaptation and Innovation and the COVID Effect 1

Adaption will occur 2

Three meters at a time 4

Chapter 2   The 4th Age of Change 9

Fired up cooking and storytelling 11

Opportunity is always in the room 15

Chapter 3   Perspective – Yesterday and Today 27

The boom time – an open door to the other side 27

The "hole in the candy" 32

Today isn't looking too good 33

Timing is everything 36

Drinking from the firehose 39

The cat food conundrum 42

The domino effect 43

Cities under siege 54

Chapter 4   Looking Toward Tomorrow 65

Accentuate the positive 65

Coach the Team 66

Growth is possible 73

Hint, hint. It's Mint, Mint. 75

Let's get together   80
Could suburban hotels become hot again—
Those urburbs?   80
Hey! Wait a minute. What happened to the cities
under siege?   81
Regeneration is a "Thing"   82
Defining regeneration   82
The COVID mountain and the three-meter method 90

Chapter 5   Adaption & Innovation Cycle   99
PART 1: Firefighting and Blazing a Trail   99
The New Reality   100
Adapt to stay relevant   102
Take a peek over the fence   103
Adapting is easier than you think – Look for
opportunities   105
What holds so many travel and hospitality
enterprises back when it comes to adapting?   108
Become a Transformist   112
Avoiding adaption and innovation distractions
and traps...   114
Tomorrow's Reality   118
Watch out for traps!   122
Adaption and innovation do not always occur at
the Corporate Office!   127
T.I.M.E: The fuel that drives Adaption and
Innovation   127
Don't bet the house   129

**Chapter 6   Adaption & Innovation Cycle – The
               Adapters' Formula   143**
PART 2: Emotional Intelligence   143

Three dominant themes became apparent from chatting with The Adapters   143

Back to the A-B-Cs of our GGTs.   147

So why is Emotional Intelligence awareness growing so rapidly?   151

Managers, listen up!   152

Managers, what EI key learning is revealing itself?   154

EQ skills translate to employee-business connection   157

How not to write a business memoir   159

Chapter 7   Adaption & Innovation Cycle   171

PART 3: Business Intelligence   171

Business Process and Business Intelligence: the 35,000-feet cruising altitude view   172

What is Business Process?   172

BP's Architectural Plan   173

4 Traits of a Business Process   174

What is Business Intelligence?   179

The P O'C filter   181

An industry head-scratcher   182

BP and BI in action   185

Looking beyond travel for inspiration: Business Process and Business Intelligence   189

Go on walkabout!   192

Understanding your employees and customers – it's the intelligent thing to do   195

Chapter 8   Adaption & Innovation Cycle   201

PART 4: Community Engagement   201

Here Comes the Omni RV   203

Community involvement and your employees   206

The Core Business Equation   208

Chapter 9   The Wrap   **215**

Macro Short-Term Outlook Q4 2020 – Q4 2021   220
Macro Medium-Term Outlook Q3/Q4
2021 – Q1 2023   222
What might lie ahead   224

Chapter 10   GGT UPDATES – December 2020   **235**

**Chapter 11   Work Zone – Tips, Takes, and
                Stuff to Do**   **287**

Now *You* Take the Wheel!   287
Learn more by key topic? Listen to the GGTs.   287
The Adapters' Tips & Takes – Topics for Meetings
and Discussions   290
The Adapters' Tips on Alignment of Concept to
User Experience   294
3.0 The Adapters' Tips on Alignment of Processes
and People   295
4.0 Adaption and Innovation – How Well are You
doing?   296
5.0 Emotional Intelligence – 10 Qualities People
with High EQ Share   302
6.0 Business Intelligence – 10 Common Uses of
Business Intelligence   304
7.0 Work from Home (WFH) Trend Data   307

References, Reads, and Notations   **311**

End Notes   **315**

*Teasers and Trailers – What's Next?

**Next Adapters edition, and spin-offs –
Regenerative Tourism**

Preface

2020 is a year that most people want to forget, but like the Great Fire of London in 1666, the stock market crash of 1929, or the events that sparked any global conflict, catastrophes actually need to be remembered and lessons learned—and adaptions and innovations triggered. That's exactly why two guys, inhabitants of the Travel, Tourism and Hospitality (TT&H) world, decided to push forward with a project that they'd been kicking around pre-coronavirus (can anyone remember that far back?).

Sean Worker and Glenn Hausmann operate their own individual enterprises. Glenn is an accomplished and well-known journalist, editor, podcaster, and speaker. His online show, *No Vacancy,* was already a thought-provoking and informative voice for the space even before C-19 hit town. Now, Glenn's broadcasts are even more relevant as he provides a forum to hear directly from the most influential members of TT&H and relay their responses to the crisis we are all trying to navigate.

Sean is also a contributor and commentator in the space, including spots on Bloomberg, speaking engagements on industry-related panels, authoring articles and lecturing. He scaled his career through hospitality and travel tech over the last twenty-five years, from restaurants, nightclubs, and hotels to alternative accommodations, holding senior management roles in operations, sales, development, brand development, and travel tech. As CEO of BridgeStreet, he and his team pivoted the company to an innovative, global agency platform model to connect Business-to-Business clients (BtoB)[1] and scaled from about four thousand apartments to over seventeen million accommodation choices across six categories. Most recently, he became the founder of T5 Strategies, a business transformation advisory firm. He is working with both established companies and start-ups,[1] in particular helping them weather the COVID storm so they can emerge in the best conditions possible, ready to get back up to speed and then accelerate forward.

These two individual trailblazers decided to explore the same path for a while. Together they went on a hunt to seek out the **Adapters and Innovators** in the TT&H universe and to dig into what makes them tick, to find out how they have succeeded, and most importantly, how they create and employ adaption in their organizations and in their own lives.

The idea was to become story collectors and *business anthropologists*, capturing *real* unplugged conversations with these **Gutsy Genius Thinkers** (GGTs) who are forging a New Reality in the space. By recording and sharing their stories and insights, their experiences, their failures, and their successes in their own words, we can chronicle them for the benefit of us all—and draw a few conclusions of our own.

So, Sean and Glenn went to work, starting with conversational interviews with twenty leaders from hotels (franchisors, franchisees, and management companies from economy to luxury), alternative accommodations, channel managers, academics and educators, founders and entrepreneurs, conference developers and hosts, executive search firms specializing in the field, financial advisors and investment bankers, data specialists, hospitality TV hosts, association leaders, and experiential tour operators. Phew! That's a lot of exploring!

Why such a diverse collection? Because Sean and Glenn see all of these "pieces" of TT&H as part of what completes the whole industry puzzle. Both agree that it's time to look at these elements holistically. They are not stand-alone entities. Instead, they all rely on each other. In today's unusual times, it may be that their reliance has come to be more than a fluid partnership; it might even be their mutual survival—even if they don't always want to acknowledge their symbiotic relationships.

Soon after the interviews began, Art Lewry, founder of production company HunterGatherer, was asked to join in the "expedition." He is an acclaimed digital storyteller and creative director. Art was tasked with "cleaning up" the "mess" that

Glenn and Sean made while doing their anthropological digging, packaging it up and sending it back out as a professional video and magazine-style presentation, adding in his own unique, well-known professional tweaks, guidance, and digital wizardry.

Did you think that was it? That the project was then done and dusted? Of course not. Where would be the adaption in that?

Sean, being the "gotta find the next level and take it there" guy that he is, then envisioned a pretty major upgrade to Phase I of the project, even committing to his *own* adaption as an author.

One of the themes uncovered in the conversations with the GGTs was that they knew when to look for assistance, so Sean rallied the team, some tech experts, and the editors at Gatekeeper Press as he headed into the unknown territory of serious, lengthy authorship.

As the book was taking shape, it was time to add another partner even closer to home—Andrea Worker. In addition to just plain putting up with "next-level" Sean over the years, Andrea was recruited this time to dust off her journalism and writing skills (largely mothballed since the Worker household shipped themselves off to Barcelona, Spain, for their own next chapter).

Andrea served as critic and idea-bouncing wall, (yes, it *was* painful, at times!) doing some rewriting and clean-up, adding a bit here and there, and giving the manuscript its first major edit before it was placed into the hands of our publisher, Gatekeeper Press, for the professional scrub and the layout, design, and legal stuff we know nothing about!

And so, Sean and company took the videos and mag-style presentation and turned it into what might be today the printed book in your hand or the digital version on your computer or tablet or smart phone. The treasures unearthed from this conversational excavation have been wrapped up in *The Adapters* and tied with an innovative technological ribbon—*The Adapters Hub*. (More on the www.theadapters.net later on.)

So. The first round of *The Adapters* has arrived. Your turn to *dig in!*

What to look for!

 Gutsy Genius Think Zone

 Adapter in the house

 Idea to grab

 Useful stuff

 Insights

 Scribble along the way

 Bit of work

 Work from Home

Notations and Quotes

The Adapters: Gutsy Genius Thinkers

Piers Brown

Founder & CEO, International Hospitality Media. London, United Kingdom

Click or use SmartPhone

James Blick & Yoly Martín Medieta

Cofounder & COO Devour Tours & Founder SpainRevealed. The Flamenco Guide. Madrid, Spain

Click or use SmartPhone

Leonardo di ser Piero Da Vinci

Engineer, Artist, PolyMath Anchiano, Vinci, Republic of Florence, Italy

Click or use SmartPhone

Sloan Dean

CEO & President, Remington Hotels. Dallas, Texas, USA

Click or use SmartPhone

Daniel del Olmo

President, Sage Hotel Management. Denver, Colorado, USA

Click or use SmartPhone

James Foice

Chief Executive, Association Serviced Apartment Providers. Gloucester, United Kingdom

Click or use SmartPhone

Benjamin Franklin

Founder, and
Founding Father
of the USA.
Boston and
Philadelphia, USA

Click or use SmartPhone

Mark Greenberg

Managing Partner &
Founder, Silverstone
Capital Advisors.
Cincinnati,
Ohio, USA

Click or use SmartPhone

Cindy Estis Green

Cofounder &
CEO Kalibri
Labs, LLC.
Rockville,
Maryland, USA

Click or use SmartPhone

Greg Juceam

President &
COO,
G6 Hospitality.
Chicago,
Illinois, USA

Click or use SmartPhone

Alexi Huntley Khajavi

President,
Hospitality &
Travel Questex.
London,
United Kingdom

Click or use SmartPhone

Keith Kefgen

Managing Director
& CEO, AETHOS
Consulting Group.
New York City,
New York, USA

Click or use SmartPhone

Raul Leal

CEO,
Virgin Hotels.
Florida, USA

Click or use SmartPhone

Guy Lean

Managing Director,
Madison Mayfair.
London,
United Kingdom

Click or use SmartPhone

Vanessa de Souza Lage

Cofounder & CMO
Rentals' United
Channel Manager &
Founder Vrtech Events.
Barcelona, Spain

Click or use SmartPhone

Anthony Melchiorri

Hospitality
Expert and
TV Presenter.
New York City,
New York, USA

Click or use SmartPhone

Cait Noone

Head, Galway Inter-
national Hotel School
& Vice President Inter-
national Engagement.
Galway, Ireland

Click or use SmartPhone

Dr. Peter O'Connor

Chaired Professor
of Digital Disruption,
ESSEC Business
School. Paris,
France

Click or use SmartPhone

Mitch Patel	**Mitch Presnick**	**Paul Slattery**
President & CEO, Vision Hospitality Group. Chattanooga, Tennessee, USA	Founder Super 8 Hotels China and Investor. Raleigh, North Carolina, USA	Director, Otus & Co-Advisory. London, United Kingdom
Click or use SmartPhone	Click or use SmartPhone	Click or use SmartPhone
	Jacob Wedderburn-Day	
	CEO & Cofounder, Stasher.com. London, United Kingdom	
	Click or use SmartPhone	

Insights - Key Contributors

Jim Alderman	Vivi Cahyadi & Karolina Saviova	Tracy Lowy

CEO, Radisson Hotel Group, The Americas. Minnetonka, MN USA	CEO & Cofounder, COO & Cofounder, Alto Vita. London, United Kingdom	Founder & Director, Living Rooms. London, United Kingdom
	Bob Hecht	
	Business Transformist Founder & Managing Director, Unimark, UK Ltd. London, UK	

"Hospitality is more than just heads in a bed. Travel is more than just booking the window seat and racking up points. It is in the very fabric that makes us human; to travel, go around the bend, explore some uncivilized places, shake someone's hand, break some bread, and make connections, so the idea that it's not coming back is an absolute falsehood."

Alexi Khajavi
President, Hospitality & Travel
Questex Events
London, United Kingdom

Introduction – Hi There!

Welcome to *The Adapters* experience! We are here to share stories and insights from some Gutsy Genius Thinkers (GGTs) who are forging our New Reality. Capturing their experiences, their successes, and their failures in their own words, we then crack the code of their revelations to decipher what characteristics and skills are required to excel, particularly in this distinct new era.

The project actually started pre-COVID—hard to believe!—in late 2019. The arrival of the pandemic forced adaption on our team. The words and wisdom of our GGTs were what we aimed to gather even before we had heard of what the scientists officially named SARS-CoV-2 and what we have all come to call the novel coronavirus, or COVID-19. Compiling and analyzing such information has always been of interest to Travel, Tourism and Hospitality (TT&H) veterans Sean and Glenn, but it seems now that the "capture, examination, and release" of experiential information is more important than ever.

The world is facing an inflection point. It's a time rife with challenge. For many, it's been overwhelming; for some it still is. But not for our GGTs. Well, in all honesty, they may have been overwhelmed or still struggle with instances of semi-paralysis of thought or action, but they have sucked it up and are still moving forward. Even in the fog of uncertainty that surrounds us all at this moment, this group sees unbridled opportunity and continues to adapt *and* innovate.

Sean and Glenn have brought some of the thoughts, passion, and purpose of these GGTs to life in *The Adapters*, shining a light on just how their adaptions and innovations came to be—and how they are now utilizing their experiences and their strategic methods to confront the previously unknown challenges that COVID-19 has brought.

Our team at *The Adapters* are lifelong learners. As a former adjunct professor at New York University, educating others and himself is in Glenn's DNA. He keeps dialing up the energy and the scope of topics on his online show, *No Vacancy*. If you want the latest news from the TT&H world, Glenn's got it and the experts who can give you the backstory, as well as what's coming next.

Sean has taken his business acumen and travel tech skills to a new level. Lately, through his T5 Strategies business transformation and travel tech advisory firm, he's been offering insight and practical suggestions on how to approach so many of the issues facing both start-ups and established companies alike during this time of stress.

You're going to read a lot about the 4th Age of Change in this work. The 4th Age of Change is upon us. George Friedman's recent book, *Storm Before the Calm,* offers the theory that highly disruptive institutional and socioeconomic cycles occur every fifty and eighty years, respectively, in the United States, and that other countries experience the same types of disruptions but along different timelines. The big difference today is that all this change and upheaval is happening concurrently with a global pandemic.

With all of the tumult that we have experienced since the start of 2020, it's hard to remember that this age of change, and our turn on the change wheel, predates C-19—by a lot! Let's reflect for a moment.

A few years back, the decision by the UK to initiate its withdrawal from the European Union (the so-called "Brexit")[3] raised awareness of a growing distrust in governments and institutions. The consequences of the protracted decoupling from the Eurozone have yet to be revealed, but it's already proven to be a destabilizing and disruptive force. The election of Donald Trump to the presidency of the US upended the norms of conventional presidential behavior and the traditional interactions the US had with both its own citizens and other nations. The divide between the inhabitants of both the left and right of the political scale in countries around the world has only widened. Couple all that with C-19, economic crises, protests around the globe, concern about the environment as natural disasters become more frequent and more severe…well, you get the picture.

Now add in other drivers of change, such as the acceleration of automation, instant information (Instagram), and Artificial Intelligence (Alexa!), and robotics (iRobot, Roomba). The 4th Age of Change may have started a relatively slow journey about 500 years ago in the time of Leonardo DaVinci, but all of these factors, and more, have certainly kicked things into high gear—and we are nowhere near the apex of this age, yet.

We expand on this topic in chapter two to contextualize why the 4th Age of Change has already begun, as the transition from one age to another is part of the process. This is the foundation upon which we will be building for many years, however murky and soft-footed it may be. After all, we homo sapiens have been adapting and innovating for epochs, evolving from caves to the three-bed semi-detached; from huddling around the accidental fire to decorative, remote-controlled fireplaces; from grunts to Shakespeare; bison bones as chisels to complex machinery; from foraging to farming; isolated groups of hut dwellers to cities of every size; from cautiously wandering off a bit on our own two feet to far-flung journeys by motorized transport for the sake of learning, experiencing, or just plain fun; from looking to the stars to exploring them. If all that incredible change and growth weren't enough, it's near-impossible to even come up with comparisons from the past to really highlight today's innovations in knowledge, efficiency, and cryptocurrency.

The mission of *The Adapters* is to enable you to "meet," listen, and learn from those who adjusted as the need arose and who are adapting and innovating for the times that we live in ***now*** that shape the future. Oftentimes, business-oriented books choose to feature only the "giants" of industry and focus on businesses with significant resources to deliver innovation. How many books are written about icons like Bill Marriott, Brian Chesky, Ray Kroc, and others in comparison to

> *"The capacity to learn is a GIFT; the ability to learn is a SKILL: the willingness to learn is a CHOICE."*
>
> **Brian Herbert**

the books that spotlight and explore the paths of the GGTs that inhabit our normal stratosphere, where *we* live or from where *we* can discover the next steps toward our own success or to the ultra-elevated?

Our GGTs like **Raul Leal** (Virgin Hotels), **Greg Juceam** (G6), **Vanessa de Souza Lage** (Rentals United), and **Professor Peter O'Connor** (ESSEC) are no doubt heading for even greater things, but to our good fortune, we've caught them at a time when they are just a bit more accessible. We're lucky enough to hitch a ride with them for just a little while, at a moment in time when we can better relate, understand, and *benefit* from their insights.

The "icons" will get their mention, of course, but we are focusing on speaking to this exciting group that includes leaders from the ecosystem that supports the TT&H world: suppliers, property developers, small and large brands, technology innovators, brokers, educators, universities, entertainment content providers, and many others.

We are seeking out the **entrepreneurs**[4] that are breaking the rules and paradigms, wherever or at whatever level they may be. Through their conversations we can look for patterns and relate them to the business world at large. Separately, we have a passion for finding the entrepreneurs and innovators *inside* companies. These internal innovators are too often overlooked and even squashed by the forces that do not reward free radicals. We feel compelled to find and share their stories, as well.

BTW, you industry giants—don't feel left out. We appreciate your achievements! Feel free to hop on board with these adapting GGTs and see what might be coming up behind you, around you, or that may have even moved up front! More than most, you all realize that adaption and innovation can come from anywhere.

The arrival of the 4th Age of Change also requires new tools to collect stories like those that form the basis of *The Adapters*—and an entirely different way of presenting the information.

What sets *The Adapters* apart from other offerings on the bookshelf in the "Business" section? In addition to the book(s), *The Adapters* is a *continuing* series of short-form commentaries, videos, podcasts, and extended interviews, collectively labeled "**The Adapters Hub.**" In the 4th Age of Change, we have simply moved our critical storytelling from around the caveman's firepit, Gutenberg's press, and the wireless, to the computers, tablets, and mobile devices of the modern era.

> *"Learning never exhausts the mind."*
>
> **Leonardo da Vinci, GGT**

The content within *The Adapters* is super easy to access digitally or in print. In addition to the memorable sound bites from our GGTs that are woven throughout, *The Adapters* includes the full text of the interviews with several of our guests, and there are Profile Pages for each—substance pieces that capture the essence of the conversations we've had with these thought leaders across the industry. We strongly encourage you to grab the beverage of your choice and watch the long-form interviews at www.theadapters.net or use the QR codes to hear "firsthand," and in their own words, just what's been on the minds of all our featured GGTs as they navigate adaption and innovation in their business spheres.

Too often, business books outdate themselves quickly. We look back on them with some fondness but think to ourselves, "Wow, did so-and-so get that one wrong!" or "I wonder how that strategy turned out?" or in the case of some of the industry icons, "How did they get from there to here?" **It was always the intention of the Adapters team to produce something designed to be dynamic, published about every ten to twelve months, with updates on how the previous interviewees are faring, while also adding new thought leaders to continue our learning adventures.**

Frequent updates to the Hub ensure an accurate reflection of the state of the ever-evolving business of travel.

Our user groups influenced our format: hi-tech, easy access, and more than a nod to what happens next. That's a game changer in today's world. Following up, touching base with the GGTs, and updating their stories means these conversations aren't static. They are not stuck in time with little relevance to what is occurring at this moment. People want to match up what a GGT thought *then* versus *now,* discover what changed *in between,* and learn what adaptions or innovations have been the results.

So, *The Adapters* isn't a traditional business book to be flipped through, only to become a background prop for your next Zoom meeting. Instead, we're providing a deeper understanding of how leaders are thinking during specific moments in time as they plan for the future.

> *"Keep training and keep learning until you get it right."*
>
> **gymquotes**

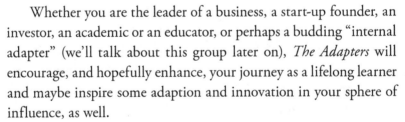

The Adapters Hub is designed for *active* use. Visit www.theadapters.net

Especially because of its up-to-date nature, *The Adapters* materials can be used by anyone, including:

- Those in school
- Newly minted graduates
- Young professionals
- And even people that have been in business for decades.

Whether you are the leader of a business, a start-up founder, an investor, an academic or an educator, or perhaps a budding "internal adapter" (we'll talk about this group later on), *The Adapters* will encourage, and hopefully enhance, your journey as a lifelong learner and maybe inspire some adaption and innovation in your sphere of influence, as well.

No matter your age or experience level, it's always a good time to adapt, if circumstances so dictate. After all, especially in Travel, Tourism, and Hospitality, accelerated dysfunctional times demand accelerated thinking. **Yes,**

COVID-19 has given new meaning to the terms *dysfunctional and disruptive*. Whether you admit it or not, you have already been forced to adapt. Are you **Working** (or YIKES! *managing* others) **from Home** (WFH) while learning to work with a wife/husband/ partner also at home *and* helping your kids learn remotely? Has your morning (and afternoon and evening!) routine vanished? Are your days now dysfunctional at worst and disruptive at best? Well, when your routine and your traditional functions are upended so dramatically, you bet you are adapting, and no doubt stressfully so.

Simultaneously, with all of this disruptive change, those of us in Travel, Tourism, and Hospitality have witnessed the Great Destruction of our industry's ecosystem. Who would have thought that 60–80 percent of major hotels, alternative accommodations, restaurants, and attractions would still be partially or completely closed eleven months into a pandemic? Individuals and companies are having to adapt to survive, as well as to deal with the destruction of lives and jobs.

While interviewing and researching for this project, it became apparent that many leaders had a strong sense of self, of community, and a desire to make a positive difference. Many spoke about charities and issues such as homelessness, food instability, and environmental matters that negatively impact our society, if not our very continued existence on this planet. They focused on their concerns about employee welfare. Would they be able to offer support, even in some small way, to employees who had been furloughed or left unemployed? They worried about the impact on the families of those employees.

As business leaders, they are fighters and are determined to restore jobs. They have a high self-awareness of their "emotional intelligence" (EI) in addition to their strong business intelligence (BI).[5] Effective leaders actively use *both* to create an environment where adaptation and innovation can thrive. EI and BI are complex topics. We will offer some thoughts on how to expand *your* awareness of why both EI and BI are critical and explore some ways to find a balance between them.

> "There's a way to do it BETTER— FIND IT."
>
> **Thomas A. Edison**

The Adapters Team is centrally focused on the topic of *adaption and innovation* and on capturing real people's business insights. We are passionate about sharing all we can with you on these topics to ensure that your business thrives. Along with the words and wisdom of the GGTs that we have gathered, this book will also offer some history on change, adaption, and innovation in the space and beyond. There will be commentary and opinion based on our own expertise and research, as well as the conversations we have had with our GGTs, and we will offer some of our own predictions and suggestions on how to adapt to today's evolving events.

Most importantly, this is a book to be written *in* (**No, seriously! Look out for the Scribble Zones along the way!**) as thoughts pop up while reading. It's probably a read that will **stimulate more questions than provide answers** and may even frustrate you at times…if so, great! Gather friends and colleagues at work (Zoom, Teams, and Hangouts) and hash through the questions in the exercise centered around EI and BI in the "Work Zone." Tease out and debate our thoughts on macro short and medium trends that may affect us. Explore *Tips and Takes* and reference materials from excellent subject-matter experts that may add to your lifelong learning commitment, or serve as guidelines for business survival or preparation for what comes next. Better still, spread the conversation out. Use the topics to address *adaptation and innovation* as an inspirational platform to build *your* culture and convert the fear of change into the enthusiasm of making a difference and helping to create our New Reality.

The Path We Will be Taking

The first few chapters you'll be tackling make up the backstory to adaption, focusing more on history. After all, as English philosopher (and interestingly, historian and archeologist, as well) R.G. Collingwood said:

"History is for human self-knowledge...the only clue to what man can do is what man has done. The value of history, then, is that it teaches us what man has done and thus what man is."

- R.G. Collingwood[6]

After our historical foray, we'll move into a bit of a synopsis of what's *been* going on in TT&H before we discuss how things look in the space today. Then it will be time to talk about "tomorrow"; some of the positives already on the horizon, and some adaptions and potential responses to the threats to our industry and our world.

Finally, we'll get down to the guidelines, Tips and Takes, reference materials, and practical steps to take to either start or enhance your journey toward being a Gutsy Genius Thinker with the help of a Super Formula for Success.

All along the way you'll be "hearing" from our GGTs and will find QR codes to link you directly to their interviews at www.theadapters. net. We've also included an "Update" section to bring you up to speed with how our GGTs have been faring since we conducted our initial interviews. **DON'T CHEAT!** See how *this* chapter of their story ends, how they got there and what they originally thought when facing the pandemic before you experience where they are today. It makes for a much better read—and a more meaningful experience if you follow the plot!

Ready?

We are about to do a bit of wandering through time, so to borrow an invitational welcome from a fictional "doctor" who calls an extraordinarily roomy blue British Police Call Box his home and his fantastic method of time travel and transportation—"Allons-y!"

CHAPTER 1

Today's World – Adaptation and Innovation and the COVID Effect

"It was the best of times, it was the worst of **times**, it was the **age of wisdom**, it was the age of **foolishness,** it was the epoch of **belief,** it was the epoch of **incredulity,** it was the season of **light,** it was the season of **darkness,** it was the spring of **hope,** it was the winter of **despair.**"
Charles Dickens, A Tale of Two Cities *(1859)*
[7]https://www.youtube.com/watch?v=Wb9_y3MGuRk

The interesting thing about Dickens is that he spoke to and captured the sentiments of both the elite and the general populace because they all related to how he told Life's story. He included them all to paint the whole picture of a world caught in a vortex of change.

Much of *our* world is in a state of flux and confusion. There is significant political unrest, with citizenry around the globe demanding to be heard. To add to the scenario, institutions and governments are being tested on how to handle a global pandemic. As of yet, no solution has been found other than trying to keep COVID-19 out of the house with a series of "sandbag" protocols to stop it from seeping underneath your door.

People and systems are stressed. Change has steamrolled over us. Many of us are fatigued and even overwhelmed by lockdowns, erratic pronouncements, and clashing directives from governments and institutions. In geographical terms, this is the time when the flowing freshwater river of change is meeting the saltwater ocean at the estuary. The estuary is rich with nutrients, but it swirls and swirls with heavy currents and lots of mud. Maybe not the best spot to weigh anchor.

Some people are fighting to swim back upstream and go back from where they came. At least there you had already found a berth and you could usually see to the other side of the waterway. Others are stuck in the mud, paralyzed and uncertain. Should they stay put, try to make it back to familiar waters, or head for the ocean with its equal potentials for life-threatening riptides or the discovery of new worlds of opportunity? It's the rare few who decide to brave the currents, adapt, and head out to sea to embrace the new vastness and develop their own "Blue Ocean strategy"[8] **https://www.youtube. com/watch?v=8cVS7YEW2Fk**. Many will stay stuck in the mud, but for others, those new worlds await.

Adaption will occur

Upstream, downstream, or stuck in the middle, adaption will still occur[9]. Since the beginning of time, humans have evolved, adapted, and innovated—sometimes in slow increments, sometimes at a dizzying pace. And then came our time, our turn at accelerated change, starting about sixty years ago. This period has delivered a vast array of technological advancements, leading to our increasing dependency on its offerings. Leaving your smartphone at home—or worse yet! losing it somewhere—isn't only inconvenient; it can result in an actual sensation of emotional loss for some. Our Apple watch or our Fitbit reminds us when to stand, move, and even breathe. Netflix gives us license to binge-watch. Uber offers the freedom to roam, and there can be dinner on the doorstep with Deliveroo, while Amazon delivers everything else!

These advancements (BOX 1) saw most of their creators building more on digital technologies rather than physical materials, beginning their hyper-acceleration in the 1990s. All of these developments

> *"The BEST way to predict the FUTURE is to INVENT it."*
>
> **Alan Kay**

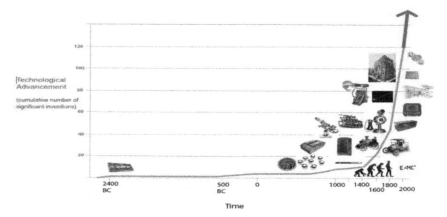

BOX 1 As this chart highlights, we have lived through an incredible velocity of change in the last fifty years, more than any other point in our history.

[10]What Are the Most Important Inventions of the 20th Century? - YouTube

https://www.youtube.com/watch?v=XyAJ_kbdNIE

have crept into the fabric of our daily lives, almost without our notice; C-19 just highlighted our dependence on "platforms" to facilitate life's necessities, with Amazon drivers now defined by some in the same "essential worker" category as other frontline workers.

The COVID pandemic has brought with it a superabundance of doubt and insecurity. It's something that continues to cause unease in daily lives, in the operation of business, and on the floors of the global stock exchanges. A little bit of confusion here and a bit of chaos there can actually stimulate adaption and positive change, as we will discover as we progress through *The Adapters*, but an excess of uncertainty can be a confidence killer, shaking the very foundations of societies around the world and, for many, casting a substantial shadow on their confidence in the future.

For better or for worse, the C-19 effect is getting a little easier to bear as we come to accept our new uncertain state and begin our personal adaption to the situations we face. These are the worst of times for millions of middle- and working-class citizens and students, with jobs being lost and college life being upended. Equally, these are, if not the best, at least better times for many, who have essentially recovered initially lost wealth as the stock markets have rallied or whose businesses have profited by providing much needed and/or desired products and services during this upheaval.

This team has long questioned the use of the terms "return to normal" or "finding the new normal." Both Glenn and I wrote a number of pieces during summer 2020 that challenged those phrases and presented the case that we are actually entering a **New Reality** and need to find our energy to adapt and move forward rather than chasing yesterday's "normal." Better still, be like our GGTs and become an active participant in shaping that New Reality.

Three meters at a time

I am an active cyclist (Lycra included) and have referenced that sport in articles to describe a recommended response to the near paralysis that threatened many during the early stages of the pandemic.  Staying fit and focused is hard work, whether that's athletically or mentally, as the terrain changes with lightning-fast speed. New politics, new global relationships, new job-killing technologies, new life-enhancing medical therapies, change, change, change! It's no wonder that when COVID joined in, some of us were sorely tempted to just come to a grinding halt and hop off that "bike." For sure, physical fitness—and decent gear and kit—is key to climbing a mountain as a cyclist, but *emotional* strength is what wins the day. Most cyclists maintain it by focusing on just the three meters directly before them to stay in a kind of cycling "bubble." You are still aware of the race and your teammates, but you do not worry about that 1800-meter climb when you're at the base, or else you'll mentally wash out before you turn over the first pedal. It's easy to be overwhelmed with change and challenges, new technologies and systems. Like successful cyclists, start by focusing on the next three meters and your plan to attack the "mountain"; your plan to move forward, *adapting* as you progress.[11]

Alexi Khajavi, President of Hospitality & Travel at Questex, and one of our GGTs, couldn't agree more with this strategy. Describing his approach to business operations and life in the time of C-19, Khajavi says, "You have to have both the short view and the long view. The short view is necessary to break it down into bite-sized bits of 'this is what I've got to do to survive the day-to-day.' Because if you start to think about the enormity of this crisis, it's going to overwhelm you. It's going to cause indigestion at its best, and it's going to kill you at the worst."

> *"When the legs scream stop and your lungs are bursting, that's when it starts. That's the hurt locker. Winners love it in there."*
>
> **Chris McCormack**

> Forced by the pandemic, the travel industry is at an *inflection point*. After a decade-long bender of growth, it's facing multiple crises and an uncertain future. Can the organization that's tasked with representing the global commercial travel industry (WTTC) *adapt to the new challenge?*
>
> **— Rosie Spinks, SKIFT, September 28, 2020**

Alexi Khajavi
President, Hospitality & Travel
Questex
London, United Kingdom

"I think the crisis actually brings this opportunity for all of us to start asking questions which were otherwise completely unorthodox and ludicrous just four or five weeks ago."

Credentials and street smarts really help in life, especially as one develops one of the most valuable human attributes: *perspective*. Having worked in tech in the early days in San Francisco, then airlines and independent hotels in Costa Rica for ten years, followed by a digital travel marketing agency and now the Business-to-Business (B2B) Questex, Alexi has the experience to support his "tell it as it is" opinions, and he also has a deep international vantage point that few others can match.

B2B companies such as Questex depend on their people surviving through downturns and introducing new-wave entrants to the old guard. Alexi's opinions on the space are clear. "We are a highly fragmented industry, from consumer to operator to owner to lender to landlord to the technology that fits in between each of those tranches *(a French word meaning "slice" or "portion." In the world of investing, it is used to describe a security that can be split up into smaller pieces and subsequently sold to investors)*[verticals]. I mean, we are so fragmented that the consumer is confused as to who is who." He is a keen advocate for nudging operators and brands to use technology to create a single point of access for the consumer. They've done this at Questex, which is effectively a single-use platform for all content they create.

Questex owns some of the largest conferences in the hospitality space. As an events management and digital media company, the company has been hit considerably hard as a result of C-19. However, Questex continues to expand with conferences like Berlin's "Adjacent Spaces," events that will drive the "change conversation" regarding the best use of space, and which will therefore drive thought leadership, as well.

Adaption Tips:

- It's paramount to bring people together, whether virtually or in person.
- Remember what Winston Churchill said: "Never waste a good crisis."
- Make your product/service/experience easy for the consumer to consume.
- New investors are joining the space; know how to pitch to them.
- The pandemic provides the opportunity to express ideas that were considered crazy pre-C-19, like "Why do we need an office?" Start asking "why?" about a lot more procedures or ways that you have been conducting your business. ***Crazy Bob in the corner, questioning everything, sounds pretty smart right about now.***

LinkedIn: https://www.linkedin.com/feed/
Company: https://questex.com/

Take the time to learn more

Click or use SmartPhone

CHAPTER 2

The 4th Age of Change

To talk meaningfully about today—and to bring a sizeable and much-needed portion of hope to our current situation—we have to flash back and put our "now" into historical context. We

have been evolving, adapting, and innovating since the beginning of our time on the planet, sometimes in almost imperceptible increments, sometimes at breakneck speed, and often during times in the midst of significant challenges.

The 4th Age of Change started to emerge about five hundred years ago. (Although, for most of us, it feels like it just started in the spring of 2020!) The transition point between the 3rd and 4th Ages of Change began around the time of that Renaissance GGT, Leonardo DaVinci. **In his day, DaVinci effectively *was* Google, albeit not as accessible to the masses.**

It's been suggested that he was the last individual to amass the most complete compilation of knowledge about everything knowable at one time. By the time DaVinci died in 1519, the Gutenberg printing press had been around for almost seventy years and was gaining momentum, much like a single-page Kindle. The printed word—and thus

> "As soon as the fear approaches near, ATTACK and DESTROY it."
>
> **M Vilan**

knowledge—was well on its way to changing everything. The greatest obstacle to capitalizing on the target market of that era was that most of those potential consumers could not read what was being printed! The user base was a little behind the tech. Sounds familiar.

Our path out of the Dark—*literally*-—began even before the millennia that we humans label the Ages of Change, with the controlled use of fire. There's lots of scientific arguing about just where to place the consistent use of fire on the timeline of evolution. The bulk of the evidence indicates fire was frequently in use beginning about 400,000 years ago, but paleontologists and other scientists have found sites in Israel that suggest fire was being purposefully used 800,000 years ago! The findings in the Wonderwerk Cave[12] **https://www.youtube.com/watch?v=SdDy_Vru470** have scientists theorizing that there were already isolated regions in South Africa and elsewhere where our early human ancestors had learned to either build a fire or maintain a natural fire for their own use.

Wherever or whenever that adaption to their environment occurred, it was the mastery of fire that really got the whole thing started for humans. The scientists who can't quite agree on dates or places seem to come largely into alignment on the *importance* of fire to evolution.

Ian Tattersall, a paleoanthropologist and curator emeritus of human origins at the American Museum of Natural History in New York, noted in an August 2020 article published on LiveScience.com that control over fire gave humans the ability to move out of the cave and explore further, even into colder climates. In addition to keeping its users from freezing to death, controlled or constructed fire offered a space to gather around, possibly encouraging socialization, the sharing of ideas and discoveries, and maybe even the beginnings of uniform communication. After all, if you are going to be sitting around the fire together, you have to have some way to tell those tall tales of the day's adventures.

The experts also seem to agree that cooking with that controlled fire laid the ground-work for the increase of human cognition, allowing for brain growth, "something

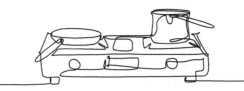

that requires a lot of energy," which Tattersall and others postulate was largely enabled by Homo erectus's ability to cook food; his gut was shrinking, but his brain was growing.

Fired up cooking and storytelling

OK—so now we have that fire to keep us warm, give us a meet-up spot, and make that wooly mammoth steak taste a whole lot better than straight off the bone (so folks like José Andrés and Gordon Ramsay can tell us how to *really* prepare it). What came next?

- 1st Age – A hundred thousand years ago, we developed language to communicate and story-tell.
- 2nd Age – Around ten thousand years ago, organized farming extended our life expectancy and enabled our cities to grow.
- 3rd Age – We made a huge leap about five thousand years ago when we figured out how to make a *wheel,* and mass tourism began (Kind of. At least to the next village!). Writing captured and transferred knowledge.
- 4th Age – In 1703, Gottfried Leibniz pioneered the binary system used in almost every computer today.

Isaac Newton, Louis Pasteur, Alexander Graham Bell, Thomas Edison, and many others took us from the 1700s to the 20th century, where things really started cooking! (Like microwave ovens in the 1950s.) During the first half of the last century, technology kept advancing at an admirable pace, then, starting in the 1960s, it's like someone flipped the switch! Fiber optics, space exploration, e-commerce, the CAD system, the first computers, and cellphones all made their debuts in the 60s and '70s. Since about 1989, when the World Wide Web came into existence, technological, medical, and sociological change—*adaption*—has been arriving so fast and so furiously that, blink!, and you will surely miss something amazing or get seriously left behind. Don't worry, though. Your Artificially

The Four Ages of Change
(From a human's perspective)

Fourth Age - 500 years ago

Robots and AI

• Technology changes have evolved rapidly in 500 years with major leaps in the 20th century
• Rapid Tech changes from 1990 to now
• It is inferred by Historians that leonardo da Vinci was the last man to know everything. He died in
• Multiple advances largely built on incremental change and evolution of memory capacity known as Moore's Law (the notion of doubling of capacity)
• Humans to use computers and thus Robots to outsource more and more thoughts and actions- for the first time in Homo Sapiens history, systematic change and innovation, independent of human action

First Age - 100,000 years ago

Fire and Language

• Mastered Fire and Language We learned to Cook and use fire as a defense and a clear technological advance
• As a result of evolution we developed language and thus story telling and knowledge transfer
• Hunting and gathering era

Second Age - 10,000 years ago

Agriculture and Cities

• Agriculture was the next Tech advance where crops and feeding systems increased leading to a doubling of the population
• Agriculture started to become organized and towns and cities developed as the population could be supplied
• Cities promoted efficiency and exchange of ideas and division of labor. No longer had to work the fields but could be a weaver in town

Third Age - 5000 years ago

Writing and Wheels

• Sumerians invent writing about 5000 years ago in modern day southern Iraq
• Writing enabled ideas to survive with some accuracy
• This enabled rules and laws to be written down including the 282 laws known as the CODE of Hammurabi
• Currency emeraged during the third age and the Wheel mobilized humans

Source: The 4ᵗʰ age—Byron Reese

BOX 2

[14]https://www.youtube.com/watch?v=sQFgzz3xvTY

Intelligent[13] assistant—in whatever shape or format it takes—will bring you up to speed.

All these "tech leaps" along the timelines have enabled humans to live longer, to experience more, and to transfer goods and services and document wealth in even greater detail.

Fast-forward to 2020, and welcome to the next transformational phase of this "4th Age of Change." Remember: *our* time and *our* turn at accelerated change began about fifty to sixty years ago. (Think computers, DNA sequencing, cellphones, GPS, fiber optics, space travel!) Now that our target market is more literate and we are not relying on one amazing individual—Leonard DaVinci, that true GGT—to be the repository of all current information, we have been able to democratize knowledge, with much of it available through Google (effectively ruining many good conversations and Pub Quiz Night contests with "Are you sure? Let's Google it!"). Most people on the planet have a smartphone, connected in a way that instantaneously moves news, updates, information, and knowledge universally, even *with* filters and the curse of misinformation and opinionators disguised as experts.

This development has afforded new status to those with *expertise* and *knowledge*. In some opinions, expertise and educational degrees have created a whole new class in our societal structure. This is a debatable supposition, for sure, but let's save that for another day.

Today's advancements are based more on digital and other technologies rather than on physical materials or machines. Bryon Reese, author of *The Fourth Age, Smart Robots, Conscious Computers and the Future of Humanity,*[15] explored this territory and mapped how humans have arrived at an age where artificial intelligence and robotics will accelerate at an exponential pace. Somewhere in the midst of this 4th Age of Change, we are experiencing the front end of the digital awakening, *and COVID-19 just put its foot on the gas pedal of change*!

We are in the midst of significant change; nothing new about that headline. There is a realization, however, that much of what we thought was constant is being questioned, and in  some cases, downright disproved. Have you ever asked yourself any of these questions? Bet you have.

- Is where I live safe, or should I move out of the city?
- Do I know if I can trust my news/information source?
- Do I like my job or boss?
- Does what I do make a difference?
- Am I an "essential worker"? Am I treated as one?

C-19 is now shaking the foundations of aging belief systems. To be clear: this book is about adaption and innovation, not politics. However, today's politics are omnipresent and omnichannel. With access to twenty-four-hour news cycles and the instant feeds of Twitter, Facebook, and the like, politics and its purveyors not only drive policy, but they also significantly shape the views of large slices of the electorate that change and morph depending on the issue and the narrator. Even as it struggles to keep up with adaption and innovation, politics is disruptive to a large extent in ways similar to how technology has impacted communication.

Equality itself is far from equal. Governments and institutions are being pressured by their citizens to rethink and make choices. It is intriguing to us that it took a pandemic (C-19) to expose major gaps in the economic and social constructs of societies around the world. They were always there, but COVID has put them on display.

Values and monetary and social systems are all being tested, as well. What we are all sensing and experiencing is just as George Friedman[16] observed in his well-timed book, *The Storm Before the Calm,* published in February 2020. As we mentioned previously, Friedman identifies a phenomenon where institutional and socioeconomic changes in the United States occur approximately every eighty years and fifty years respectively (with similar patterns occurring in other countries). Unlike other periods in modern history, though, both cycles appear to be converging within the same decade—which is unprecedented.

Government, social norms, and the social contract between government and its citizenry are being fundamentally questioned, and in some cases, forced to change. The world has become accustomed to America being a major voice at the table, except that the table of old has been rejected in favor of a fast-paced drive-through by some, and an organically produced and locally sourced buffet by others. The tumultuous rise in Trumpism, Johnsonism, and others, evidenced by the support of almost 50 percent of the electorate in the recent US presidential election, and the support for Johnson and his push for Brexit, is an emerging political and cultural voice that will impact the New Reality for many years to come. There are those who see the Trump campaign's efforts to invalidate the election results as a real threat to Democracy, in the US and beyond. Others see it as the opportunity to examine the gaps and modify the structure going forward. Governments will experience fundamental change in response. Possibly scary, but Democracy has perpetual change built into its DNA, much the same as business. Adaption is fluid.

What history is teaching us is that these "norm-breaking" changes often lead to adaption, innovation, and periods of immense growth.

The effects of C-19, coupled with the pre-COVID societal, institutional, and technological transformations that were already underway, suggest we should expect to live through a dramatic and possibly highly disruptive period for quite a while. In any case, we bunch of humans may have to begin adapting in earnest. In this era, the change curve is climbing more steeply than you might think, and although one might perceive C-19 as a massive *pause*, it is more likely an accelerant of global change. ***Anthony Melchiorri, GGT,*** (TV personality, creator of *Hotel Impossible*) thinks of the acceleration of C-19 change in this way:

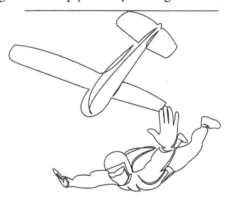

> *"[You] should feel liberated to do what the hell you want to do. Now we all realize we're walking around with masks and gloves on, and we're not leaving houses. So, if you're not doing what is in your heart now, what the f**k were you waiting for?"*

Opportunity is always in the room

Innovation, invention, and adaption can occur at any point in history and under any circumstances, even in "less-enlightened times" and during periods of enormous upheaval or economic stress. Just a few examples to give you a bit of hope:

- Framed magnifying lenses for reading were already in use by the time inventor Roger Bacon mentioned them. The first subject to be painted wearing eyeglasses shows up in Italy in 1352. Benjamin Franklin found time—in between involvement in a Revolutionary War and the establishment of a new country—to take this invention a step further, creating **bifocals**!

- The GGTs of the Middle Ages gave us lots of useful stuff like the **heavy plow, mechanical clocks**, the aforementioned **printing press, blast furnaces, coffeehouses,** and improvements on **alcohol distillation**!

- The 14th century also gave us a less-welcome concept: **quarantine**. Apparently, the local Venetian powers-that-be figured out that ships returning from eastern Mediterranean maritime trade were escorting back the plague and other diseases along with their boatloads of goods. Originally ordering citizens into isolation for thirty days to try and keep the spread under control, the municipal governance then extended the isolation period to forty days—*quarantena* in the local tongue. Do we say "Grazie!" for this adaptation that we are now making use of today?

Further along the timeline, the Great Depression certainly saw great darkness and despair for millions around the world. It was also an age that brought us:

- **The car radio** – Called the Motorola to trade on the name of its popular cousin, the Victrola record player. A 1930s invention that brought fame and fortune to brothers Paul and Joseph Galvin when they made a distribution deal with Ford Motor Company! No matter that it would be another thirty years before the invention received its next great adaption, allowing listeners to actually take control of the dial and choose their listening experience.

- **Monopoly** – Charles Darrow adapted "The Landlord's Game" and repackaged it with a few extras in 1935, including the new name of "Monopoly." Darrow took a page from the game itself and became the first millionaire game developer after striking a deal with Parker Brothers for the rights to the game. Poor Lizzie Maggie, who invented the original game, was eventually paid $500 in a nod to her "contribution." Lesson to be learned there. Follow through and protect your adaption or innovation.

"Remember, dark times don't turn the lights out on adaption or innovation."

Sean Worker

Scribble Zone: What are the three adaptions or innovations that have inspired and motivated you?

_____

_____

_____

_____

_____

_____

_____

_____

_____

_____

_____

_____

_____

_____

_____

_____

_____

_____

_____

_____

_____

_____

_____

Gutsy Genius Thinker
Leonardo di ser Piero Da Vinci
Engineer, Artist, Polymath
Anchiano, Vinci, Republic of Florence

Leonardo is a GGT who embodies the notion of "have-a-go," and before you know it, you've invented the flying machine (on paper). As he said, "I have always felt it is my destiny to build a machine that would allow man to fly."

It's not unusual for a GGT to envision a product ahead of its time, or in Leonardo's case, before the material and manufacturing process were available or even in existence. According to sources at Wikipedia, "Some of his smaller inventions, however, entered the world of manufacturing unheralded, such as an automated bobbin winder and a machine for testing the tensile strength of wire. He is also sometimes credited with planning the inventions of the parachute, helicopter, and tank. He made substantial discoveries in anatomy, civil engineering, geology, optics, and hydrodynamics, but he sadly did not publish his findings, and they had little to no direct influence on subsequent science." Lesson to all GGTs—write and publish your ideas and stories!

Although Leonardo had no formal education, he's regarded as *The Renaissance Man* or a universal genius. It is said that he may well have been the last man that knew all there was to know in the world until Google appeared. He was not known for staying still and moved from patron to patron (Venture and Private equity) as he sought funding for his ideas. No easy feat to secure Series A funding in those days. Leo (to his friends) was unorthodox and deeply curious. In 1472, at the age of 20, this GGT qualified as a master in the Guild of Saint Luke—the guild of artists and doctors of medicine. He went on to have a colorful personal life and gained fame as one of the greatest doers (Get Stuff Done—GSD) of all time. He died at Château d'Amboise, France, on the 12th August 1519, aged 67.

Although Leonardo was not available for a video interview with Glenn and me, we improvised, and hope that you QR to have a listen.

"I have been impressed with the urgency of doing. Knowing is not enough; we must apply. Being willing is not enough; we must do."

Leonardo Da Vinci

Adaption Tips:

- Learning never exhausts the mind.
- There are three classes of people: those who see, those who see when they are shown, those who do not see.
- In rivers, the water that you touch is the last of what has passed and the first of that which comes, so with present time.
- He who wishes to be rich in a day will be hanged in a year.
- Simplicity is the ultimate sophistication.

Wikipedia profile @ https://en.wikipedia.org/wiki/Leonardo_da_Vinci
Biography @ https://www.leonardodavinci.net/

Take the time to learn more https://www.youtube.com/watch?v=nrV91kOn-ao&t=18s

Click or use SmartPhone

Gutsy Genius Thinker
Anthony Melchiorri
President of Argeo Hospitality, Keynote Speaker,
Host and Executive Producer.
AnthonyMelchiorri.com
Hospitality Expert and TV Presenter
Creator and Host – *Hotel Impossible*
New York City, New York, USA

Energy and grit, that's Anthony. This guy is an Adapter on steroids and a must-listen. Working his way up to hotel general manager, then learning how to be a "different brain" as SVP Asset Management at Tishman Hotels was transforming, but not enough. As he says himself, he's an "emotional guy," so doing "stuff" by the book was hard for him. After about twenty-five years in the business, he was itchy, bumping up closer to fifty (forty-five), and his daughter suggested he get on TV. He took her advice, and thus was born the *Hotel Impossible* TV series, along with other related shows. Of course, he didn't just wait around for that next iteration of himself to be accomplished. He actually worked as the executive producer and appeared in a movie before his first TV series hit the small screen.

As he commented, "If you notice, over the last probably eight, ten years, you're a founder of this…Before, we used to call that 'entrepreneurs,' and it's much cooler to be a founder." Fast-forward, and Anthony developed a "sizzle wheel" to pitch his new show (think pitch for start-up funding), and the show did not get picked up at first. So Anthony kept pivoting until it did. No giving up for Anthony.

This is a story of tenacity, energy, and focus on the endgame. For many of us, transitioning careers is tough, let alone changing your entire life to follow a dream in or around middle age; this takes guts with a bit of genius thrown in. He connected with so many of the shows' participants because he understood that some were on the edge of losing their dream, but with effort and *adaptation*, anything is possible, not *impossible*. Anthony is a vocal advocate for the Travel and Hospitality sector. Click through to watch and listen to a passionate fella.

> *"I've always stayed close to that desperation. I've never felt like I got too soft because I'm always feeling like I'm going out of business."*
>
> *Anthony Melchiorri*

Adaption Tips:

- Drive revenue.
- Hunt for mentors.
- "Don't piss off the hedge-fund guy in New York."
- "I got thrown out four times, and we still got the show." Adapting is painful.
- "We should feel liberated to do what the hell we want to do. Now we all realize we're walking around with masks and gloves on, and we're not leaving houses. So, if you're not doing what is in your heart now, what the f**k were you waiting for?"

LinkedIn profile @ www.linkedin.com/in/anthonymelchiorri/
Company @ www.anthonymelchiorri.com/

Take the time to learn more

Click or use SmartPhone

Gutsy Genius Thinker
Benjamin Franklin
Founder, Polymath, and Founding
Father of the USA
Boston and Philadelphia, USA

We were lucky enough to connect with Ben Franklin recently. He referred us to his extensive archive of ideas and inventions, which says a lot about this GGT. Much like our other GGTs, he is always _Adapting_ and _Innovating_. As a media visionary of the scale of Ted Turner or Rupert Murdoch, he leveraged the notion of franchising through "silent partnerships" (franchisees) with printers up and down the East Coast of America. Not unlike Ray Kroc (Founder, McDonald's) or Chris Nassetta, CEO Hilton, Ben leveraged his _approved_ supply chain to his franchisees by manufacturing and distributing ink and paper, as McDonald's does with brand-standard burgers. He stepped down as CEO of his printing business at the age of 42 and continued to live off the proceeds for the rest of his life.

As GGTs are never satisfied with the status quo, his next 42 years (BF died at 84) were hectic and varied. He went on to disrupt business markets, invent and contribute to his community by establishing the first public library, fire company, hospital, militia, night watch (police), and university. He invented the lightning rod (more money), served as a Colonial Governor, Ambassador to France, attended the USA constitutional congress, and contributed to and edited the American Constitution. In his spare time, Ben led a very colorful personal life, became a significant philanthropist, and learned to speak French fluently.

"You may delay, but Time will not."
                    Ben Franklin, CEO and overachiever

Adaption Tips:

- "Use facts and reason to support your ideas. Passion is important, but it doesn't give people the reason they need to give you their support."
- Check yourself to determine whether you rely more on force or reason to get things done as a manager.
- *He who waits upon Fortune is never sure of a dinner.*
- *Well done is better than well said.*
- *Seek first to manage yourself, then manage others.*
- *Create solutions for seemingly impossible problems.*
- *Become a revolutionary for experimentation and change.*

Wikipedia profile @ www.en.wikipedia.org/wiki/Benjamin_Franklin

Biography @ www.biography.com/scholar/benjamin-franklin

Take the time to learn more https://www.youtube.com/watch?v=FGx2PBgVSG4&t=6s

Click or use SmartPhone

Scribble Zone– List 3 major adaptions, inventions, or innovations that have inspired and/or motivated you in your career and explain why.

CHAPTER 3

Perspective – Yesterday and Today

"Yesterday, all my troubles seemed so far away."
Paul McCartney, John Lennon

The boom time – an open door to the other side

About a year ago, most companies in TT&H were preparing to present their perpetually growth-driven budgets. 2020 was being forecast to be another BOOM year after seven-ish years of bubbly and fun. Why not? Many in the space—or even adjacent to it—had been posting record earnings. Airbnb's Brian Chesky and many others have been rattling the status quo. Google has been quietly getting into the travel business, and everyone has been buying something.

The events market has also been enjoying record years. Cruise ships have grown so enormous they can now boast their own post or zip codes. Speaking of cruise ships, Barcelona, a major port for the cruising hordes, was whining about all those tourists, and Venice was whinging while submerging itself under the weight of all those gondolas poling about, loaded down with the same tourists. Yurts became a thing. And suddenly, everyone wanted an "experience"—and they were willing to pay well for the privilege.

Apart from all that, one of the best trends that came from all this "irrational exuberance" (Alan Greenspan—Fed Chair during the Clinton era) was

> *"Boom Hoka shakka – boom times."*
>
> **Hooked on a Feeling (Guardians of the Galaxy)**
>
> **https://www. youtube.com/ watch?v=_ZKZ_ IQ5FWQ**

27

that TT&H *professionalized*. Brands expanded, travel tech emerged, "experiences" became a real category, Serviced Apartments and Alternative Accommodations woke up the BIG 6 Hotel Brands and attracted the attention of investors—*yes*, investors. TT&H became an investable class of assets!

The ecosystem attracted new talent from across other industries like Fritz van Paasschen from Nike, Coors, and other companies and Sébastien Bazin, a fearless banker who is bold, alternative, and tells it the way that he sees it as he leads Accor to its new frontier.

Chefs and mixologists became celebs. We found our inner design "self and sense": bespoke restaurants, micro-brands, mini-brands, macro-brands—*everyone had a brand*. In order to have a proper wedding, depending on faith and tradition, it could cost the price of a small car or an entire town. And through it all, we kept learning and growing and enjoying our Boom.

These last years have been *the best of times for* Travel, Tourism, and Hospitality. All our troubles of today certainly did seem far away yesterday, and because we've been most recently living in the relative Boom Times, it makes it that much harder to face today, let alone imagine a brighter tomorrow after C-19. The good news? As opposed to other "dark times" that our industry has endured, the positives we bring with us from yesterday, and the fact that the TT&H industry has a much stronger baseline from which to rebound means there will be vast opportunities once we cross through the Open Door.

> "I previously worked in Switzerland, and there, if you work as a server in a restaurant, it's just as important as the local doctor because you're providing an invaluable service."
>
> **Cait Noone, GGT Head, Galway International Hotel School, Vice President International Engagement**

GGT Raul Leal, CEO Virgin Hotels, may not be ready to confer medical degrees on the inhabitants of the Travel, Tourism, and Hospitality domains, but he is proud of their contributions and of the place that the industry holds in the societal scheme. Leal said,

> Gosh, I wish I could figure out a way…to make the people that work at the hotels incredibly proud of what it is that we do. I think what we do is incredibly important. I say that to our teams. What we do is amazing. You know, we take care of people like me that travel over a hundred thousand miles a year. You make me feel safe. You make me feel secure, or you make me feel that I can call my family and it's all okay. And I don't think we get enough recognition for that globally, for the importance that our industry has on the travel segment.

Don't underestimate your position on the economic wheel. The travel, hospitality, restaurant, and bar space matters. The industry contributes between 8–15 percent of many countries' Gross Domestic Product (GDP).[a] The majority of tax revenue, such as bed, property, food, airport, and rental car taxes, drives many cities' local economies, while the national and federal government systems receive little or nothing.

Boxes 3 and 4 show the dependency of many economies on TT&H and do not consider the multiplier effect [17]https://www.youtube.com/watch?v=RqWYmQQzXxs of a dollar/euro/pound as it is spent throughout the economy. For example, the chart counts a hotel room rate but does not count the associated payment for goods and services, such as buying sheets and towels, petrol for the vans, or new bar installations in a new pub. Although the USA leads the table in gross GDP dollars, the Travel industry is a relatively low contributor in that country at 2.8 percent of GDP, while France is

---

[a]   GDP is the monetary value of all finished goods and services made within a country during a specific period.

ranked number eight for gross dollars but takes the honors with 89 million visitors annually and 10 percent GDP. Spain has slightly fewer travelers than France, but their numbers contribute in excess of 15 percent of Spain's GDP.

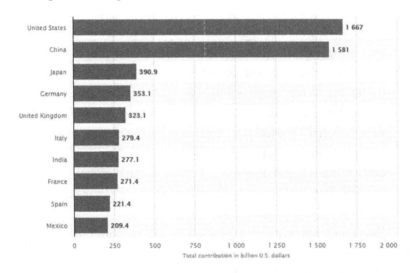

BOX 3

Total Contribution of Travel and Tourism to GDP in Selected Countries Worldwide in 2019 *(in billion* US *dollars)*

BOX 4

Number of Visitors to the Top 5 Countries Globally

Country	Number of Annual Visitors in Millions	% GDP
France	89m	10%
Spain	83.7m	15%
USA	79m	2.8%
China	62.9m	9.3%
Italy	51.1m	13%

Source: Statistica 2020, Visit Britain, USA Department of Commerce Sources, Far & Wide, French Finance Ministry, USA Department of Commerce -2.8% Travel and Tourism Sector Supports 7.8 Million Jobs and Accounts for 2.8% of U.S GDP in 2018 |Nov 20, 201979m visitors to USA 9Far & Wide) Number 3, Wolfstreet, Visit Britain

As we mentioned earlier, *The Adapters* project was set in motion with no awareness that a pandemic was about to hit. Long before the arrival of C-19, we were already examining the interconnected Travel, Tourism, and Hospitality industries and their ecosystems of suppliers, measuring their *React versus Respond* quotients both as a business sector and within individual companies. With so much rapid technological, social, and political change taking place around the space, we were already questioning "yesterday." Was the industry even keeping up (**adapting**), let alone moving ahead (**innovating**)? Are today's business leaders even aware of the need to adapt to maintain a competitive edge and to foster innovation, and if so, do they know how to go about it?

Sean's T5 Strategies had already been engaged in assisting companies to assess the *Response versus React* quotients in their organizations within the previous "normal" realm of business doings. Glenn's *No Vacancy* podcast guests were already talking about what was going on in the world of TT&H, pondering the industry's ability (or too often lack thereof) to look beyond its own backyard for inspiration. C-19 then added a new, urgent impetus to business strategic planning and daily operations. Suddenly, "adapters" and those who can compile their strategies are in hot demand.

So, in the pre-pandemic TT&H environment, what observations kept coming up in conversations with Gutsy Genius Thinkers, as well as in our own musings? Some noted a disturbing inability for some to see the interconnectedness of our industry's occupants, or worse yet, to view other players within the ecosystem as enemies, rather than allies. Others saw col-

leagues and competitors clinging to a potentially dangerous belief in their own position on the industry ladder, and still others observed in the industry a state of inertia that can be caused—*believe it or not!*—by long-term success.

<table>
<tr><td>

"Sacred cows
make the best
hamburger."

Bob Hecht,
Transformist

</td><td>

***GGT* Mitch Presnick,** founder and CEO of
ROOM Technology Ventures, explains the situation
like this: "Once an organization gets to a certain size,
[they think] it's not in their interest to innovate, because
to innovate, they're disrupting themselves."

</td></tr>
</table>

The "hole in the candy"

Even before the devastation of the C-19 Effect, one of the major
supposed "constants" that Travel, Tourism, and Hospitality took for
granted was already feeling the squeeze of change: *"Of course, tourist
destinations, particularly major cities, will always serve as a bedrock for
the industry!"* was the mantra of many in TT&H and pretty much
how they conducted their operations.

Smaller and suburban communities will certainly share in the
economic suffering that follows in the wake of C-19, but it's the
recent shifts in the dynamics of city living that may make today's
urban areas even more vulnerable as the COVID Effect takes hold.
As **Chris Holer,** a successful property investor friend, put it:

> *"The ring around the cities is surviving, while the core of the
> city is emptying and dying like a candy with a hole, hollowed
> out and half as sweet."*

We have all experienced the hustle and bustle of "the city." In the
case of tourist-magnet cities like New York, Orlando, San Francisco,
London, Paris, Venice, Madrid, and Barcelona, it turns out that the
*hustle was being disproportionately generated by tourists rather than
natives.*

With a population of about 1.7 million in 2019, Barcelona
accommodated 2.7 million passengers disembarking from some
800 cruise ships in their port that year. More than 47 million
travelers were recorded that same year at the city's El Prat Airport,
and more than 9 million made overnight stays in the city. It's no

wonder that the TT&H-ers who ply their trades in Barcelona and its environs never imagined an end to the boom times. Read any travel magazine or Trip Advisor review from pre-COVID, and you will see that Barcelona consistently ranked as one of the world's top tourist destinations.

But for years prior to COVID, Barcelona and Madrid had already seen their citizens begin moving out of the city center to local barrios (neighborhoods/suburbs) as developers and brands moved in to meet the demands of booming tourism. Rents soon skyrocketed beyond what many non-branded hotels, restaurants, and bars—and the staff that run them—could afford.

Ok. That's "The Way We Were." Where are we now?

Today isn't looking too good

We now know that the travel, tourism, restaurant, airline, and hospitality space, as well as retail, have been hammered by the effects and the restrictions of the pandemic. By all accounts and according to Nicolas Graf, Associate Dean, Jonathan M. Tisch Center of Hospitality, the Hospitality Business School, NYU, the recovery to stability "could take until 2024" and may never truly be achieved in most countries without substantial government support.

Chip Rogers, president and CEO of the American Hotel and Lodging Association (AHLA):

"We are incredibly worried what the drop in demand will mean for the industry and the millions of employees we have been unable to bring back. The job loss will be devastating to our industry, our communities, and the overall American economy. We need urgent bipartisan action from Congress now." September 2020

> Rogers recently indicated that more than eight thousand hotels could close in September if business travel does not pick up and funding from the Paycheck Protection Program runs out. According to AHLA, only 20 percent of hotels have received any debt relief from commercial mortgage-backed security lenders on Wall Street. Without aid from Congress, the industry association expects massive foreclosures.

The traditional platforms that arguably drove demand during crises over the last twenty years, such as Booking and Expedia, are themselves struggling. So, what do they do? Up their game to drive share of wallet and market share!

What is interesting is that Booking's merchandising algorithms and add-on offerings have improved considerably. Since the start of the pandemic, in an effort to drive basket size, they have enhanced pop-ups with upgrades for room types with detailed side-by-side comparisons. Rentals United (with GGT **Vanessa de Souza Lage** on board) has become the information center for best-practice sourcing for alternative accommodations and experiences. As a channel manager,[18] https://www.youtube.com/watch?v=_nFVXaiSoAE https://rentalsunited.com/ Rentals United makes it easier for businesses to connect with distribution platforms such as Booking, Expedia, Agoda, and so on.

The airline industry has already reduced capacity by 50 percent or more. United Airlines recently announced that the company will fly at 50 percent capacity until a vaccine has been widely distributed—possibly as far out as 2022 or 2023! Marriott announced that 17 percent of its corporate staff will not return to work, and thousands of others face the same consequence. Cruise ship lines, furniture manufacturers, restaurants, event venues, and the learning institutions that support these industries have all been affected.

For context, in 2019, there were five thousand airlines globally, based on ICOA codes,[19] https://www.youtube.com/watch?v=t1jhFOJTrwE that ferried over 4.5 billion passengers. In 2004, 1.9 billion flight seats were occupied. Astonishingly, by 2019, 4.7 billion human butts were hurtling through our skies. That's over half of today's global population of 7.8 billion people! (Sept 2020 Worldometer)[20]. Now consider all the freight and bags that were jammed in there, too. No wonder the 25 major[21] cities of the world were heaving!

Airlines reacted quickly to the C-19 Effect and reduced capacity. The next phase for them now is shrinking fixed overhead. It appears that they are adapting their Hub model and either eliminating entire routes and/or closing some hubs. This may help airlines survive but will certainly impact capacity to deliver that tourist or business traveler into the system.

Number of scheduled passengers boarded by the global airline industry from 2004 to 2021*(in millions)*

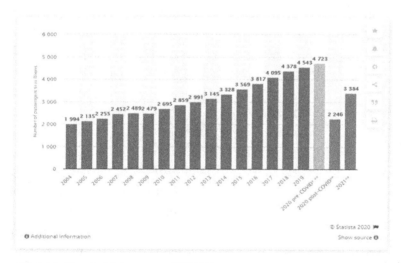

Global air traffic - scheduled passengers 2004-2021
Published by E. Mazareanu, Jun 10, 2020
In 2019, the number of scheduled passengers boarded by the global airline industry reached over 4.54 billion people.

BOX 5

Rank	City		Rank	City		Rank	City
1	Bali		11	Istanbul		21	Dubai
2	London		12	Jamaica		22	Grand Cayman
3	Paris		13	Hoi An		23	Kathmandu
4	Rome		14	St Petersburg		24	Bora Bora
5	New York		15	Roadtán		25	Cusco
6	Crete		16	Marrakech			
7	Barcelona		17	Ambergris Caye			
8	Siem Reap		18	Rio de Janeiro			
9	Prague		19	St Maarten			
10	Phuket		20	Playa del Carmen			

TripAdvisor's list of the TOP 25 Destinations

Source: The PointsGuy - Clare Lanaux, 2017

BOX 6

Timing is everything

So many have "expert" views on timing. For instance, on March 1, 2020, the *Financial Express* interviewed Vistara Airline's CEO, **Leslie Thng**, who said the [pandemic] *"would have a short-term impact on the aviation industry* and airlines need to remain flexible and nimble while dealing with the situation," while back in 2017, **Doug Parker**, CEO of American Airlines, famously told investors that given the structural improvements to the airline industry in recent years, *"I don't think we're ever going to lose money again"*(Motley Fool, Jan 2020). However, today, as one of the most dynamic leaders in the airline industry, Parker has predicted that it could take two to three years for the airline and tourism industry to return to some sort of normality—around 2024! In this, Graf and Parker are clear: it is going to be a long hard road to find stability and confidence again in the space and maybe make some profit.

> "Once you have tasted flight, you will forever walk the earth with your eyes turned skyward, for there you have been, and there you will always long to return."
>
> **Leonardo Da Vinci, GGT**

In a recent *Business Insider* piece, journalist David Slotnick noted, *"Corporate travel budgets are expected to be very constrained as companies continue to be under financial pressure even as the economy improves."* According to the International Association of Travel Agents (IATA), surveys indicate that the link between GDP growth and business travel has frayed, as videoconferencing makes in-person meetings less necessary.

IATA's revised timeline represents the beginning of a new wave of pessimism from airlines about the travel recovery and forecasts a similar recovery window of late 2023 to 2024. This sounds ominously similar to the protracted 2007 financial crisis.

In the early months of the pandemic, many carriers suggested a two- to three-year time frame for recovery. One exception was Southwest Airlines CEO Gary Kelly, who offered a five-year timetable in April. *"Based on history, in a recessionary environment, it is a long recovery period for businesses,"* Kelly said on his first-quarter earnings call. *"This one feels like it could be worse."*

With a "second COVID wave" now racing across many countries and regions that thought they were finally out of the pandemic woods, (and there's already talk of a possible *third wave* in the spring of 2021 and variant, more transmissible virus strains being discovered) some of those timelines will probably have to be rethought— again! At the time of this writing, restrictions and lockdowns have been reintroduced in Great Britain, Ireland, France, Spain, and elsewhere. The more disruption, the heavier the economic and social toll. Curfews from 10:00 p.m. to 6:00 a.m. and stay-in-your-own-municipality orders are now the norm here in Barcelona. Our friend in France can't make his usual visit to us. The border between the two countries is open—but the restriction on his side to stay within 50 kilometers of home means the border is out of reach. And even where movement between borders is allowed, pricey COVID PCR tests, onerous paperwork and difficult-to-achieve timeframes to produce the lot, make travel a near impossibility for many.

As the cliché goes, **"Rules are made to be broken."** (And are too often for the lazy to hide behind, was General Douglas MacArthur's addition.) The conventions of economics, fiscal tools, and political policy are being heavily tested. As a result of Band-Aid fiscal triage to ensure the survival and short-term well-being of countries' populations, we have seen an odd suspension of reality. *While these financial injections and numerous recovery schemes have allowed us to survive long enough to breathe and learn, nothing has been solved.*

Earlier we noted that the AHLA[22] https://www.ahla.com/ predicts in a recent November 2020 survey that, without government assistance, there is a chance that 71 percent of hotels won't survive for another six months without further government COVID relief. (At the beginning of 2020, there were about 57,000 hotels across the US. Up to 38,000 are at high-risk for potential closure.)

Northstar Meetings Group reported as of November 5, 2020, "The states of California and Florida have been particularly hard hit—with hotel-related job losses as of September numbering more than 234,000 and nearly 173,000, respectively. Without additional aid from Congress, those numbers are predicted to climb to nearly 470,000 in California and more than 336,000 in Florida."

Those are numbers that are hard to fathom. This will cause a massive displacement of employees, with an attendant ripple effect. Add others facing similar displacement like the airline industry, convention and catering services, tour operators, etc., into the equation, and the numbers and potential damage are almost incalculable. However, China appears to be recovering much faster, with major brands reporting markets returning to reasonable capacities. There is hope!

We may well be facing a new economic collapse as unsustainable government subsidies, like payroll protection schemes in various countries, come to an end. We will eventually learn exactly where the foundations of society are stable enough—and where they are not. Fiscal rules had to be broken, and governments and their institutions, for the most part, rose to the occasion to buy society time, funding vaccine research at an unprecedented scale. But we will soon be faced with how to put those broken bits of society and industry back into a sustainable whole.

> *"Hope is seeing light in spite of being surrounded by darkness."*
>
> ***anon***

Throughout the pandemic, the United Nations World Tourism Organization (WTO) has continued highlighting the severe economic impact the COVID shutdown has had on GDP, employment, and the like. Striking statistics include the potential loss of 197 million jobs and $5.5 trillion in travel and tourism-related gross domestic product due to prolonged travel restrictions. In addition, the US may lose $155 billion in 2020 from the loss of international visitors. The picture is bad, and the WTO has helped show just how bad it is.

A report from the *Wall Street Journal* suggests 20 percent of New York state's total hotel supply (about two hundred and fifty thousand rooms) could close permanently. Hospitality data provider STR expects US hotel demand will not fully recover until 2023.

The rest of Europe reflects a similar trend, while China is performing relatively better with reopening. STR also reported that occupancies ranged from 18.5 to 57 percent in China for July 2020, with an upward trajectory over the previous months. Nevertheless, this remained their worst July on record.

All these numbers represent real people that spend, and, at present, a only a fraction of those people are on the move.

Drinking from the firehose

Right now, liquidity is certainly a challenge. Very few news outlets and authors have spoken about the pending liquidity crisis that we may well face from Q2 forward in 2021. Nick Corbishley of WolfStreet.com wrote, *"If the situation of generalized panic continues, thousands of businesses, especially small ones, will first enter a liquidity crisis, then close their doors."*

The importance of cashflow management

"The pandemic was a disaster for Stasher's revenues. Fortunately, we run a lean organisation, and we're asset light. I'm proud of how quickly we went into crisis mode, slashing all surplus expenditure. Our burn rate has never been this low since we took on VC funding back in 2018."[and utilized a 13-week cash flow approach]

Jacob Wedderburn-Day, GGT
Cofounder and CEO, Stasher.com

Corbishley's prediction is highly likely to be proven correct, as the Association of Bankers in the US noted that bankruptcy filings were already up by 27 percent year-over-year in July/August 2020, and the worst may yet be around the corner. CMBS loans (commercial mortgage-backed securities[b])[23] https://www.youtube.com/watch?v=oosYQHq2hwE are a vehicle to mortgage hotels, multifamily apartments, or properties.

According to Lindsey Wright, senior managing director, asset management, at Greystone & Co., when interviewed on HNN on July 10, 2020, *"CMBS loan servicers are drinking from the fire hose now."* She added that her company has been overrun with different types of requests over the last few months.

Based on the data above, we may be facing a deluge of defaults across all categories of asset ownership. This situation is magnified by the number of leases much of the broader Travel, Tourism, Hospitality, airlines, and rental car space holds. There is little public

---

[b]   CMBS are fixed-income investment products that are backed by mortgages on commercial properties rather than residential real estate. CMBS can provide liquidity to real estate investors and commercial lenders alike.

information on this. T5 Strategies' client interactions indicate the problem appears acute. Unlike an owned asset, where a "work-out" or forbearance (possibly deferring interest to the back end of the loan) is an option, leases and rents, even if deferred, become due immediately once the rent deferral period ends.[24] https://www.youtube.com/ watch?v=yxIh6-8KUHc

Leased and rented assets such as hotels and serviced apartments (SAs) all are facing this dilemma. It must be noted that generally, at the front end of COVID, SAs had higher occupancy in the 50–60 percent range and up to 20 percent higher than hotels. The SAs may be able to weather this storm better than hotels due to longer-term stays and the ability of their occupants to maintain social distancing in the work/life environment of the serviced apartment. For example, London serviced apartment occupancy stood at 61.8 percent for Q1 2020, down 21.5 percent compared to Q1 2019 as COVID-19 started to take hold in March. Hotels reported a larger decline of 23.0 percent over the same period, with average occupancy at 59.4 percent according to STR.[25] https://str.com/

The key action for operators was/is managing liquidity and working with banks and landlords to secure deferral, rent-free periods, turn over rents, and/or forbearance to save a mass exodus of these assets. Some headline examples are malls and large shopping centers offering limited openings to try to stay afloat, with rents oftentimes not being paid at all by tenants.

This period could leave communities in dire straits since many hotels and landmark local eateries act like shopping mall anchor stores[26] within their locales, and those retail centers, already suffering losses pre-pandemic, are now under serious threat. According to the US National Retail Federation, the average mall[27] https://nrf.com/ supports five to eight other businesses as the anchors drive foot traffic (circulating shoppers). CNBC reported on September 22, 2020, that Brookfield and Simon Properties, both significant mall operators and owners, have laid off 20 percent and 30 percent of their workforces, respectively, due to the reduction in foot traffic and rent payment defaults. An empty conference center leads to an empty convention hotel. It's not rocket science:

> *No food trucks, no shoeshine, no taxi services, no souvenirs, etc.*
> *= local suppliers and tradespeople at risk*
> *= higher local unemployment*

The cat food conundrum

Supply chains have also been impacted, with everything from electronic equipment to canned goods being delayed. Case in point. My wife loves tuna fish (Yuck!), and our cat loves a certain brand of wet cat food. Neither item has been easy to find of late. We have been on scavenger hunts to grocery stores  and pet supply shops to find enough of either to hoard. (You can keep your toilet paper. We will trade you for a can of Poesie cat food, beef flavor, mousse style!)

We finally asked a number of these retailers just what was the problem. Turns out that the contents of the tins can be found without a problem. It's the tins themselves that are becoming scarce as materials run short and as factories have shut down or been forced to operate on reduced hours and staff levels. Now take that response and think about other items that may become harder and harder to find.

We asked GGT **Mitch Patel**, President & CEO, Vision Hospitality Group, for his take on the supply chain issue.

> Yeah, there's definitely a challenge there. I talked with my fellow hotel development companies and they are having similar challenges…FFE (furniture, fixtures, and equipment)…

and sheetrock; hotels use a lot of that. A lot of these products come from outside the US, specifically China [and are getting harder and harder to source]. Fortunately, in the last few years, we bought a lot elsewhere. We wanted to diversify, because this is not the first time we're dealing with this. Remember the strikes? But it could be tariffs too. There's always something to disrupt the supply chain. I think we'll get some delays on some of our hotels, but unfortunately, yes, there is going to be an impact on the supply chain.

Many of our GGTs share the belief that supply chain disruption could become a serious threat, especially if C-19 and its effects linger, but some, like Mitch, had already been addressing this danger. Good planning!

The domino effect

Let's broaden the definition of "supply" for a moment. The major hotel chains are dependent on franchisees building and opening new hotels to fuel their pipelines. Although existing projects appear to be moving along, many new projects have slowed or stopped. There are approximately 600,000 rooms in the USA pipeline (LE-Lodging Econometrics July 30, 2020, as reported in Hotel News Network).

Interestingly, analysts at Lodging Econometrics report that at the close of the first quarter of 2020, Europe's hotel construction pipeline expanded to near-record highs with 1,840 projects and 294,047 rooms, a 10 percent increase in projects, and a 15 percent increase in rooms, year-over-year (YOY). (June 4 Hospitality.net).

Although pipelines are strong, the real net growth is far from predictable—and there has been rising tension between asset owners and franchisors.

As GGT and featured Adapter **Paul Slattery** of Otus Advisory put it, "If I'm a franchisee at the moment, my hotel is shut up. What are the good reasons why I should pay franchise fees to franchise all for nothing, right?"

Paul believes, "Two out of the five big hotel franchisors need to consolidate, and the three major contract-catering companies should do the same." He went on to reference the cruise industry and predicted, "The cruise ship industry, given what has happened with them, will probably take longer for them to combine than anyone else, but should."

This is putting pressure on the current investor, asset manager, management company, franchisee/franchisor system to question itself. Who is driving value? The asset owner or the franchisor?

Insights - Key Contributor

Leading Hospitality Brand

The Adapters comment: Radisson Hotel Group certainly had to adapt during a time of crashing demand and a travel industry on its knees. As a large hotel group, they are competing with the likes of IHG, Marriott, Wyndham and others in a super competitive landscape. Their approach has a high degree of Brand Emotional and Practical intelligence as they "reimagine" the future of the hotel market and hotel branding. Learn more about how Radisson is responding versus reacting.

"Radisson Hotel Group is one of the world's largest and most dynamic hotel groups with seven distinctive hotel brands with more than 1,100 hotels in destinations around the world. Our portfolio of hotel brands includes Radisson Collection, Radisson Blu, Radisson, Radisson RED, Park Plaza, Park Inn by Radisson and Country Inn & Suites by Radisson."

Jim Alderman
CEO, The Americas
Radisson Hotel Group
Minnetonka, MN USA

Market: What segments of the market does Radisson focus on and why?

Radisson Hotel Group in the Americas is focused on upper-upscale, upscale, mid-scale select service, and the more reasonably priced end of the limited-service market.

Problem: What gap in the market do you think Radisson is aiming to address in the next 2-3 years?

We have specifically kept our brand offerings narrowed to one brand per segment, so we do not offer similarly priced rooms that are +/– $5-10 in RevPAR but drawing from the same reservation system and customer base. We hope as the recovery takes hold, owners will recognize the clarity of not competing within their chosen brand family. Additionally, we plan to re-adapt our Park Inn brand to accept well located and exceptionally operated exterior corridor hotels. That segment has been abandoned by most of the larger global major hotel companies, and with 500,000 rooms in the US exterior corridor inventory, we see a huge opportunity.

Obstacles: What obstacles do you expect the Company to face in the next 2-3 years and why?

The existential threat to the industry, not just Radisson Hotel Group, is the unknown timing or tactical path that AirBnB, Google, and/or Amazon choose when it comes to entering the hotel market in a different manner. Should any or all choose to become that direct booking engine, it will be a problem. They have the eyeballs. I think with the new administration, if they lean towards forcing a Ma-Bell type of break-up of the behemoths of Google or Amazon, it will accelerate this eventuality. After all, the maxim "excess profit breeds ruinous competition" might never be so easily applied when the ease of entry due to the technological and marketing dominance, along with the sheer financial power of those three entities, is so absolute, in comparison to almost all global major hotel companies combined.

The other primary obstacle I see for our Company is continuing to stay on the absolute cutting edge of technology and everything related to the IT infrastructure. **We have no choice but to continue to spend for security, but that is table stakes.** The complexity and rampant evolution of our IT functions in the hotel industry make it an imperative to keep pace, and it is a huge impact on operating margins.

You just cannot ever see to get to a place where your *
CRS, RMS, GDS, and the other four major platforms are all
bleeding edge at the same time. An emerging technology
that is demonstrably better than existing systems seems to
emerge in our space, almost quarterly.

**Adaptions: What are the 3-5 major Adaptions you made
to your business to stay relevant? What was the result?**

We have not had an extraordinary amount of time as
a new team at Radisson Hotel Group to do everything
we have planned given the current climate of a global
pandemic. However, this does present an opportunity to
assess how to best emerge stronger.

1. The first thing we are doing is a re-imagining of
    Park Inn in the Americas. I think the pandemic has
    highlighted that exterior corridor properties have
    a place in the future of hospitality. We have come
    up with a conversion package to radically change
    our Park Inn brand to expand with exterior corridor
    properties.

2. The second area we are tackling is to improve
    the ROI for our powerhouse brand, Country Inn
    and Suites. We need to improve the cost model,
    starting with the 'bricks and sticks.' We are using
    a great deal of the advances made in our other
    theaters, especially in China and throughout
    greater APAC, to reduce the size of the hotel and
    increase the revenue-producing areas. Size is the
    only variable that dramatically changes your cost
    model. Drywall, concrete, steel, and wood-framing
    are commodities that cost the same for everyone.
    It is only by rationalizing the size of our offering to
    exactly what our target guests need and what they
    will pay for that we will improve our ROI for owners.

3. The last thing we will be adapting in the next year is a complete overhaul of our IT platform. We currently operate on architecture named for the founder of Radisson called 'Curtis-C.' It was revolutionary technology when it was introduced in 1999. Can you possibly even imagine the amount of annual investment it takes to keep 1990's era technology relevant and functional today? We are making those investments every year, but it is time to embrace the full-scale overhaul and re-platform for the future. We are working with the leading technology providers to build a best-in-class suite of technology beginning next year.

Perspective: What are the 3-5 issues that you feel the Hospitality Industry should address in the next 2-4 years?

1. We need to improve how we showcase our inventory. With the availability of technology, there is no reason a guest should not be able to see the inside of their exact room choice, the view from the window, the situation of the hotel and the precise location on the street as well as exactly where the closest restaurants and attractions all are and what they have to offer. We all do bits and pieces of this now, but there is such a more natural flow that can be integrated into our main landing pages for hotel booking.

2. **I think the industry needs to embrace a better labor model** where the rewards of property success flow through to everyone, on a reasonable basis, within the hotel. All owners do an annual budget and set financial performance targets they intend to achieve. Every employee at the hotel has a hand in

the success or failure of achieving that budget. The global impact of this pandemic, more than anything ever before, has highlighted the essential front-line workers. One of my mentors and an early boss of mine, Lew Miller, had a terrific performance-based operating model that provided for bonuses for all hotel personnel. While it might not be completely applicable for all hotels or owners, it certainly aligns a team to focus on the guest experience and the hotel's performance.

3.   We also need to find an effective balance between convenience, efficiency, and security. Our industry struggles as one of the unfortunate destinations for human trafficking. We all, as hoteliers, stand united against this horrific crime, and each of us have taken extraordinary measures to continually combat the issue of trafficking. However, as we all rush headlong towards contactless check-in and electronic check-in, I for one am not convinced that bypassing the front desk is always going to be the best course of action. There is nothing like having an eye-to-eye personal interaction with a guest to facilitate the personal experience of hospitality. It is at these key moments where we also have the ability for trained front desk personnel to have a sort of 'gut-check' to make sure that everything is above-board with the guest they are registering. No one wants or expects our front desk agents to be Sherlock Holmes; however, our colleagues, generally, have such a deeply developed level of experience interacting with the traveling public that they can often spot when something is not right. Being able to bypass that key interaction is something I see as potentially problematic if not handled properly.

What are some of the technologies/other industry trends that you believe the Hospitality space should embrace?

Innovative in-room technology that already exists should be deployed more robustly throughout all segments of the hotel industry, including motion or thermal detection, to regulate in-room HVAC controls and save energy. Low-flow plumbing and water-saving technology should be more widespread. Constant recirculating fresh air is certainly on the mind of all the traveling public after the pandemic.

What are the 3-5 Adaptions or Innovations that have caught your attention that you feel should be incorporated into the Hotel space and why?

I feel like there should be more blending of consumer/retail brands in the hotel space. Consumers' affinity for retail brands and emerging trends could be and should be able to be translated into hotel space much faster. Sometimes our industry is one of the slowest to adapt to new trends.

What consumer trends are catching your attention and why?

Number one would be influencer-based marketing. You do not see the level of engagement throughout social media platforms with hotels as you do with consumer brands. When a celebrity or pseudo-celebrity who became famous purely on social platforms can sell a half million units of a product with a 60-second endorsement, why are we not leaning into this phenomenon as hoteliers?

What are the 3-5 major key learnings/failures that propelled your personal growth/thinking?

1. The first would be that you cannot stay on top, as a hotel brand, without constant re-investment

and re-invention/innovation, which might include wholesale change of your operating model or brand offering. The brand leaders of today are not entirely the same as the brand leaders of 20 years ago. Given the massive level of capital investment in securing a site and building a hotel or buying an existing hotel, you would think that the ability to stay a leader within your market would be easier if you have selected the right brand partner and/or operator. **Brands should be able to adapt better vs. simply inventing a new brand to bring change** when you identify changing market conditions or realities. As we keep inventing new brands, we tend to relegate older ones to become less desirable. Why not follow a better consumer model where we re-invent older brands versus leaving so many of them to eventually go fallow? That is the direction we are following at Radisson Hotel Group as we learn from our experience around the world to adapt our brands.

2. Additionally, today you never underestimate the power and speed of changing consumer sentiment. Unfortunately, hotels are extremely expensive to completely renovate and re-tool to keep up with today's shorter attention span when it comes to design and expectation. However, we can quickly adapt how our staff interacts and changes the guest journey both digitally before arrival and during their stay, as well as with the post-stay interaction.

3. As far as personal choices or failures that have propelled me forward, I would probably say a lack of patience. I have had 14 different jobs in the industry or parallel industries such as real estate or lending. My desire to advance has probably been

as much of a detriment in the long-term analysis as it has been a benefit. I have had the good fortune to work for the same person or company more than a few times at different points in my career. However, jumping to the next best thing too soon has also cost me a great deal financially and from some interesting missed opportunities. I have followed more of a millennial path than that of a boomer (I was born in the last 'boomer' year), and I get restless when I feel like I can find a better use of my talents in a different position or organization.

What were the best practices that lead to your success?

The primary things that account for my success to date would be that I remain highly accessible to our customers, and I am constantly networking. I am still in relatively close contact with all the key people that have influenced me from my first job out of college and before that with professors from my University and classmates in my real estate major. I make myself available to our owners and franchisees and return every email or phone call from them. Additionally, I try and always give credit to my colleagues and teammates for everything we accomplish as a team. I believe strongly that allowing others to be recognized for their contributions says more about a person than the accomplishment itself. I would rather deflect the spotlight from myself to illuminate others. You will be rewarded with loyalty and commitment. However, when it comes to accepting responsibility for failures, I view that as a singular issue. I share credit but not blame. I learned some lessons very early in life from my mother, who was a multi-sport coach, that only players with teamwork win, but losses belong to the coach. Very rarely will you witness singular accomplishments or lone-fought victories in our industry. Even professional golfers have caddies, coaches, and sponsors.

*CRS/GDS - **Computer reservation systems**, or **central reservation systems** (**CRS**), are computerized systems used to store and retrieve information and conduct transactions related to air travel, hotels, car rental, or other activities. Originally designed and operated by airlines, CRSs were later extended for use by travel agencies and global distribution systems (GDS) to book and sell tickets for multiple airlines. Most airlines have outsourced their CRSs to GDS companies, which also enable consumer access through internet gateways. Modern GDSs typically also allow users to book hotel rooms, rental cars, airline tickets, as well as other activities and tours. They also provide access to railway reservations and bus reservations in some markets, although these are not always integrated with the main system. These are also used to relay computerized information for users in the hotel industry, making reservations and ensuring that the hotel is not overbooked.

Linkedin@ https://www.linkedin.com/in/jim-alderman-7422aa6/

Company@ https://www.radissonhotels.com/en-us/

Cities under siege

Now that many cities have far fewer tourists (cruise ships were banned entirely from Barcelona Port when the country's lockdown began on March 14, 2020, and the restriction has been indefinitely extended as of November 2020), their city vibes have practically vanished in many cases, leaving the centers to seriously become the "hole

in the candy." It's an acknowledgment of the power of COVID's punch that the virus could turn Barcelona's famed main promenade, Las Ramblas, into a virtual ghost walk at times; even the 2017 terrorist attack on that street couldn't stifle its vibrant attraction for long. It may be nice to get into Barcelona's Sagrada Familia, or the Prado museum in Madrid or the Louvre in Paris without waiting in a two-hour queue, but there are also far fewer cafés or restaurants to enjoy before or after the cultural experiences and city activities, and virtually no live performances like concerts, flamenco shows, or Broadway or West End theater productions to improve the situation.

> *"The skillful leader subdues the enemy's troops without any fighting."*
>
> **Sun Tzu**

It is reasonable to assume that many countries around the world will have proportional closures and foreclosures as a result of the erosion of travel and its byproducts.

Now consider the implications of Work from Home (WFH), and the problem is compounded as companies close urban headquarters and hubs and workers flee the city centers and industrial complexes for the office in their spare bedroom or down in the basement.

Since the coronavirus struck, there has been significant demand for homes outside the cities. Who wouldn't prefer to be in lockdown with at least a small garden for relief? Who doesn't worry that the very density of the inner city might make you an easier target for virus-laden droplets? City life, the center of opportunity for thousands of years, is now being questioned, looked at with a new suspicion, and as a result, home sales are posting record numbers.

"Not since 2004 has the number of home sales been this high during the month of October in our Northern Virginia footprint," says Nicholas Lagos, 2020 president of the Northern Virginia Association of Realtors® (NVAR). "And for the first time since April 2016, the number of monthly active listings has reflected a year-over-year increase. Realtors® in the NVAR region sold nearly $1.5 billion dollars in real estate for the second month running in October, a 42.53 percent increase over October 2019." This represents 2,220 homes sold, which is the highest number of homes sold in the NVAR region in 16 years.

Similar trends have occurred in the United Kingdom and Ireland. Even the sluggish property market in Spain has seen a bit of an uptick since the strictest portion of the national lockdown has eased.

This is not a new phenomenon in the scheme of the historical timeline. Plagues, social unrest, and even crime rates have caused a similar exodus from the more densely populated places throughout the course of history, but again, this is all new for *us*. For many of us, it's a complete reversal of what we have experienced in our lifetimes, where the revitalization of inner cities was the norm as demand for an in-town, low-commute lifestyle grew.

Add another twelve months or more to deliver a vaccine that covers most of the globe, and it might be that some cities will struggle to ever regain that same vibe.

While the migration from urban settings may be looking grim, we're going to leave those cities to fend for themselves for just a moment, but we will check in on them again soon!

Even as country after country enacts border shutdowns and entry restrictions, C-19 has actually proven that we are globally interdependent. As we've shown, the travel sector is a major contributor to the GDP of most countries. Governments are stretched; businesses have essentially stopped their employees

> "ALERT! ALERT!
> Tomorrow is
> Monday again.
> QUICK! Run…
> FAST."
>
> **The Minions**

from traveling; and with so many fewer airplanes in the air, it is reasonable to fear that many innovative ideas may never see the light of day if we cannot meet in person. Inspiration is often sparked when your mind is at ease with a golf club in hand, enjoying a beer, engaged in some other leisure activity, or meeting casually with friends or work associates.

 Sitting in a meeting room surrounded by peers and following the agenda is not always the ideal setting to ignite the innovation spark. Travel enables "workcations," and a great night's sleep in a Heavenly Bed (Westin) may release those brilliant ideas. More than likely, the multitude of distractions associated with your Work from Home (WFH) efforts, coupled with possible family and financial concerns and the learning curve we are all adjusting to in this new environment, might easily impede our path toward innovation brilliance.

But the TT&H tribe have proven resilient over the years— they know how to overcome adversity.

Glenn and I LOVE this space and celebrate that our global clan are a positive, optimistic, and adaptable bunch. We have lived the "Best and Worst of times"—and we're still here.

Scribble Zone: *Jot down the gaps that are in your business strategy. Are you ignoring growing "holes" at its center?*

_____

_____

_____

_____

_____

_____

_____

_____

_____

_____

_____

_____

_____

_____

_____

_____

_____

_____

_____

_____

_____

Gutsy Genius Thinker
Cait Noone
Head Galway International Hotel School
Vice President International
Engagement, GMIT, Ireland

Cait is known in her community as a powerhouse promoter of Travel, Tourism, Hospitality, and the Arts. Prior to arriving in Galway, she was the Dean of Les Roches Jin Jiang International, the first international hotel management school in China, with stints at Les Roches, Switzerland, and other educational institutions around the world. Like many of our GGTs, she gives back to her community and represents the University on the Galway 2020 Steering Committee and the Galway European Region of Gastronomy Steering Committee. With her participation, Galway earned the European Capital of Culture in 2020 designation. She also volunteers her time towards tackling community issues.

We checked in with Cait recently and learned that her university, and indeed the entire Irish higher education sector, are adapting the delivery of curriculum due to fall out of C-19. In addition, GMIT is working with global partners in Canada, China, and South Africa to co-develop programmes that will support local tourism enterprises while also providing mobility opportunities for students and faculty.

In a recent interview with the _Irish Times_, recalling her early days as a hotel receptionist, Noone says, "I liked the industry, but I found aspects of it quite difficult. In the late 1980s in Ireland, the industry was very male dominated at managerial level, and I didn't see many opportunities available for young women to progress their careers." Fast-forward, and approximately 51 percent in the Travel space are female, but with a continued imbalance on

Boards and in senior leadership roles. Cait and many others are driving the space to evolve rapidly.

"It's not about showing up; it's what you do when you are there that makes the difference."

Cait Noone

Adaption Tips

- Educators must be innovation nurturers.
- Diversity matters—Be a change Leader to ensure that your teams represent the make-up of your community and customer base.
- Social and communication skills must evolve faster to thrive—hunt and find mentors to help develop those skills.
- Be a lifelong learner or become extinct.
- Business leadership, both style and skills, will have to change dramatically to adapt to the C-19 aftermath.
- Every level in a business must influence the culture—workplace culture reflects the effort of all employees.

LinkedIn profile @ www.linkedin.com/in/cait-noone-fihi-a2aa32b/
Company @ https://www.gmit.ie/

Take the time to learn more

Click or use SmartPhone

Gutsy Genius Thinker
Raul Leal
CEO, Virgin Hotels
Miami, Florida

Developing a well-recognized hotel brand that has a wide range of disparate brand affiliates from trains, planes, and spacecraft could have been a nightmare. As Raul said, "We didn't want a big red box Virgin Hotel." The end result was a design that could transform over time, that is a comfortable place to hang out, with technology taking a role but not dominating the experience. Richard Branson noted during a visit that there was a "lack of Virgin in your face," with a dash of red via a SMEG fridge in each room; essentially the essence of Virgin.

Adapting is nothing new to this GGT. As a first-generation Cuban immigrant, Raul developed his career in hospitality while he was based in Miami with Desires Hotels and Tecton Hospitality. "I have been fortunate to grow up through the ranks and eventually become a hotel owner, a partner in a progressive hotel management company, and now CEO and partner for one of the world's most progressive brands." Glenn and Sean interviewed Raul when C-19 was gaining momentum with a follow-up on Glenn's show "NoVacancy" in April 2020. Ever consistent, his perspective is long and positive that there are opportunities for the Virgin Hotel brand to grow as the property market is reshaped. Never miss an opportunity to *adapt* and take advantage.

Adaptation Tips

- If you have a different point of view on something, follow it through to the end and see if it's viable or not.

- Don't just focus on eliminating consumer dis-satisfiers—take time over the concept phase to develop something utterly unique.
- Don't nickel-and-dime the consumers. They always know they are being nickel-and-dimed.
- The devil is in the details. Consumers notice the details, and they know when you're paying attention.
- You can walk into a hotel and right away know if there is love in the hotel. "Love" is somebody taking care of the details.
- We need to think of the hospitality sector as an "experience," not just a commodity.

LinkedIn profile @ www.linkedin.com/in/lealraul/

Company @ www.virginhotels.com/

No Vacancy additional content about Raul - www.youtube.com/watch?v=JpkhzyVvwxQ

Take the time to learn more

Click or use SmartPhone

Gutsy Genius Thinker
Mitch Patel
President & CEO
Vision Hospitality
Chattanooga, Tennessee
U.S.A

It's been a tough year for Mitch and his family-owned business, founded in 1997. Vision owns and manages over 45 Hotels, with a further 9 under construction with multiple brand flags. Like most hoteliers, the start of the year looked like it was going to be another banner year, and then C-19 hit. He has had to lay off or furlough hundreds of their 1,600 employees. Based on his empathy for his team, this was obviously hard on so many levels. When we caught up with him, he was calm, positive, and optimistic that they could weather the tsunami that is COVID. Again, another common trait of a GGT: stay calm, think, and *Adapt*.

Culturally, they are clear on their Vision Values of Integrity, Respect, Excellence, Community, Teamwork, and Spirit. They are some of the few that make it clear publicly where they stand. We wish more companies would be that clear.

His company is branching out in other brands, such as ACE Hotels, to diversify, and is also developing an in-house brand (although these projects are on hold until they see a clear pathway forward). Even during these times, Mitch looks for inspiration. He admires the Chick-fil-A brand for building a loyal following. They treat their people and customers consistently well. He is an active voice in the Franchisee community to encourage the major Hotel Brands as a Franchisor to aim for simplicity. Simplicity, just like Chick-fil-A. "We have got to look outside the space for inspiration."

I (the author) have listened to Mitch on various industry panels, and he is a very polite thought agitator, promoting a dialogue to inspire others to be more entrepreneurial to drive evolution and adaption. Click through below and enjoy our interview with this GGT.

"Let's admit it. The hotel industry is slow to adapt."
Mitch Patel

Adaption Tips

- Look outside your comfort zone for inspiration.
- Culture matters—We wrote a book about our Culture (Vision).
- Number one is ensuring the team knows that they are appreciated and respected.
- It's not easy to be consistent; that is why it's worth doing.
- Meetings need to be short. We're all busy; get to the point; offer solutions and outcomes, and be optimistic.
- Simplify process—We have 18 different Apps to make our business work; far too many.

LinkedIn profile @ www.linkedin.com/in/mitul-patel-a8aa1213/

Company @ www.vhghotels.com/

Take the time to learn more

Click or use SmartPhone

CHAPTER 4

Looking Toward Tomorrow

Accentuate the positive

"You got to ac-cent-tchu-ate the positive, E-lim-i-nate the negative, And latch onto the affirmative; don't mess with Mr. In-Between."
Johnny Mercer and the Pied Pipers (1944)

Now is not the first time that employees and businesses have been stressed and stretched across the 4 Ages of Change (1944 was most assuredly a time when the future wasn't looking too bright), but it is the first for many of us—and that's all that really matters. It's *our* New Reality. The problem is *now,* and it is real. Stress can lead us to curl up and play the dangerous possum game, huddling in a ball until the danger goes away.

Unfortunately, *playing* dead in the business world can mean the real death of your business. It's not such a useful tactic in our personal lives, either. Thankfully, as our GGTs demonstrate—and as Johnny Mercer and his Pied Pipers sang—these problems and this time we live in can also serve to motivate us to *do*; to take action to find ways to adapt and innovate.

Believe it or not, there are some positives to be found in the admittedly daunting vision that many paint of the post-COVID world. For starters, there are some topics that are finally getting the airtime they deserve, like mental well-being—a subject once banished to the "let's not talk about it" zone. With so many experiencing symptoms of anxiety and depression as a result of the pandemic, mental health is now moving to "Let's talk about it on Zoom."

> *"Life is short. SMILE while you still have teeth."*
>
> **Not salmon**

I recently participated in a call hosted by HoCoSo Hospitality Consulting Solutions that dedicated time to this issue. Led by HoCoSo Cofounder and Chairman **Jonathan Humphries** and **Chris Mumford**, Head  Leadership Services, it was refreshing to hear a wide range of emerging experts speak to the stress levels being experienced by the Travel, Tourism, and Hospitality workforce and their fear of becoming part of the long-term unemployed. Speakers shared recommendations on how to chat with employees. Operational leaders spoke about holding Zoom calls with employees to meditate together and to be completely transparent about the state of the company, learning to strengthen, or even rebuild trust. They presented ideas that were not particularly expensive or taxing to already strained resources. Mostly all that's needed is a bit of time and the employment of some emotional intelligence. (A topic we will soon examine at length in chapter five.)

In addition, some sectors of the economy have actually thrived during the COVID era. Online commerce has plowed on as we order everything from food to furniture, all from the same desk that was delivered and set up by IKEA last week. (Talk about supply-chain problems! Try buying a desk today or a printer, a bicycle, or audio equipment. The list goes on, although I hear that toilet paper is back in stock!)

Adapting and innovating. It's the human story, and if there really is a constant left standing, this one is it. There *are* businesses adapting quickly to manage their workforces in offices and homes offline. Many companies have already taken advantage of replacing employee functions with robots and artificial intelligence to increase efficiency—sadly, hugely impactful for many.

Coach the Team

In the case of the COVID Effect, the disruption revealed structural as well as temporary gaps and weaknesses. As in other periods of change, the 4th Age of Change demands that people stand up and adapt, embrace the opportunities, and do more than fill the gaps—*fix them!* Not all leaders are built for such protracted periods of adaptation and innovation. The challenge to boards and investors is to be brave enough to make the required "updates." Sports teams do this all the time; they build teams around a point in time, against current and anticipated competitors versus their legacy. Think about the American football team, the New England Patriots. They let Tom Brady, their legacy quarterback, leave the team for another NFL franchise.

In spite of winning a record six Super Bowl championships during Brady's tenure, the Patriots decided to let their legendary team leader depart, choosing to focus on building a new team for the future. They are feeling the pain this season, but they know they must pivot in order to position themselves for another run at sustained success. That's also how Liverpool F.C. won the 2020 Premier League under a dynamic and agile-thinking Adapter, Jurgen Klopp. As the new manager of Liverpool F.C., he focused on the future and built his strategy and team to win. In the words of world-renowned football/soccer coach José Mourinho[28], "you coach teams to win, not individuals."

Some hotel companies, cruise ship operators, and others have centralized many accounting and back-office functions across their portfolios, thus reducing employees, while some hotels, restaurants, and the Big Red Tour Buses have been parked or closed. Hospitality is not alone. Many other industries have done the same in their respective sectors. As painful as this is, technology and a demand drop have an effect, possibly long-term. The irony here is that C-19 enabled this to change so quickly, especially in a sector that, as **GGT Prof. *Peter O'Connor of ESSEC Business School, Paris,*** puts it, "frequently suffers from organizational inertia." Some of the changes come with real pain, but they also promote new growth, and sometimes even a more tantalizing landscape.

Gutsy Genius Thinker
Peter O'Connor, PhD.
Chaired Professor of Digital Disruption
at ESSEC Business School
Paris, France

Peter is a world-renowned expert on e-commerce and online marketing. He has over thirty years' experience in educating the managers of tomorrow. As you might expect from a GGT, he is sought-after as a speaker at industry events, where he specializes in challenging companies' inaction regarding the digital revolution. I have seen Peter at his best, asking the tough questions on stage, challenging many of the leaders across the Travel, Tourism, and Hospitality space to justify their digital approach to revenue generation and automation. He knows no fear. To compete at similar speeds with other industries, ours needs that level of clarity and energy to drive Adaption and Innovation.

His insightful views into the effect of "operational inertia" in businesses (a tendency to do nothing or to remain unchanged) inspired us to label this term as the "POC Filter." This notion is explored in chapter four—"Looking Toward Tomorrow."

According to "Google Scholar," Professor O'Connor has been cited 6,874 times because of his prolific publishing through books, academic and industry-focused articles, and his Coursera MOOCs (Massive Open Online Courses through Coursera, a large online learning network site).

"May the Force be with you." (P O'C is a *Star Wars* fan.)

"Let's say travel, tourism, hospitality is just, well, in denial. Okay. It's in denial as to the effect that digital is having on this sector. We talk all the time

about the fact that, yes, digital is important, but we don't actually invest the resources in digital to actually be able to take advantage of it." (The C-19 effect may well accelerate this.)

Dr. Peter O'Connor

Adaption Tips

- Take a *start-up* attitude to your business. A Singaporean bank started hackathons with groups of students and required their managers to participate in developing fresh thinking. As a result, they started a digital bank in India.
- Read this book—*Don't Make Me Think* by Steve Krug.
- You need to have a brand that means something, that develops a real relationship with consumers.
- Make it so easy for them [customers/users] to do business with you that they won't think about doing business in any other way.

LinkedIn profile @ https://www.linkedin.com/in/peter-o-connor/

Company @ https://www.linkedin.com/school/essec-business-school/

Take the time to learn more

Click or use SmartPhone

Scribble Zone – *Who do you think are the most dynamic leaders in Travel, Tourism, and Hospitality?*

"Alignment of mission may be the new adaption for many companies for the near future for many years to come."

Sean Worker – T5 Strategies

[29]**Invent TOMORROW by Learning From TODAY**, Sean Worker T5 Strategies July 30, 2020, IHM Media https://www.servicedapartmentnews.com/features/setting-a-new-course-invent-tomorrow-by-learning-from-today/

It is refreshing to see that many of the trade industry organizations have made efforts to align their message. C-19 is undoubtedly an imminent threat to humanity; it's also a pandemic of industrial destruction to the travel, eating, and entertainment categories. Indeed, other sectors are hurting, but on aggregate, these make up about 8–15 percent of many countries' GDP. The majority of their workforce earns a lower-than-average income and constitutes the fabric that holds many communities together, from the "agony aunt psychologist" bartender to the stress-relieving spa masseuse and the waiter who delivers your Special of the Day with a flourish and a friendly smile. There are signs that some of the organizations that represent them are "banging a drum." Hopefully they will get in rhythm and adapt their own organizations to reflect their members' very new and urgent needs.

The major industry associations and representative bodies need to educate governments to recognize Travel, Tourism, and Hospitality as foundational to a community's infrastructure. Some of the voices that need to be heard from include:

- Chip Rogers, American Hotel and Lodging Association
- Clive Wratton, British Travel Association
- Dawn Sweeny, CEO of the National Restaurant Association USA (NRA)
- Kate Nichols, UK Hospitality
- James Foice, CEO at the Association of Serviced Apartment Operators (ASAP)

- Capt. Joe DePete, Airline Pilots Association
- Gloria Guevera, President and CEO World Travel and Tourism Council (WTTC)

Media companies such as Skift, International Hospitality Media, Questex, and *No Vacancy* have taken up the banner through excellent storytelling. They have reinforced the message that the travel industry needs funding to avoid total collapse. Their methodologies are evolving quickly to adapt and innovate, hosting online forums, conferences, and debates. All this has contributed to scaling messaging and best-practice sharing, a critical element of speed-driven survival and adaptation to a very unique problem.

It was encouraging to see that Skift assigned investigative resources to question the efficiency of the WTTC (World Travel and Tourism Council) during this pandemic in their article "It's Time to Rethink Travel's Global Leadership – Starting with the WTTC." (Rosie Spinks, Sep 28, 2020) They interviewed a wide range of travel leaders on and off the record. They concluded that there is a need for the WTTC because it's the "best hope the private sector has for global cooperation and representation."

In our view, this challenge thrown down by the SKIFT Team is a challenge to many organizations to pick up the pace of evolving their companies and associations. For those that remember Y2K,[30] the fear of possible embarrassment by not reacting to the threat of potential digital annihilation pushed companies to upgrade their technologies. https://en.wikipedia.org/wiki/Year_2000_problem. Enterprises such as IBM, Oracle, and others reaped the rewards from an equipment installation and consulting angle, but businesses everywhere were forced to upgrade. It's probable that the upside did not reveal itself until much later. Think of the companies that flourished after 2000, such as Google, Apple, Amazon, and others; could they have flourished without that broad capital investment in technology innovation and process improvement?

Growth is possible

Nearly all countries depend on Travel, Tourism, and Hospitality—in particular, business travel to grease the wheels of the local economy and provide revenue sources. As IATA noted, GDP and growth depend on people *moving*. Furniture suppliers, chemical manufacturers, and companies such as Samsung need to demo their products to the hospitality space; they need to *meet* to show the latest gel dispenser, flat-screen TV, or their other adaptions or innovations in person. Hotels and convention centers depend on people to meet, greet, eat, and drink while they close the deal. People *must* travel; it's one of our innate needs. Bums in seats matter, be it on an airplane, train, or hotel barstool. Growth will occur from a low base, but it will occur.

The US Federal Reserve has indicated that low or near-zero interest rates will be the norm for years. The new growth is adapting to the current state and planning for growth that can arise from the adaptions and innovations made today.

But first we have to get people on the move again.

Our data has shown that in Europe, the countries of Spain, France, and Italy, with their higher dependence on tourism as a portion of their GDP, may continue to bear the brunt of this pandemic as a result of that statistic.

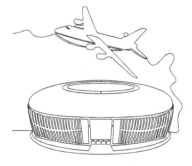

We expect Spain and France, as well as other countries, to negotiate adaption agreements between governments to enable visitor numbers to return. Some countries, like Spain, the UK, and Ireland have already begun imposing negative COVID PCR tests, to be conducted no less than seventy-two hours prior to a departure time, as requirements for entry via air and seaports. Ironically, in the birthplace of the GDPR, the cost may be less traveler privacy in return for a suntan, some tapas, and a bottle of wine! But I think these days most of us would be willing to pay that price.

Encouraging people to get back on planes and trains and put their heads in beds again goes hand in hand with the next big problem to solve: proving the safety and efficacy of the fast-tracked inoculations, instilling confidence so that enough people will get the jab. Sufficient numbers of the vaccinated in the general population are essential to bring the pandemic under control, and for a sense of trust in travel and related-hospitality industries to be restored. Then once the vaccination is in demand, getting supplies in sufficient numbers, and rapid distribution will be the next hurdles.

It is likely that in the very near future, passports will double up as vaccine verification documents. Artificial Intelligence, "AI," will play a major part in tracking that, and other information. As is common, governments seem to rely on the Travel and Hospitality sector to act as Tax Collectors. Now we may become vaccine trackers and enforcers. You can hear it now at the Hertz counter or hotel front desk: "Hi! Checking in? Can we see your Passport and vaccination verification and a current COVID PCR test, please?" This adds another level of complexity to the duties and responsibilities of travel and hospitality frontline workers but may be the price of getting people back in cars, trains, planes, serviced apartments and hotels, restaurants, etc.

Travel, and those who use and work in it, *will* change. The only question is, how will you participate in that change? *React or Respond?*

Hint, hint. It's Mint, Mint.

Business travel—the butter on much of TT&H's bread—will likely be reshaped considerably down, the effects of which may be dramatic. Corporate business travel budgets are being cut drastically, with no window as to returning until 2023–2024. Even then, they may not return to pre-COVID heights. According to airline industry pundits, the mega aircraft that had been slowly invading the skies are being phased out, to be replaced by smaller models. TT&H Tribe, take note! This is an indication of future passenger volume into your market! But even though predictions are that the first and business class categories are over as we know them, Jet Blue may be taking off now to get ahead of the curve—if you will pardon the pun. The forecast is for lower-cost premium class to become the norm. Jet Blue has doubled down and may be ahead of trend with an upgrade of their MINT class amenities. This lower-cost "lux" seat has been adjusted for smaller aircraft A321LR (two hundred seats) and will commence its New York to Stansted and Gatwick UK routes around Q2 2021.

> "You cannot stay on top without constant re-investment and re-invention/ innovation."
>
> **Jim Alderman**
> CEO,
> The Americas
> Radisson
> Hotel Group

Insights - Key Contributor

HOTEL ALTERNATIVE - Hotel & Serviced Accommodation Services

The Adapters' comments: Living Rooms is a specialist in delivering a luxury hotel and serviced accommodation experience. They are loved by a loyal following of household-name movie actors, artists, global creatives, and high-end business brands. 2020 was not an easy year, but Living Rooms outperformed relative to the market. Learn how Living Rooms still had loyal guests traveling and staying with them despite the collapse in travel.

Living Rooms (1992) was founded on a desire to meet the needs of the modern traveler, offering a hotel alternative that combines the luxury and services of a hotel with the privacy and space of one's own home.

 With 5 properties, totaling 90 hotel rooms and apartments across West London, each part of the Living Rooms collection reflects the needs of our customer in terms of location and practicalities as well as their expectations when it comes to high-end design and exceptional service.

Each property is unique, curated with the same care and attention to detail as would be paid to a private home.

Tracy Lowy
Founder and Director
Living Rooms
London, UK

Market: What market did Living Rooms decide to disrupt and why?

The traditional hotel and serviced apartment market.

Wanted to represent a move away from corporate, soulless environments into a more considered, tailored approach that appealed to the growing 'creative corporate' clientele.

Problem: **What gap in the market did you identify in the Hotel and Serviced Apartment space and how did you tackle it?**

Identified a need for an alternative to London's traditional hotels and serviced accommodation.

I conceived the Living Rooms hotel alternative, a unique brand philosophy that reflects the needs of our customer in terms of location and practicalities as well as their expectations when it comes to high-end design and exceptional service.

Lifestyle to me is about experiences and feeling a sense of place, so every one of our properties has an individual personality that is connected to the surrounding neighborhood—to encourage our customer to live, not just stay.

Obstacles: **What challenges did you encounter and how did you push through them?**

Our considered, tailored approach to each project means that we spend more time, but this is a long-term investment that pays off in the long run in terms of rate and guest satisfaction.

Being a London-based company, international affairs affect the business—9/11, the 08 crash, COVID etc.

We push through by ensuring we keep our finger on the pulse, staying ahead of the curve and remaining agile.

Expanding an existing business:

- *What are the 3-5 tips you have for owners and leaders in the Luxury bespoke space?*
  - Small details make a big difference
  - Work with people who get it
  - Listen to your customer; luxury is all about bespoke service. That's how you build loyalty and trust
  - Remain adaptable
  - Be brave
- *What are the 3-5 major key learnings/failures that propelled your growth/thinking?*
  - To stand clear on where we want to be positioned in the market and who we are as a brand
- *What were the best practices that lead to your success?*
  - The cultivation of a unique brand philosophy that flows through everything we do
  - We don't sell; we tell
  - Stay relevant
  - Finger on the pulse
  - Understand the DNA of your customer
  - Stay connected with your surrounding neighborhood
  - A foundation of loyalty and trust in team and clients

How did you determine your "design" approach and attitude?

Wanted to do the complete opposite of what was currently offered by the traditional hotel and serviced accommodation brands by creating environments that encourage guests to live, not just stay.

Understanding the DNA of your customer/client is key. Our target market is those that are turned off by the corporate and traditional. Our approach, everything from design to service, is less corporate, more considered and creative.

Adaptions: What are the 3-5 major Adaptions you made to your business to stay relevant?

- Strategic Relationships – working with the most relevant people in the industry: bookers/agents, consultants, travel writers, influencers—they are our army of LR Brand Ambassadors.
- Introduced curated events – retail pop-ups and partnerships with local stores, album launches, book launches, talks and food and beverage experiences.
- Wellness – partnering with industry-leading wellness company to introduce Wellness Rooms at The Laslett.
- Sustainability – socially responsible within the industry. Allowing travelers to make informed decisions that have a positive impact on the planet. The more we talk about sustainability and what's good for the guests and good for the hotels, the more we will all benefit.
- When curating our look and feel we seek out art directors, photographers and architects that operate outside of the hospitality industry. The end result is unique and reinforces our brand philosophy.
- Utilizing new and adapting technologies to enhance and streamline the customer journey, engage and encourage new business.

Company@ https://www.living-rooms.co.uk/

Let's get together

> "If I'm a fran-
> chisee at the
> moment, my
> hotel is shut up.
> What are the
> good reasons
> why I should pay
> franchise fees to
> franchise all for
> nothing, right?"
>
> **Paul Slattery,
> GGT**

The next trend around the corner may be mergers. Firms such as Intercontinental Hotels and Accor allegedly are engaging in merger talks; a move largely calculated to cut cost and drive liquidity during an anticipated protracted recovery. Even if this one does not occur, expect mergers in 2021 as forecasted by **Paul Slattery,** *GGT.*

It is to be expected that as spending contracts and travel remains elusive, everything from food trucks to banks specializing in loans to the Travel and Hospitality space will also need to adapt and innovate to survive. At the end of the day, this is an interdependent ecosys- tem. **We are all connected and in this rowboat together. But are we ocean-bound or pad- dling like hell back upstream?**

Could suburban hotels become hot again— Those urburbs?

While not strictly a suburban player, the properties that are president of G6 Hospitality, *Greg Juceam's,* responsibility, may fare better than others in both environments, according to that particular GGT.

First of all, the G6 portfolio is firmly and proudly committed to its position as an economy accommodation provider. Named "Best Budget-Friendly Hotel" in 2020 by *USA Today*, the properties had already done some adapting to make themselves better prepared for times like these. In his interview with the Adapters team, Juceam explained that their two brands—Motel 6 and G6 Suites—are being combined where possible into a single structure:

"The rooms are all the same size when we build. If you want to be 60 percent extended stay and 40 percent nightly stay with Motel 6, it's fine. But maybe we get into a situation, a downturn in the economy, and you want 80 percent extended stay. It's modular. You just pull out the nightly amenity package and you put in the kitchenette and you put in the pots and pans when you slide in the new cabinets and off you go. Now you're 80 percent extended stay. Same cost."

Ironically, the suburbs and the "urburbs" could have the edge against their town/city cousins if hotels, serviced apartments, restaurants, and even commercial property owners do some serious adapting to capture the expanded WFH market. The "master-planned" communities where towns were built from scratch outside of the city centers evolved in the 1960s to become towns of some magnitude in their own right. Examples of the planned "Urburb"—the urban suburb—are Reston, Virginia (possibly the first of its kind), and The Woodlands, a "new" town outside Houston, TX, USA. Both were started by entrepreneur property developers; Robert E. Simon (Reston) and George Mitchell (The Woodlands). These early pioneers developed the concept, and their "urburbs" have been copied around the world. They understood that community is central to the experience with minimal density, now more than ever.

 ## Hey! Wait a minute. What happened to the cities under siege?

Nope. We haven't forgotten about them. For starters, why not look at the "Hole in the Candy" from a completely different angle, rather than just filling the middle back up with more of what started the problem in the first place?

> *"Sustainable tourism is sort of a low bar. At the end of the day, it's just not making a mess of the place,"* said Jonathon Day, an associate professor focused on sustainable tourism at Purdue University. *"Regenerative tourism says, let's make it better for future generations."*

Regeneration is a "Thing"

There has been a lot written about, spoken of, and put forward in the arena of sustainable tourism in recent years, but a movement has been stirring to promote the concept of *regenerative* tourism[31]—a *big step* beyond sustainable.[32] https://www.nytimes.com/2020/11/12/travel/travel-tours-experiences-virus.html) Elaine Glusac wrote an excellent piece on the subject in the New York Times in August 2020, providing much food for thought and the source of much of my inspiration for this section.

Defining regeneration

Regenerative travel has its roots in regenerative development and design, which includes buildings that meet the U.S. Green Building Council's Leadership in Energy and Environmental Design (LEED) standards. The concept has applications across many fields, including regenerative agriculture, which aims to restore soils and sequester carbon.

For her article, Glusac interviewed Bill Reed, an architect and principal of Regenesis Group, a design firm based in Massachusetts and New Mexico that has been practicing regenerative design, including tourism projects, since 1995. "Generally, sustainability, as practiced today, is about slowing down the degradation," Glusac quoted Reed. "A slower way to die" was how Reed described efforts like fuel efficiency and reduced energy use. "Regeneration is about restoring and then regenerating the capability to live in a new relationship in an ongoing way," he added.

Professor Day advocates for the construction of a circular economy, designed to eliminate the waste in the system, keep materials in use through reuse, repair, and upcycling, and regenerate natural systems. No reason this concept can't be applied to Travel, Tourism, and Hospitality and all the elements of their ecosystem. "Tourism is just at the beginning of this process of how we can apply circular economy ideas to the system," said Day.

> *"The regeneration of society is the regeneration of society by individual education."*
>
> ***Jean de la Bruyere***

Chris Holer's "hole in the candy" analogy, describing the "hollowing out of the city center's core," applies here, as well.

GGT **James Blick**[33] https://www.youtube.com/user/jamesblick78) is a well-known YouTuber. A native New Zealander, Blick moved to Madrid and cofounded Devour Tours, then launched Spain Revealed, offering specialized experience tours based primarily around local food and beverage. He is an active voice in nudging along the dialogue to apply the regenerative tourism principle to Madrid, Barcelona, and other "tourist cities." In a recent YouTube upload, Blick wandered the almost-deserted streets of the center of Madrid, commenting on the local retail and culinary landmarks that were hovering on the brink or that had already shut shop. As the designer and leader of many a food-and-drink-related tour (he tells us that a lot of personal research went into choosing the best eating establishments and watering holes!), Blick and his wife-partner Yoly Martín, a well-connected and locally engaged Spanish native with her own tourist-centric enterprise, are walking encyclopedias of what's happening on the local tourist scene. Both say that even before 2020, much of what was unique about Madrid's center had been noticeably hollowed out by tourism and the flight of the locals to the suburbs. C-19 has just made matters that much worse.

Blick admits they had just "kind of got a handle on the concept of sustainable tourism. And really," he noted, "that sets the bar fairly low." Regenerative tourism is something beyond that. "It's more than just don't burn down the forest. It's why don't we plant some trees?"

Martín sees regenerative tourism as an exciting challenge; not sure what it will entail, she does know that governments need to take some responsibility, as well. "They need to help, too, take some control, and put some sensible limits in place." In the meantime, she and Blick are planning to "bring" their online tourist guests to less-populated spots in Spain to spread the tourist load a bit once travel restrictions are lifted and the pair can "take their show on the road" once more.

In the case of Madrid, and other cities like Barcelona, without some intervention, there are fears that, effectively, the heart of the city will have moved.

> "La vida es aspirar, respirar, y expirar."
>
> **Salvador Dalí**

Blick is advocating for developmental support to encourage family-run businesses to return and to incentivize entrepreneurs to come back, including the bakers, tapas bar owners, butchers, and grocers. Tourists come to see the "street life." Blick and others think that's not possible without the local people that inhabit and bring the life to that street. **Blick** and **Martín**, by the way, are prime examples of Travel, Tourism, and Hospitality folk who faced the ultimate "disruption" as a result of the COVID restrictions. With social distancing, travel bans, and bars and restaurants originally shuttered, then partially opened, then closed again, then sort of semi-opened…you can see where this story was headed. Pretty tough to run a tour/experience business in that environment. You can learn more about their story and how they have adapted to today's uncertain times, pivoting nimbly to keep their business better than just afloat, by reading their GGT profile and visit them on the Adapters Hub.

In Glusac's piece, she noted that Tourism New Zealand, the country's tourism organization, is talking about measuring its success not solely in economic terms but against the well-being of the country, considering nature, human health, and community identities. Similarly, travel leaders in Hawaii are discussing repositioning the state as a *cultural* destination in hopes of reengaging islanders, many of whom are fed up with over-tourism.

So, what might a "regenerative tourism" project look like? Possibly like Playa Viva. Bill Reed's Regenesis Group worked on the development of Playa Viva, a small resort south of Zihuatanejo, Mexico, on the Pacific Coast, which opened in 2009. The firm's assessment of the two-hundred-plus-acre property considered the beaches and the surrounding ancient ruins, the bird-filled estuary, and the problem of local turtle poaching. They also considered the local *human* inhabitants; in particular, the poor schools in the village. Ultimately, the small town of Juluchuca became the gateway to the property. An organic agricultural system benefited both the property and local residents, and a 2 percent fee added to any stay funds a trust that invests in community maintenance and development.

The notion of regeneration is a linear cousin to adaptation and innovation. This 4th Age of Change can include virtual reality tours of tapas bars, pubs, and historic landmarks, and a foot-stomping evening of flamenco. From your living room, you can enjoy a walk through Central Park, Hyde Park, St. Peter's Square, or St. Mark's Square. If you think that's a poor substitute for the real thing, check out Julian McDonnell's informative (and sometimes irreverent) Joolz Guides "private" London walking tours on YouTube.

And really, do cruise ships have to be jammed with five thousand of your closest friends and relatives, all descending down a gangplank to invade the city or storm the beach?

Of course, it would be perfectly reasonable to argue that Rome or Barcelona or Paris or [fill in the blank] could not exist without tourism and the euros those pesky tourists generate for the local economy. Maybe it's time for the cities and countries to step up to manage this, to limit travel as New Zealand is suggesting, ensuring that the experience is sustainable, even regenerative for all. City councils and governments may also be asked to adapt to what their populations are asking for: **balance.** You might be surprised; travelers might actually agree with the approach! Let's try something like a regenerative, friendly, virtual, and immersive reality tour with every major site in the world, www.everycoolplace.com, for $10.00 per month, with 10 percent of profits divided up between the sites. Now that's the *4th Age of Regeneration* and a great way to research your next in-person vacation!

Other players are poised to amplify their presence in major urban hubs, doing their part to fill in the "hole in the city" and beyond.

citizenM[34] https://www.citizenm.com/) is a Netherlands-based hotel chain that came on the scene in 2005, describing itself as the creator of a "luxury hybrid hotel for today's modern travelers...one who values a luxury hotel experience in central city locations, but at an affordable price." The first property opened at Amsterdam's Schiphol Airport, followed by hotels in Amsterdam city center and other central city locations and transportation hubs, featuring the "Living Room"—a modern twist on a hotel lobby, with open computer stations where guests can check themselves in and out. Proud of its commitment to environmental and social governance (ESG) policies and practices, citizenM has development plans in the works around the world, designed to conserve the inner-city vibe.

Futurists like Bernard Marr, Thomas Ermacora and others—like the Adapters Team—are optimistic about the future of cities as we enter the New Reality. Some of the pre-COVID urban design trends that were already in motion (more mixed-use housing, more ground-level shops and services, more dedicated pathways for pedestrians and bicycles, more last-mile connections to public transportation, more green space and urban gardens, etc.), bringing new, sustainable life to urban centers, will be accelerated as those spaces re-invent themselves yet again—just as they have since the first collection of houses, shops, pubs, and eateries circled the first village square.

It may seem contrary to expectations, but the increase in Working From Home may actually benefit cities and urburbs, in particular. For one thing, traffic may actually be able to flow with so many fewer cars on the roads. That should also improve city air quality. True, city center offices may be left behind now that businesses realize that their workforces don't need to be housed in the human equivalent of a beehive, but many companies are already exploring the notion of smaller, neighborhood, suburban, and even urban regional "work hubs," where groups of employees can take a break from their home offices, utilize company resources and materials, and collaborate—and socialize—with coworkers.

These "work hubs" bring new life to their surroundings. Existing services and social offerings are fortified, and new businesses find fertile ground to get their starts. Even the emptying mega-structures can find new life. There have been plans afoot already to repurpose some of the largest office buildings into housing sites, with the creative inclusion of smaller, independent retailers and services, artisan work zones, and more. And can you just imagine rooftop gardens in numbers to provide truly locally sourced produce for those new, better connected "neighborhoods"?

With some regenerative initiatives, especially in the teaming tourist destinations, and some adaption in the centers of human population, it is possible that we can fill the "hole in the candy" with some pretty healthy and wholesome mixtures.

Of course we will travel again. We *will* fly to all things fun and wonderful and experience them in person. But surely we can adapt our travel and tourism model to ensure that we can attend a world business convention or New Zealand's Maori Kororipo Heritage Park and contribute positively to regeneration, leaving the place better than when we arrived.

Putting some thought into what your organization can do to participate in regenerative tourism could lead to a whole array of socially honorable adaptions or even innovations, as well as earn your enterprise a host of new loyal clients/users/customers—and employees!—while preserving your business environment for continued success.

Scribble Zone: Take 3 minutes and jot 2–4 ideas on how your organization can become a champion of regenerative tourism.

Scribble Zone: Write down the 2–3 brilliant ideas you came up with.

The COVID mountain and the three-meter method

Taking action to try and make sense of all that's happening, what's come before, and how to adapt for tomorrow will take a lot of personal discipline and energy. Be assured that the previous three Ages of Change, and the opening five hundred years ago of the 4th, were not as comfortable as a night on a Westin Heavenly Bed. So, find that inner entrepreneur and gutsy innovator. Be a GGT and get out there and make the 4th Age of Change come alive—because if you do not, others will. Crisis breeds opportunity.

Humans are traders and hand-shakers. We are highly tactile, sentient, and require the use of most senses, most of the time, to make our decisions. Travel and Zoom are necessities, but the timing of this recovery will be protracted, taking more than two to three years to regain its footing—possibly even longer—and to test the highs of 2019. Many of the observers and commentators have shared where the pitfalls are. These include:

- Dependency on single markets to single customers
- Over-optimistic forecasting and projections
- Time-frame risks as to when travelers might actually start moving again at volumes that matter
- Traits of poorly run businesses, for whom adaption was an underused strategy, even before the pandemic.

However, the industry's optimism remains ever-present, and rightly so. Some are reading the road signs along the way. Some have already made it over the first COVID mountain using the "three meters in front of you" method and can now pause to really examine the route that lies before them. We are already seeing adaption in the market; true innovation should follow as some motor toward the deep blue ocean.[35] Blue Ocean Strategy https://www.youtube.com/watch?v=8cVS7YEW2Fk&t=13s). Others will stick in the muddy estuary, and others will try to swim back upstream to where "normal" lived. The **New Reality** will eventually become the New Normal. ***It's time to choose.***

Scribble Zone:
Digital pen at the ready: *List two concepts that you disagreed with in this chapter and why!*

"In challenging times, look to how you can adapt and engage. Remain positive."

Cait Noone, Head Galway
International Hotel School
Vice President International
Engagement, GMIT, Ireland

Gutsy Genius Thinker

James Blick   Yoly Martín
Cofounder & COO   Flamenco
Devour Tours & Founder Tours
SpainRevealed
Madrid, Spain

James Blick and Yoly Martín are true founders and entrepreneurs in the classic sense: they saw gaps in the market and filled them! James cofounded Devour Tours, a platform for tour experiences, and he also founded SpainRevealed. Let's also add YouTube stars to the list of their accomplishments. Yoly founded a unique flamenco experience company; the Flamencoguide.com brings guests behind the scenes of this centuries-old "gitanos" dance to "feel it."

James embodies the definition of an Adapter. He went from lawyer ("Yeah, there's the other side of the spectrum!") to travel writer and producer of TV commercials to today's iteration as cofounder. James will freely admit that he didn't really know employing a [business] formula was what he was doing in the beginning. *"I started a business before I knew how to run a business,"* confessed the transplant from New Zealand in their interview for The Adapters. "It was pretty organic," agreed Yoly, "but everything seemed to work; we got customers, and we grew."

Devour's mission is to "connect curious travelers with local food and community in a way that helps culture thrive." This is a resounding theme echoed by our GGTs—that sense of being part of the community, regardless of the size of the organization. James and Yoly are media experts and have a keen sense of how to ignite your curiosity while offering so many options to immerse yourself in the local community.

So, just how have James and Yoly adapted when face-to-face tours and the research opportunities for more experiential tourist offerings have pretty much "fallen off a cliff," in James's words?

"Start by pulling back the curtain, letting people in, and sharing the worries and hardships," says James. The two have produced numerous "at home" videos, sharing tips on moving to Spain, doing cooking demos of popular Spanish dishes, and even walking their own neighborhood during lockdowns to just talk about the situation.

Yoly noted that their followers, and even the new visitors to their sites and channel, have reacted positively to that genuine sharing. "It keeps the trust going with those we know, and starts that relationship with new people, potential clients."

The Adapters have challenged the Travel, Tourism, and Hospitality community to "look over the fence" for inspiration for ways to adapt and innovate. James and Yoly have an infectious level of calm confidence that the C-19 crisis will actually broaden their respective product lines and grow their businesses off a strong foundation. They have already published a cookbook, a travel guide, and are branching into bespoke "how to move to and live in Spain" content. Why? Because their YouTube followers told them what content they want. Amazing what happens when you *LISTEN* to your customers!

QR and listen to James and Yoly telling their stories. Many much larger companies can learn a thing or two from them about adapting and innovating to prepare for the New Reality.

"Examine the taxonomy of your business now more than ever."

James Blick

Adaption Tips:

- If you can triage cash flow and your financial obligations, now is the ideal time for a review of the basics of your business.
- You can pivot product and methods of delivery, but not your brand or your values—who you are and what made you a success.
- Don't be afraid to partner with others in your space. "A rising tide sinks all boats."
- I can never imagine working for someone else. How about you?

LinkedIn profile @ https://www.linkedin.com/in/jamesblick/

Company @ www.spainrevealed.com/

Company @ www.devourtours.com/

Company @ www.theflamencoguide.com

YouTube @ www.youtube.com/user/jamesblick78

YouTube @ www.youtube.com/watch?v=ohSl61Y-7iQ

Take the time to learn more

Click or use SmartPhone

Gutsy Genius Thinker
Greg Juceam
President, G6 Hospitality
Chicago, Illinois, U.S.A

As President and COO of G6 Hospitality, which was purchased by Blackstone in 2021, Greg Juceam is transforming the business that owns Motel 6, Studio 6, and will be known internationally as Hotel 6 and Estudio 6. "The real story for us is that we're a 58-year-old brand that everyone knows, which has had a renaissance over the last two years." In addition to transforming and adapting his business, C-19 has had an extraordinary impact on the community that he serves.

Greg is a humble, energetic leader that has little or no inclination in sugar coating his message. For context, we chatted with Greg early in the rise of the pandemic. G6 is an economy brand and was witnessing a rise in demand from families that were already being displaced from their homes due to financial difficulties. He spoke at length about the displacement issues. "We are passionate about serving our community; we can help families transition until they find their footing again due to being a high-value economy brand. Our Teams really feel we are helping."

Juceam, in addition to his day job, is Chairman of the American Hotel Lodging Association foundation. Created in 1953 as the charitable, not-for-profit affiliate of the American Hotel & Lodging Association (AHLA), the foundation has distributed more than $27.5 million. As Greg noted when asked about the mission of the foundation, "We keep the industry's talent pipeline filled by funding scholarships, workforce development programs, and school-to-career outreach that launch careers and provide our member hotels with the talent they need to succeed over the long term." This is a powerful way to nurture and inspire the future of TTH.

Prior to joining G6 Hospitality, Juceam served as CEO of BRE Hotels and Resorts, a non-listed real estate investment trust focused on the ownership of upscale, extended-stay, and select-service hotels.

"Be part of your Community and the Community will be part of your business."

Greg Juceam

Adaption Tips

- As a brand, there's a lot you can learn through failure.
- Value equation is something that we absolutely must deliver; otherwise you're not going to be differentiated from all the other low-cost providers.
- With customers, we want to understand not just what they wanted, but what they were willing to pay for it.
- It's simple: today, investors are looking for an opportunity to meet an unmet demand.

LinkedIn profile @ https://www.linkedin.com/in/greg-juceam-7540915/

Company @ https://g6hospitality.com/

Take the time to learn more

Click or use SmartPhone

CHAPTER **5**

Adaption & Innovation Cycle

"It is not the strongest of the species that survive, nor the most intelligent, but the ones most responsive to change.[1]"

Charles Darwin

PART 1: Firefighting and Blazing a Trail

I think we can all agree that Darwin knew a thing or two about adapting. The GGTs that are featured here have experienced life's tragedies, financial collapses, and other bumps—business-related and personal—over the years, but they kept adapting and *Responding* versus *Reacting* to the situations they've faced. On occasion, some have taken their adaption to the next level and created innovation.

Their ability to adapt is a large part of their success, one of the keys to the achievement of the positions they now hold. If we subscribe to Darwin's theory, then adaptability may be the most important charac-  teristic they possess as they take on the challenge of life during a global pandemic. C-19 is an event where we must choose to React, Respond, or freeze in place. You can be super smart from your chair in the living room or a shack on the beach (which sounds okay sometimes, by the way) and get nowhere, *or* you can respond.

Across the twenty interviews that we conducted for Phase 1 of *The Adapters*, every single person was positive about getting on with it. Some have children, from the youngest of tots to the grown-up kind. Some do not. They run large, medium, and small businesses, organizations, or educational institutions. They hail from multiple states in the USA and from countries around the world, and all had the common mission of calmly responding to the C-19 crisis for the enterprises in their trust, for their families, and for themselves.[36] Their charge comes with the fatigue and the anxiety of hours spent in meetings, whiteboarding ways to manage cash flow, address employee concerns, investor expectations, and the safety of customers and guests. Usually armed with only sporadic and often-conflicting official information, like many of us, they are juggling their business responsibilities as well as the needs and concerns of their own families and personal situations.

> *"The art of life is constant readjustment to our surroundings."*
>
> *Kakuzo Okakaur*

In a very candid interview, *GGT* **Anthony Melchiorri** shared that he'd "had a moment or two." It's "not something I [would normally] admit…but I had that moment…I had to get in my car and clear my mind. It was like, 'what's going on?' And one of the words that came to my mind is 'stamina.' This is stamina. I need stamina."

But Melchiorri did find stamina that day, and he and his fellow GGTs have persevered, devising some rapid adaptions to combat a ravaging "fire" that threatens their businesses and institutions. It must have felt a lot like Churchill trying to lead through the early days of World War II: establish the War Office, assess damage, gauge supplies, and estimate financial capability, all while also assessing the enemy. Churchill and his team were rapidly adapting to a reality that was vastly different from the relatively predictable one they had operated in up to that point in time.

The New Reality

As of December 2020, we have more insight into our situation, and adaptation has fired up into full swing to bridge from here to the New Reality. We have more knowledge of the enemy, and we have learned to essentially "hold the line" and in some places "slow the offense"—although the "orders" to do just that are not often uniformly issued, accepted, or executed. Much like conventional warfare, there has been carnage. The damage is not immediately apparent—no buildings burning, no shell casings—but the impact, both emotionally and financially, sadly still comes with a death toll, much like any other conflict.

Governments today have struggled to adapt quickly, but so did Churchill's government when it was faced with the possible invasion of Britain by Germany. It took immense energy, diplomacy, motivation, and vision to find a way through such a crisis. The irony is that so much adaption and innovation occurred during the period that was World War II, from jet engines to the development of efficient supply chains. Remember those Dark Age and Great Depression advancements?

The GGTs have established their war offices and are adapting based on what they can control and influence. Being clear about your Circle of Influence[37] https://www.youtube.com/watch?v=DVNpd7E7ltU and focusing your attention and efforts on what you can control in that circle is paramount to establishing clarity and effectively deploying energy and resources. Let's check in with **GGT Jacob Wedderburn-Day,** CEO of Stasher (start-up), to see how he responded in the early days of the COVID crisis.

> "There's nothing more fundamentally disruptive to the status quo than a New Reality."
>
> **Umair Haque**

For starters, he communicated up and down his organization every day to inform and *include*. He communicated openly with his investors, presenting scenario-based cash flows (13-week increments) and long-range forecasts out to 2023. He needed to know early on if he could survive with the cash they had raised. He felt confident he could. Armed with this confidence and the data to support it, Stasher went about scaling their business to the projections and continuing to STASH (store bags) in third-party locations such as retail stores and hotels for those that were traveling. They adapted by developing an entirely new SaaS model[38] https://www.youtube.com/watch?v=R5q_RXk_t7A).

As the world starts to reopen, Stasher has a software app[39] https://stasher.com/ that hotels, retailers, or other clients can self-administer as a White Label[40] moneymaker. Thus far, it's been very well received, and Wedderburn-Day envisions this as an opportunity to truly scale his business as travel returns. This next-phase technology wasn't planned to be introduced at this stage, but the situation called for adaption, and Stasher answered the call.

> "The complexity and rampant evolution of our IT functions in the hotel industry make it an imperative to keep pace and it is a huge impact on operating margins."
>
> **Jim Alderman**
> CEO,
> The Americas
> Radisson
> Hotel Group

Adapt to stay relevant

Before we race much further down Adapter row, we should probably take a moment and ensure that we are all on the same page regarding "adaption" versus "innovation." We have found that there is some confusion in understanding the important differences between the two.

Box 6

Adaption is the forerunner to Innovation. You can have Adaption (and Success) without Innovation, but hardly successful Innovation without Adaption.

Adaption is: Modification of a task, concept, or object to make it applicable in situations different from originally anticipated. Source: business dictionary (modified)

Innovation is: The process of translating an idea or invention into a good or service that creates value or for which customers will pay—generally considered a new idea, method, a novelty. Source: business dictionary (modified)

Beyond just incorrectly interchanging the two terms, there are even occasional grammatical skirmishes over the correct form of "adaption." Although the short form is acceptable, tradition still favors the longer version, "adaptation." But, of course, in this 4th Age of Change, we are choosing to get right to it and adopt "adapt" for our discussions.

So, was **Stasher's** app an *adaption* to a current product or an *innovation/invention*? Based on the definitions above, this was a response to an event; **Stasher** effectively *adapted* an existing concept *and* produced a potential game change*r for* his company. However, when they formed the company on September 21, 2015, as the world's first luggage storage network, that was innovation. Jacob and his partner Ant saw a gap in the market and went for it. www.stasher.com

> "Whether you think you can or you think you can't, you're right!"
>
> **Henry Ford**

Take a peek over the fence

The Adapters team has broadcast and written frequently to encourage the Travel, Tourism, and Hospitality space to gain inspiration outside of their typical domain of expertise—it's a good tactic to get you started on charting your own path to adaption.

About a decade ago, hoteliers began to realize that generally, they were good at servicing groups and vacationers in their restaurants, but the independent restaurants and chains had the edge. The restaurant operators and brands had been forced to innovate so that the "experience" was as important as the food. They created concepts at all price points, from Shake Shack to the Cheesecake Factory, the Michelin-starred Clove Club in London, to the myriad amazing local tapas bars/restaurants in Barcelona.[41] https://www.cntraveler.com/

gallery/best-restaurants-in-london) Condé Nast Top 30 Restaurants in London, Elizabeth Winding Oct 31 19).

Independent hoteliers and franchisors realized that consumers wanted the quality and experience that restauranteurs offered. Some adapted and redesigned accordingly. Canopy by Hilton Washington DC, The Wharf, truly adapted to deliver a breezy, waterfront second-level combo restaurant and cocktail bar with brilliant food, equal to or better than a stand-alone restaurant brand. (*Sean and Andrea Worker lived in DC and frequented the bar! For the view, of course!*)

TIPS & TAKES

Nippon, Singapore, and Taiwanese Airlines are introducing "flights to nowhere"—and people are paying to take them.

In late August, Japanese carrier All Nippon Airways flew a 90-minute scenic flight on one of its "Flying Honu" Airbus A380 aircraft. Passengers were treated to a Hawaiian resort-style experience in the airport and onboard the plane, which normally flies between Tokyo and Honolulu.

Taiwanese air carrier Eva Air launched a sightseeing flight on one of its Hello Kitty jets. Departing from and landing at Taipei's Taoyuan International Airport, the 2-hour 45-minute flight traveled at an altitude of 20,000 to 25,000 feet to give passengers a closer view of Taiwan and Japan's Ryukyu Islands.

Taiwan's national carrier, China Airlines, flew two flights that took off and landed in Taipei in August. A representative for China Airlines told CNBC that the initiative has received a positive response from the local market.

Royal Brunei Airlines launched a no-destination flight last month. The national flag carrier for Brunei, a Southeast Asian country on the island of Borneo, flew an 85-minute "Dine & Fly" sightseeing tour along the coastline of Brunei and Malaysian Borneo. The flight, which included brunch and pilot commentary, sold out within 48 hours, and hundreds have registered interest for future flights.

Why and where it works
Though a flight for the thrill of flying isn't for everyone, no-destination flights may thrive in locations that have low COVID-19 infection rates and limited travel opportunities otherwise

Add in the business lounge and The Adapters are all in on the flight to nowhere—in a C-19 bubble, of course.

Source: Airline - Monica Buchanan Pitrelli – Sep 15, 2020-CNBC

Adapting is easier than you think – Look for opportunities

Adaption and innovation can be thought of in simple terms. It is not uncommon for people and businesses to wait around for a eureka moment (*innovation/invention*). This passivity could mean possibly discounting that *adaption,* with even the smallest of changes, could make the biggest difference. In some instances, adaption today may mean continued survival.

The legend goes that a UPS driver suggested that UPS change their routes to remove as many traffic lights as possible as a driver was constantly having to stop and start. Adjusting to avoid turning across oncoming traffic (left-hand turns where they drive on the right and vice-versa) would also speed things up. UPS adopted this suggestion. Nowadays, UPS delivery vans don't always take the shortest route between stops, but it is a more efficient one, saving lots of money in gas/petrol/diesel, as well as reducing nonproductive idling time. A simple adaption made a significant difference.

> *"The greater danger in times of turbulence is not the turbulence; it is the act with yesterday's logic."*
>
> **Peter Drucker**

Nurturing and rewarding a culture of adaption is critical to staying relevant. The UPS example speaks to the demands on an established business to adapt, sometimes in spite of workplace politics, regulations, and all the other influences. In cases such as start-ups backed by Venture Capital funding,[42] the approach is usually to innovate first, coming forth with the new way, the new idea, the new technology, etc., then to adapt as they scale. Along the way, adapting reinforces the foundation of the business while it pivots toward product development and experiences; think Airbnb growing from an extra airbed on the floor to aggregating millions of accommodations and experiences delivered via a global platform. These issues affect businesses of all sizes.

TIPS & TAKES

True Story of Adaption in the Time of Covid

Andrea and I love going to the gym. Okay. That might be overstating our feelings just a tad... but, in truth, after the lockdown began in Spain on March 14, 2020, it wasn't long before we found that we actually did miss a session on the cardio machines or at the cable stations.

Being innate adapters, we dug out the elastic exercise bands from storage and had our neighbors gawking as we attached them to the wrought iron gate at our front door and did our best to simulate some of the lats and triceps pulldowns, back rows, and wood-chop twists. All in all, better than sitting on the sofa while pounds of take-home tapas and the results of our newfound baking skills settled themselves firmly on hips, abs, and other unwanted places.

The months of lockdown wore on. Gradually, the restrictions on movement began to ease, and shops, restaurants, and the like began to open. Of course, we were thrilled, but a new worry came with the unshuttering of all our favorite haunts. What about the gym? Would we ever feel safe again, going somewhere that seemed like the ideal place for COVID catching with all that huffing and puffing and dripping sweat? We thought not, and were resigning ourselves to a life attached to our front gate, since buying home exercise equipment seemed out of the question—there was none to be found anywhere—and even if we could find some, where would we put it, and what would we have to pawn to purchase it?

Then, one day, came a text message from DiR, our gym franchise. It seems that instead of just waiting for the lockdown to lift, the folks at DiR had spent those three-plus months doing some serious adaption evaluating, taking steps to entice members back with a combination of new hygiene protocols, some thoughtfully planned new rules and regulations, and a bit of software reconfiguring.

In addition to adding more cleaning staff and more rigorous cleaning and disinfecting of the equipment, the gym will now open at a reduced attendance capacity, broken into one hour and fifteen-minute sessions. The DiR app has been reworked so that members can schedule their sessions and know in advance how many places are already taken at each time interval. Too many people for your comfort zone? Pick another time slot.

Within the facility itself, masks are required at all times. Showers are off-limits, and equipment is cordoned off, putting enough machines out of action to allow plenty of space between us gymsters. Towels are mandatory, as is wiping down equipment with disinfectant after each use (Andrea and I did the disinfectant thing before our use, as well!), and there are attendants watching for noncompliance offenders. Wearing nitrile gloves is also encouraged, and using the rope pull and the free weights is discouraged since they are harder to clean. To top it all off, once an hour, all the gym attendees have to pause, leave the fitness salon, and allow the staff to do spot disinfecting.

From a customer service standpoint, the gym management didn't wait for members to ask about the lost time on their memberships. They sent out the notice that let us know our memberships would automatically be extended to correspond with the length of time that the facility had been closed by the Spanish Health Authority. Points there!

Moral of the story? DiR used the time of the full lockdown wisely, thinking of ways to safely bring back their existing members and enhance their recruitment of new ones. They did some Business Process Work, put the new steps into place, conducted training, and spent some euros on hiring extra staff and on adapting their mobile app and their website to better correspond with the needs of their constituents.

Masks, gloves, and scheduled sessions—we're back at the gym. Take that, tapas, banana bread, and Deliveroo, Grub Hub, et al.![43] https://www.dir.cat/en

What holds so many travel and hospitality enterprises back when it comes to adapting?

GGT Peter O'Connor, Professor, Information Systems, Decision Sciences and Statistics Department, Chaired Professor of Digital Disruption at ESSEC Business School, thinks that sometimes

"...those companies tend to be extremely rigid in their thinking and in their processes. They have the capital; they have the resources to change, but they also have a lot of *organizational inertia*...we're [Travel, Tourism, and Hospitality] so far behind, and as a result, there's the potential for people from outside our industry to come in and grab our business. You know, [it's] the 'we've never done this before. That's not the way we do things. That will never work.' Those are phrases that we hear again and again, unfortunately. As a result, what's happening is people from outside our industry are coming in. They're cherry-picking the low-hanging, usually high-margin fruit. Too often we're being left with double the cost and half the revenue."

Organizational inertia aside, **GGT Cait Noone**, *Head Galway International Hotel School and Vice President International Engagement, GMIT, Ireland,* lays a bit of the blame for the often-static environment of some of the Travel, Tourism, and Hospitality players on a tendency to get caught up in their own minutiae:

"I think we're very slow to change but very good at talking about change. We might read a textbook or a newsletter that our professional body sends out, and we think, 'Oh, I must get onto that, but I need to run down now and micromanage another group of people.' I'm not criticizing. I'm talking about reality. I'm a bit guilty of it too. I think we're really slow to change our mindset."

Scribble Zone: *Write in what you WILL do and what you will STOP doing that is getting in the way of adapting.*

START DOING/CONTINUE DOING	STOP DOING

So, the next time you hang with your teams, ask them these questions:

1. What can we improve, or what process do you think is stupid and needlessly time-consuming?
2. Is there a better way to produce a pizza or clean a room, plane, cabin?

Alexi Khajavi, President, Hospitality and Travel at Questex, observed:

> I think the beauty of a crisis is that questions that just four or five weeks ago were crazy questions—you know, if you didn't want to be the odd guy, like Bob in a corner, they're like, you know, Bob's an idiot, right? He keeps talking about why do we need an office? Well, actually, Bob's pretty sharp right now. Right now, a lot of people *are* saying, 'Why *do* we need this office?' Our employees are working from home. So, I think the crisis actually brings this opportunity for all of us to start asking questions, which might have seemed completely unorthodox and ludicrous not long ago.

We appreciate that we may be challenging you to question the conventional thinking about adaption...you know, the one where *innovation* is the sexy and highly rewarding choice, compared to its oftentimes neglected cousin, adaption. Well, of course, innovation is sexy. It's also erratic by nature and fraught with failure risk.

We *are* suggesting that adaption is the propulsion system that drives frequent incremental change and value and is often the launchpad for innovation. The hunt for innovation should always be on the radar screen, but don't ignore the benefits of adaption. Encourage both and understand their values and the likely reward of each.

Become a Transformist

Bob Hecht
Business Transformist
Founder & Managing Director,
Unimark, UK Ltd
London, UK

Bob Hecht is a well-regarded organizational Transformist. After fifteen years with Alix Partners as a Partner in their restructuring and technology practice, he has seen his fair share of adaption and failure and then was asked to come in and deal with it!

Key reflective thinking traps:

Transformation is a watchword in the evolving world of business today.

As a transformist, I ask questions around several thought patterns that can be summarized in a few two-word comparatives. Is your operational thinking based on:

- A reflective or a prospective approach?
- Are they barriers or benefits?
- Is your approach reactive or responsive?
- Do you understand the difference between disruption and distraction?
- Does planning center on participation or collaboration?
- In discussions, do you listen, or do you hear?

The inevitability of change is a constant...fear it, and it will dominate you; embrace it, and opportunity will surround you.

LinkedIn @ https://www.linkedin.com/in/
bob-hecht-9b228514/

Scribble Zone: *Capture your reaction and response.*

Avoiding adaption and innovation distractions and traps...

Don't chase "cars"

Today's news can be distracting, as well as depressing. The business world is front-loaded with data, news-grabbing headlines, and clickbait. What to look out for:

- **Skimming:** Or worse, just ignoring news and sources of information about your own sector, as well as keeping up with the adaptions and innovations of others around you. (Over-the-fence peeking.)
- **Dismissing:** "That's not about hotels or restaurants or serviced apartments, etc., so that's nothing to do with how we do business!" Boy, could you have just missed out on a major improvement that you will seriously regret later!
- **Chasing every "car":** Unless you have unlimited time and resources, don't go after everything you read, see, or hear. Some ideas can be filed away for later. If they still look good after a revisit, then give them a go.
- **Giving up too soon:** Of course, stay mindful of your company's precious resources (*woof! woof!*), but don't just sit on the sidewalk watching the cars go by, either. Don't shut down an idea—someone else's or *your own*—until you've given it its due consideration. Pay attention to "Bob in the corner."

What's the take here? Seek *perspective* from today's "news." Consider if the "headline" has meaning for you or your company. If you think there's something more there, grant it a little more of your time or resources; just don't become the dog chasing every car. Our adapters held steady if they thought an idea had merit, even in the face of opposition. But they also knew when to give up the chase. Consider *your* response to the following "cars."

- Your competitor drops a new product into the market or buys a competitor—now what?
- An airline drops baggage fees. Do you follow its move?
- A smaller firm than you just won the bid, and you lost your largest customer. Okay. That may require a whole pack of pups to go after that one.
- CoWorking and Living Spaces are equally being affected by the C-19 crisis. The Work-From-Home (WFH) effect is likely to result in a structural change. For example, Blackrock[44] https://www.blackrock.com/) announced that they expect about one-third of their seventeen-thousand-person[45] workforce to WFH permanently. Another report found that 98 percent of people would like the option of being able to work remotely for the rest of their careers. Is this an opportunity for CoLiving and CoWorking spaces? What can you offer to attract this changing market?
- According to the World Economic Forum, the average workday during lockdown was forty-eight minutes longer. Will this affect travel? Will these W-F-Homers need something your business can provide, or will this workday increase harm your business if you don't make some changes?
- Remote working and online shopping could drive fourteen million cars off US roads permanently (TWEF, Aug 2020). How do fewer cars and drivers on the road affect what we do?

ADAPTION ACTION: Analyze "today's news."

- The outcome of the React or Respond process could trigger or inspire an iterate or an adapt moment.
- Was this problem anticipated? Now what will you do about it? Iterate, adapt, pivot? Could this negative event lead to a new innovative product or process?

- How will your company react or respond to hotel supply, airline capacity, restaurants, local experiences, or rental car agencies shrinking or disappearing?
- What to do where once a large local shopping center or mall was a big draw for tourists and now it stands at half its capacity? (Think of those premium outlet malls that had coachloads of tourists needing local accommodation, filling local eateries, or checking out local attractions.)
- Your capital source gets hit badly by C-19, and losses mount. Do you React (panic)? Maybe. Carefully Respond with a sense of urgency? Better.

Do you have a process in place to internalize the issues and decide if you will react or respond?

Scribble Zone: Jot down your 3–5 action points about the above scenarios.

Tomorrow's Reality

> "You will rarely solve today's problems with yesterday's solutions."
>
> **Bob Hecht, Transformist**

Through observation, learning, and testing, a business starts to build up a New Normal/New Reality and sparks the next stage. This was as much true pre-COVID as it is today.

Staggered change often leads to rational and cost-effective pivots.

Sometimes the pivot becomes the *star performer* and your New Reality. Amazon was a bookseller, and now it's become the seller and distributor of everything. Why sell books when you can sell everything? Airbnb asked, "Why build a hotel when you can convince everyone to offer up a room on option?"

Insights - Key Contributor

Travel Tech Start-up (Alternative Accommodation)

The Adapters comment: AltoVita are on a mission to change how the modern traveler stays. Be it short or long stay, this start-up travel-tech platform has made a significant impact on the market since being founded in 2018. They are taking a new approach to disrupting the marketplace.

"AltoVita is an end-to-end solution for modern travelers. Staying with us means with us you can maintain your healthy, active lifestyle while abroad, and we'll take care of all the logistics. Create a unique stay by adding services a la carte, including cleanings, babysitting, storage, or grocery shopping."

Vivi Cahyadi
CEO & Cofounder

Karolina Saviova
COO & Cofounder
London, United Kingdom

Market: What market did AltoVita decide to disrupt and why?

AltoVita was launched in 2018 to standardise the quality inconsistency of alternative accommodation by combining technology and human-vetting. Countless marketing channel testing and product iterations later, we discovered our product market fit in the temporary housing segment within global mobility.

Problem – What market/innovation problem did AltoVita identify and how did you go about solving it?

Traditionally dominated by old-fashioned legacy models, the temporary housing sector comes with an inherent complex supply chain and multi-layered cost structure. Contracts between relocation management companies (RMCs) and corporate housing providers are often exclusive and lengthy, creating complacency and lack of incentives for innovation.

PDFs and emails are still the most commonly used tools to communicate property details to employees, while spreadsheets dominate the workflow between corporate housing providers and RMCs when it comes to rates and availability.

AltoVita's solution is designed to mindfully improve the experience of both employees and end suppliers with duty-of-care compliant instant booking features, consumer-friendly interface, and direct API integration so that data only needs to be entered once at source.

Obstacles: What challenges did you encounter and how did you push through it

Legacy models naturally inherit a legacy mindset. Change is a foreign concept with the industry players so unwilling to adopt technology. We pushed through this barrier by working with brand ambassadors, respected individuals as our spokespersons who validate and vouch for our product. The pandemic creates further opportunities in ways that could accelerate the technology adoption.

What 5 Tips do you have for young Start-ups?

1. Build a business model; flexibility and agility
2. Find the right cofounder
3. Articulate problem and market size (you cannot create problem and market, but you can iterate and refine product)
4. Demonstrate transparency and accountability to investors

5.   Disciplined product development (never build a product that no one will use)

What are the 3-5 major key learnings/failures that propelled your growth/thinking?

1.   In addition to your clients, your employees are your biggest fans. Design a compensation structure to attract top talent who believe in your vision.
2.   Keep refining and testing your product with the right target audience to solve actual problems.
3.   Engage with the industry; learn from your competitors and peers.

What are the 2-3 Marketing tips you have for Start-ups ?

1.   Thought leadership (unbiased content strategy).
2.   Test marketing channels. Laser-focus on the right ones and curate content accordingly.
3.   What gets measured, gets managed. Data-driven analytics is a must.
4.   Cross-industry collaboration on content and brand-awareness.

Innovation: What groundbreaking innovations did AltoVita bring to your target market?

The corporate housing content management and distribution are not only outdated but also extremely fragmented. AltoVita's system delivers fast and efficient consolidation of duty-of-care compliant inventory worldwide, including serviced apartments and verified private homes. Our Business to Employee (B2E) solution distributes directly to target market via AltoVita's proprietary interface and workflow completely customisable to clients' brand identity and DNA.

Adaptions: What are the 3-5 major Adaptions you made to your platform as a result of User feedback loops? What was the result?

1. Balanced combination of technology and human-centric approach.
2. Embracing duty of care via inventory vetting, content standardisation, and streamlined operations,
3. Implementation of customised Google Map API into map view search feature.

LinkedIn @ https://www.linkedin.com/company/altovita/

Company @ https://www.altovita.com/

Watch out for traps!

 TIPS & TAKES In a piece by Samuel Bacharach, the McKelvey-grant professor at Cornell University identified five common innovation traps: performance, commitment, business-model, deliberation, and short-term versus long-term gains.

1. **The performance trap**: Companies inadvertently set performance traps when things are going well. Sales are up, and the financials are solid, but the firm isn't bothering to commit time or resources toward developing the next generation of innovative ideas.
   (Think Peter O'Connor and organizational inertia. "Why would a company want to disrupt itself?")

2. **The commitment trap**: The opposite of the performance trap is the commitment trap; that is, the company sinks a lot of resources into new ideas that just aren't panning out. Rather than recognizing the mistake and changing course, leaders feel compelled to put more money into a sinking project with the hope that something will eventually flourish.

3. **The business-model trap**: This happens when a company ventures into a product or sector which may seem ripe, but the firm doesn't readily possess the competencies or materials necessary to execute. While it may seem like a good idea to expand horizons and product lines, if a company is not equipped to take on the new task, then it can fall victim to the business-model trap.

4. **The deliberation trap**: Companies embark on an endless journey to nowhere when too much time is spent analyzing, discussing, researching, and testing a new idea—without real results. Teams spend so much time processing the idea that they never arrive at real results. No one—neither team members nor the leader—is prepared to risk taking that

important first step of transforming the idea into a concrete innovation.

5. **Short-term wins are not substitutions for real long-term gains:** Short-term wins usually stem from meeting traditional customer needs and offering traditional or expected products and services. Short-term wins are usually rooted in past practices. When opportunities arise that could garner some long-term gains, companies focused on the short-term are often looking the other way. A short-term win is certainly not a bad thing, but it would be unfortunate if long-term gains were overlooked in their wake.

These traps characterize some of the factors that can stifle innovation. Organizational leaders may rationalize the existence of the innovation traps, and the organizational culture might justify and reinforce them. Innovation traps are cognitive blinders that steer leaders away from taking bold steps, from pulling the plug, from redirecting an effort, from screaming out that the goals are misguided, and that the emperor has no clothes.

> "If you have a different point of view on something, follow it through to the end and see if it's viable or not. (Learn to Fail Fast.)"
>
> **Raul Leal (CEO, Virgin Hotels)**

Entrepreneurial leaders should not ignore these traps; once they are triggered, they can lead the organization down a sinkhole. Your challenge is to identify and disable the innovation traps that can prevent your idea from moving ahead.

Author's note: While I agree with all these advisory notes, please add *Adaption* to each scenario as these traps certainly apply there, too.

(Notation - Samuel Bacharach. Mckelvey-Grant Professor Cornell. See index section Aug 14, Inc Mag)

Scribble Zone: *Write in what you WILL do and what you will STOP doing that is getting in the way of adapting.*

START DOING/CONTINUE DOING	STOP DOING

Scribble Zone: *Where are your business' traps lurking?*

_____

_____

_____

_____

_____

_____

_____

_____

_____

_____

_____

_____

_____

_____

_____

_____

_____

_____

_____

_____

_____

Adaption and innovation do not always occur at the Corporate Office!

Innovation sparks can fly either at the entrepreneur's start-up or at the established company that is sophisticated and brave enough to source and nurture *inside* "entrepreneurs/innovators."[46] This can be complex to manage, but when it comes to inspiring adaption or innovation, the UPS or hotel/rental car shuttle driver or the accounts-receivable manager is as important as a multi-degreed scientist at Astra Zeneca, toiling to find a vaccine for C-19. Think Churchill again. The war was filled with experts, but it was a bunch of code breakers in a shed at Bletchley that cracked the German's encrypted codes, fifty-two miles away from the leaders!

The path to innovation is difficult and littered with potholes, detours, and misleading signs. Resources may be scarce. Find a way to decide which ones are worthy of attention.

> "That will never work, or that's not what we do here" is never a crowd-pleaser in the arena of adaption and innovation.
>
> **T5 Strategies**

T.I.M.E: The fuel that drives Adaption and Innovation

T. Trend or Fad
I. Initiative & Investigate
M. Major Adaption and/or Innovation
E. Execution

T. Trend or Fad?

Is this product/service/experience a **trend or fad**? Many entrepreneurs and business leaders make the mistake of *creating a* *product looking for a solution versus identifying a problem and then building its solution.* For instance, in the wake of C-19, conferences and events have ceased to exist, yet we all still need to connect and communicate. Some venues could try to invent a Zoom-lookalike or simply use Zoom. (Interestingly, Zoom was the big winner over Skype.) Radisson Hotels and Resorts were one of the first to embed Zoom meetings as part of their meetings product line in September 2020, six months after C-19 hit. They are adapting using tech that already exists to solve for a new problem. It most likely will not be the final solution, but certainly will be a building block to leverage.

> **"Fads don't solve a problem.** *They sort of over-engineer a problem, maybe. Yeah. Do you remember? Do you remember the folded toilet roll in the hotel room when you folded the toilet roll over? When was that?"*
>
> **Piers Brown**

Exactly right, Piers! What a time waster! Did this add value? Save time or money? Did the guest even notice?

> "Firms need to learn how to ride a trend's wave to success. If they don't, they risk being swept away by its powerful tide."
>
> **Luc Wathieu – Georgetown University**
> **Elie Ofek – Harvard Business School**

There are other business examples that, in hindsight, were either the Fad or missed the Trend. Retail has been decimated by neither adapting nor innovating to survive. A few examples:

- Blockbuster versus Netflix
- TiVo versus Roku
- Tower Records versus Spotify and iTunes
- Toys "R" Us versus Amazon

- Nokia versus Apple iPhone
- *Any electronic* reseller versus Amazon
- Barnes & Noble versus Amazon...

Don't bet the house

Blockbuster discounted digital and home delivery, comfortably categorizing them as fads. All these companies had a lot in common. They had strong market share and ignored data that suggested that other, less than obvious competitors could compete and penetrate share faster and cheaper. Sometimes when you are losing, it's best to leave the casino rather than double down on the same number. But the odds are that most people stay! Casinos—and innovative, next-generation companies—are betting on it.

> "Ignoring trends can give rivals the opportunity to transform the industry."
>
> **Harvard Business Review**

Will hospitality discount WFH as a trend or fad? Will hotels and event spaces adapt to become "close-to-home office spaces" or embrace "digi-meeting" tech and find a way to monetize meetings with user fees? Or will they dismiss that, too, as a fad?

TIPS & TAKES

Determine if you are ADAPTING or INNOVATING—test and retest against the definitions.

Consider a wing mirror on a car. For years, the mirror was fixed, then was improved to manually swivel to a close, and finally, it became automated. Adaptation or innovation? Effectively incremental marginal improvements mean this was adaption. This required continued technical training and marketing.

However, if the car mirror was self-cleaning, and the owner could change it to a variety of colors at home—that would be a technical innovation!

I. Initiative & investigation

Take the initiative to encourage a Test-and-Learn and a Fail-Fast culture. Those of us involved in travel tech have learned that Perfect *really is* the enemy of Good. Booking.com, Expedia, and Airbnb, as do most tech companies, release a *most viable product* (**MVP**). An MVP is released to test changes and new products and let the *users* tell *you* what they do or don't like before you finish the last 10 percent of product development.

Restaurants do this all the time with menus. Add a new dish, and believe me, the guests will be more than happy to tell you what they think. A best practice is that they then either launch in existing units or build new ones as comparison prototypes. Restaurant brands commonly pick "test cities" such as Houston (USA) and Manchester (UK) to concept test their brands. These cities have a broad demographic and a lot of competition. This is the "physical" version of a website testing to assess user preferences.

- Encourage the feedback and investigate further.
- Nurture a culture of curiosity.
- Take the initiative to build a culture that is fearless about measured failure.

How else will we ever get to Mars, where someone will surely need a restaurant chain and home delivery!

Alexi Khajavi with Questex agrees with the "test-it" method. Long before a single conference attendee walks through the door of one of their events (or nowadays, clicks into a virtual gathering), the content that will be presented has been thoroughly tested.

"The content that you see at the event has actually been already merchandised multiple times in the digital ecosystem…we'll put out editorial without video. We may do a podcast, then we'll measure the engagement of that content. The content that performs well essentially becomes the content that gets brought to the live event. It's sort of a culmination of what we've been doing digitally for the twelve months prior."

M. Major adaption and/or innovation

This phase is where products are being created to solve for problems. Whether you are testing a new feature on your website or a menu to accommodate market changes (adapting) or changing your entire restaurant concept or online product to cater to a new need in the market (innovating), this work process is fraught with danger. Be conscious as to how to manage this "change" in your organization, particularly if you are changing your existing business. Start-ups have an advantage as they start clean and benefit and pivot from learning. However, remember that adaption is the foundation of innovation, but not all *adaptations necessarily lead to innovation.*

Consider beds and bedding. It's hard to believe, but there was a time that Heavenly Beds by Westin were not common. **Barry Sternlicht,** in 1999 (Heavenly Bed Store), asked why beds and bedding were not white. Previously, dirt-camouflaging floral-patterned bed quilts were the norm. As the story goes, he drove the adaption to make all beds and bedding wondrously comfortable and **white**. He did not invent the bed or the linen; he adapted the product to become an experience and subconsciously trusted as the bedding was white. Now, if he had invented self-cleaning and folding laundry, that would have been true innovation!

E. Execution

It's time to **scale or fail**. The user is the ultimate X-Factor judge. If you determine that all the effort is worth it, then the *entire* enterprise must be aligned to passionately execute—not an easy task. If you are a business owner that grew your business by expanding from one store to two, you know that this is tough. Add in a major geographical expansion to really feel some pain along the way.

- Marriott evolved from being a root-beer stand to an international hotel franchisor.
- Ray Kroc with McDonald's followed a similar pattern.
- CBRE became a multinational property expert.

These businesses all adapted and innovated multiple times to get to where they are today. Thomas Cook (Global Travel firm), on the other hand, expanded *beyond* its core product and tried to become all things to everyone, including running an airline.

While scaling, the obligation is to deliver an "experience" that *mirrors* or enhances the experience/product…The adaptors and innovators figured that out; they executed through cultural ambassadors—product adaption and/or innovation delivered by a well-honed process and people who believe in it. They captured the essence, bottled it, and consistently delivered it. Our GGTs all had this in common: they continually spoke about **culture**, **experience**, **consistency**, and the **customer**.

- *Cait Noone* spoke about her students and about inspiring her faculty to deliver a meaningful and practical education.
- *Raul Neal* spoke about the freedom of GMs to deliver the essence of Virgin at each unique location.
- *Sloan Dean*, CEO of Remington Hotels, realized that COVID-19 changed the concept of T.I.M.E, and he had to change his company's mindset. Remington is now engaged in a much-altered marathon. *"We're in a hundred-mile race, and we're one or two miles in."*

The concept of T.I.M.E applies to almost any industry. Although Noone, Neal, and Dean are leading teams from across the spectrum of TT&H, they illustrate the need to assess trends and fads to determine if a curriculum should be modified or upended, or if new travel-trend data merits changing menus, adding technology, or designing new facilities based on facts and intuition. They apply the principles of: "Observe, Test, and Learn" before scaling implementation, *then* they execute.

Scribble Zone: List three reactions to the concepts of T.I.M.E. What do you think are Fads versus Trends? How well does your company "Test and Learn"?

TIPS & TAKES

Capital Advisors' Practical Advice, Adaption Traps, and Tips

GGTs **Mark Greenberg** (MG), Managing Partner and Founder, Silverstone Capital Advisors, and **Paul Slattery** (PS), Director, Otus & Co. Advisory, London, UK, have more in common than being just long-term adapters, despite being based almost four thousand miles apart from each other.

As investment bankers and advisors to hundreds of companies over their careers, Greenberg and Slattery are both confident and clear on the traits that companies exhibit in both good and bad times and what problems can cause a company to fail. Understanding and following these basic tips may well enable your firm to be agile and adapt sooner—and avoid potential disaster!

Adaptation: 6 Business traps to be seriously avoided

1. **High *single-customer* concentration**: The company is structured and capitalized in a way to support large customers. When such customers fail or drive prices down, stress occurs. (MG)(PS)

2. **Growing beyond their balance sheet and borrowing capacity**[47]: Often it is as simple as not understanding the working capital dynamics to support the growth. The inverse is true, where shrinking revenues or costs rise faster than your balance sheet can support. This can lead to possible restructuring or even bankruptcy. (MG)

3. **A lack of financial discipline and process**: "You have to understand the company's quality of your earnings (Q of E)[48]. If you do not, trouble may loom." (MG)

4. **Lack of formal corporate governance**[49]: "I see that a lot in below-$500m [in revenue] companies. [they lack a] solid,

diverse board of directors, audit process, etc. The thinking becomes narrow with it." (MG)(PS)

5. **Less than transparent financial and business practices for investors and other stakeholders:** (MG)

6. **Lack of understanding of the core business and not having a meaningful business continuity plan:**[50]-BCP) (MG)(PS)

Scribble Zone: Write down your reaction to Greenberg's and Slattery's recommendations.

_____

_____

_____

_____

_____

_____

_____

_____

_____

_____

_____

_____

_____

_____

_____

_____

_____

_____

_____

_____

_____

Gutsy Genius Thinker
Piers Brown
Founder & CEO, International
Hospitality Media
London, United Kingdom

Piers singlehandedly brought a voice and a market-place to the serviced apartment space, which includes CoLiving, CoWorking, boutique hotels, and connected hospitality tech to the category. As a journalist, media marketer, publisher, and much more, his leadership has a community-centric connection. His business was affected by C-19, as many have been. Piers and his team adapted quickly to launch meaningful live webinars with real content. By mixing expertise and disciplines such as investors, tech thinkers, property managers, and more, his team facilitated a give-before-you-get attitude to the community he serves.

At The Adapters, we have focused on the importance of balancing EI (Emotional Intelligence), BI (Business Intelligence), and C (Community). Piers has integrated all three elements into his business. Two of his editors are under thirty years of age and have thrived during the C-19 crisis, including being promoted. Piers and his business partner George Sell, despite market pressure, *kept a level head*.

They understood that virtual or semi-virtual meetings were evolving anyway, and he noted, "I believe that the way people do business over time will be disrupted too. And you know, this technology that we're using is perhaps an example of how meetings are going, you know, online. It's what is happening with the client of ours."

A key learning from chatting with Piers is that "any business must listen and allow people to go with the ideas that they are truly passionate and care about." Hopefully with some profit thrown in.

He has now "adapted" again and aggregated many of his events under one umbrella event—"the UrbanLiving Festival." This is set to be launched in November 2020 as a hybrid in-person and digital event. www.urbanlivingfestival.com/

Click through and learn more.

"Take the other step while others hold back."

Piers Brown

Adaption Tips:

- Know your core and keep a flexible business model.
- Know your customers and put them at the center—stay nimble; sometimes small and medium-sized is ideal.
- Don't be afraid to ultimately make decisions that perhaps you don't want to. It's a business decision, and some are not popular. Focus on the profitable products, not the shiny ones.
- Listen, and allow people to go with ideas they are passionate about.

LinkedIn profile @ https://www.linkedin.com/in/internationalhospitalitymedia/

Company @ https://www.internationalhospitality.media/

Take the time to learn more

Click or use SmartPhone

Gutsy Genius Thinker
Mark Greenberg
Managing Partner & Founder,
Silverstone Capital Advisors.
Cincinnati, Ohio, USA

Mark is a passionate problem solver and operates in a world that requires the ability to make sense of complex financial and transaction challenges. As an experienced Investment Banker and Advisor, his firm is dealing with the dark days of companies facing the most complex of decisions due to C-19, including how to survive economic destruction. However, his clients have also benefited from the pandemic as Mark's products and services have satisfied new demand.

We talked with Mark about the challenges facing business, and the function and formation of Boards came up frequently. GGTs are politely direct, and Mark is no exception. "I am frequently engaged in a strategic planning capacity by shareholders and boards. They are seeking to understand company dispositional alternatives, including equity monetization, and Boards are oftentimes lacking business capability and governance skills to navigate such matters." Greenberg also observed that he sees that it is mostly men, with a "severe" shortage of women either at the Board or CEO level to offer balanced thinking. All companies want growth, and this means having a sound foundation to build off.

He is an active member of his community and sits on several Boards. Mark is also known to have an occasional glass of Italian wine in his hand!

"Be transparent with your Employees, Lenders, and other stakeholders, and build a no-nonsense business plan."

Mark Greenberg

Adaption Tips

- Strong Board—even a small company must build a strong, balanced Board.
- Deal with anomalies and problems quickly.
- Plan for leadership succession.
- Be Transparent.
- Hire a professional investment banker early in your sale process. Businesses are rarely sold to the buyer that you had anticipated.
- Be diverse.
- Manage cash aggressively.

LinkedIn profile @ https://www.linkedin.com/in/mark-greenberg-19a8119/

Company @ https://www.silverstoneadv.com/index.aspx

Take the time to learn more

Click or use SmartPhone

Gutsy Genius Thinker
Paul Slattery
Cofounder & Director, Otus & Co.
Advisory
London, United Kingdom

Paul is a real-life academic, lecturer, author, and researcher, and he studied this sector. His insights and opinions are deep, vast and prolific. As a frequent contributor and advisor to the thought leadership of the space, investment banker and cofounder of Otus & Co., Paul tells it the way it is. By clicking through below, you will listen to a wide-ranging chat about the state of most categories, including cruise lines, hotels, and restaurants.

As Paul keenly observed when we interviewed him at the peak of C-19, "The problems that we're facing now cannot be resolved within individual companies. They must be resolved sector wide. They have to be resolved internationally." In all of our interviews, we asked for the medium-term (three years-ish), and Paul was clear: "We know of [the dire nature] of this situation. We have an excess of hotel room stock in cities throughout the US and in the UK, in major city centers, and most other Northern Atlantic countries. Many of them are shut up already. There will not be the demand [created by] them [brands] for years."

It is also interesting that Paul commented frequently on the tension between a franchisor and franchisee during C-19. The franchisee is carrying the majority of the asset risk, while the franchisor has relatively lower risk as a marketer, distributor, and brand owner. However, with such a dramatic decline in fees, how long can the franchisors survive in their current incarnation? The currency dependencies may well be rewritten.

Author of *The Economic Ascent of the Hotel Business, Second Edition*, Goodfellow, 2012. By Paul Slattery ISBN: 978-1-906884-67-3.

Adaption Tips:

- Brexit is a "downer." Now, adapt, and make it work for you.
- Nice stuff on the walls won't do it; the hotels and events markets need to change radically to survive.
- With one new brand every month for the last ten years, less is more.
- "Most of us probably can't remember the holiday before last, the last movie we saw; this will pass."
- Great time to rebuild infrastructure.

LinkedIn @ https://www.linkedin.com/in/paul-slattery-b74521/

Company @ http://otusco.com/

Take the time to learn more

Click or use SmartPhone

CHAPTER 6

Adaption & Innovation Cycle – The Adapters' Formula

> "Know thy measure."
> **Greek Delphic maxim**

PART 2: Emotional Intelligence

$$(EI + BI + C) + A \times I = S$$

Three dominant themes became apparent from chatting with The Adapters

A) Emotional Intelligence "EI"
B) Business Intelligence "BI"
C) Sense of Community.

Using different terminology to describe the same elements, the GGTs referenced these three traits, over and over. All three are cornerstones of their approach to their work and their personal responsibilities, but they acknowledge that EI, BI, and a sense of community are even more important in today's world—yet sometimes more difficult to keep uppermost in mind with the never-before-encountered challenges, frustrations, and uncertainties that define the COVID era.

Gutsy Genius Thinkers. Our GGTs are certainly that—thinkers.

- They have vision.
- They know how to gather the data and analyze it.
- They develop plans.

- They seek out technology that will enhance their businesses and provide the most consumer-attractive and friendly experience.
- They have learned—sometimes the hard way—to recognize a trend from a fad.
- They have also learned, sometimes with some pain, how to create a solution for a market problem instead of wasting valuable resources developing a solution without a problem.
- They are continually seeking to learn from within their own industries as well as from external sources.
- They are dedicated to honing their business acumen and are always striving to perfect their business process and *business intelligence* (BI) practices.

In addition to critical thinking skills, our GGTs also showed us in their interviews that they had something else in common, another attribute that defines them as GGTs: *Emotional Intelligence. (EI)*

Whether it's an innate characteristic or a skill that they exerted considerable effort to recognize and cultivate in themselves, each GGT referred to it. They used different terms to describe the capability, but the conversations were laden with references to EI:

- "Don't do anything without collaboration." – *Cait Noone.*
- "Be a servant leader. Really care about the individuals in your team and empower them to make a difference." – *Daniel Del Olmo.*
- "I'm confident as an entrepreneur, but I wouldn't be able to do this by myself. Find the right partners to do the 'other side' from what you are best at." – *Vanessa De Souza Lage*
- "I think trying to find a common ground—I talk about it right at the beginning of our discussion, with trying to find some common ground that we can all agree on." – **James Foice**

Many leaders have been swept downstream while trying to determine the direction in which they wanted to bring their companies, organizations, or institutions as a result of fallout from C-19. (Actually, becoming adrift and dragging your organization along with you isn't new to the COVID era. Unwary leaders have been falling victim to this pitfall since the first caveman declared himself head honcho of the tribe!) Still, in today's chaotic times, it is difficult to judge whether it is best to scramble and swim back upstream to what once was (previous normal) or direct the company to set a course through the swirl of the estuary to the *"Blue Ocean"* of the New Reality.

> *"According to the survey from Levo Institute, 80 percent of employees consider emotional intelligence crucial for developing their careers."*
>
> **Prosky**
>
> Source How To Help Employees Become More Emotionally Intelligent (prosky. co) https:// talkingtalent. prosky.co/articles/ help-employees- become-more- emotionally- intelligent

The adapters and innovators that we interviewed spoke openly about how C-19 has tested their emotional strength as individuals, parents, spouses, employees, managers, and/or leaders. It has shaken the very ground that they stand on. Being confined has forced them to adapt and innovate at home and at work with magnified family and business tensions. This in turn has seen trends (or are they fads?) from podcast mania to "Zoomitis" and expanded homeschooling.

This would be a lot to balance in a *single* day—but here we are, still at it in an event now heading toward its 1-year anniversary. No wonder a few of our GGTs say that their commute to work is something they never thought they would miss, but actually do! However, the key learning here is to be hyperaware that EI and BI are becoming entwined. Achieving sustainable success without a healthy portion of both is less and less likely, and we have noticed that C-19 appears to be driving business to rapidly incorporate the EI and BI theories into our lexicon.

The demands on leaders to adapt and adjust to be more understanding and empathetic are rising. While this trend will create more stress on leaders to actually *lead*, embrace being out of your comfort zone; *that's where most people perform the best.* First time on stage singing? A starring role in the school play? First national final in your sport when you score? You feed off the applause and the energy in the stands. Nurture those relationships; strong interpersonal foundations are paramount to being able to receive trusted and genuine feedback, the kind meant to support and grow, rather than criticize and tear down. Look for the field and perform to your highest level; no mistakes, no progress.

EI and BI are not new concepts and have been written about extensively. We will provide a little background and some clarification, but our intention is to highlight the trending importance of EI, so we will refer you to some excellent publications that explore these concepts at a deeper level and hopefully encourage your journey of learning.

Because the terms EI and BI can be confusing and are often a major eye-rolling turnoff for many, let's jump into the geeky stuff first and define both.

Emotional intelligence (also known as "EI," "emotional quotient," or "EQ") is the ability to understand, use, and manage your *own* emotions in positive ways to relieve stress, communicate effectively, empathize with others, overcome challenges, and defuse conflict.

Business intelligence (BI) plays a key role in the strategic planning of organizations and is used for multiple purposes, including measuring performance progress toward business goals, performing quantitative analysis, reporting and data sharing, and identifying customer insight.

Contemplating these definitions, and the emphasis that our GGTs place on the EQ of their achievements in conjunction with their business skills, we felt compelled to develop The Adapters' "Energy Formula" of success.

$$(EI+BI + C) + A \times I = S$$

(Emotional Intelligence and Business Intelligence + Community) + Adaption x Innovation = Success

I don't remember this equation from Algebra 101, but it's a cornerstone to business excellence, and something our Adapters seem to have in common.

Great *teams* develop because of leaders coaching and creating a positive environment for ideas to flourish. When such an environment is nurtured, teams will most likely find a meaning, or a mission if you prefer, that feels right to most. Once a mission is identified, actions need to occur to deliver an outcome; effectively, a strong business process (playbook) needs to be developed, updated, or adapted.

Once the business process is defined and set in motion, it becomes organic. It lives, but it will need to be imbued with resilience to handle changes, be they economic or social. (Think the 2008 financial crash, COVID, and new competitors or new owners). These environmental  influences demand adaption, but with resilience and flexibility built into a well-thought-out playbook, using plenty of BI, and nurtured with the right amounts of EI, the chances for long-term survival and success multiply.

In essence, once EI is activated, a mission is identified, and the BI process is deployed, then the energy starts to multiply, and businesses can adapt and, ideally, innovate to a successful outcome.

But we're getting ahead of ourselves!

Back to the A-B-Cs of our GGTs.

We've said that our GGTs emphasized A) Emotional Intelligence, B) Business Intelligence, and C) Sense of Community in their conversations. Let's explore those elements a bit further, starting with EI.

> *Culture Energizes Strategy.*
>
> **Sean Worker – T5 Strategies**

(A) Emotional Intelligence

$$(EI + BI + C) + A x I = S$$

Emotional intelligence (otherwise known as Emotional Quotient or EQ) is the ability to understand, use, and manage your own emotions in positive ways to relieve stress, communicate effectively, empathize with others, overcome challenges, and defuse conflict.

One of the foremost thinkers on this topic is Daniel Goleman (see recommended reading in the reference section at the end of the book). A recognized leader in EI (EQ), Goleman[51] https://www.youtube.com/watch?v=Y7m9eNoB3NU) describes five main elements to drive Emotional Intelligence:

1. **Self-awareness:** This is the ability to recognize and understand personal moods, emotions, and drives, and the effects of them on both ourselves and others. This is a complex task, even on a good day. Ray Dalio (of Bridgewater hedge-fund fame) in his recent book *Principles,* references themes in his chapter titles such as "Get the Culture Right [to] Get the People right [to] Build and Evolve Your Machine."[52] It is interesting that a very successful hedge-fund manager realized that a linear equation is formed from emotion in order to hire the right people to drive a "machine."

    Many successful leaders have a toughness and drive that is less than congruent with EI. Many call a few winners "charismatic," while others that are largely BI-driven, with a smattering of EI, are characterized as "tough." Think Steve Jobs and many other GGTs. However, today many leaders may have to develop their EI muscles faster to connect to a population that has experienced an emotionally charged and sustained period of stress.

2. **Self-regulation**: This is the ability to monitor and manage your energy states, emotions, thoughts, and behaviors in ways that are acceptable and produce positive results, such as well-being, loving relationships, and learning. (yourtherapysource.com)

3. **Internal motivation**: Link.springer.com describes this as:

> Engagement in, or attraction to, an activity for the sake of enacting the activity, such that there is no known external incentive for said activity.

Simply put, it is the force that leads you to achieve a goal because of personal satisfaction or desire. Examples are starting your own business or deciding to run your first marathon. Great coaches know how to unlock this in their athletes or employees with simple motivational prods such as, "You know you can run faster. Why? Because I've seen you do it before." You just might believe that you can run faster, simply by being told you can, and then you do!

4. **Empathy.** This includes not only understanding others' feelings and behaviors, but also intelligently using that understanding to forge stronger interpersonal relationships and make better decisions—*not for the purpose of manipulation.*

5. **Social skills.** Social Intelligence/skill (SI) is the ability to successfully build relationships and navigate social environments. *Our society puts a huge emphasis on book smarts and IQ, but our relationships affect a much bigger part of our lives.*

It is interesting that the ancient **Greek maxim "know thyself"** (scio te ipsum) has had a variety of meanings attributed to it in literature, and over time, as in early ancient Greek, the phrase meant "know thy measure." (Wilkins 1927)

Self-aware leaders are difficult to come by because most of us, understandably, have blind spots. Adaptation and innovation demand that market awareness and personal awareness be crafted, even shaped by listening and curiosity.

Being aware and emotionally connecting with your environment is important. GGT **Mitch Presnick**, investor and Room Technology Ventures founder and serial entrepreneur, commented that first observing, then understanding the essence of the Chinese culture was fundamental to his success. He did not import his American business assumptions but did bring his business know-how. *"Success in China is about patience, candor, and three times the preparation than anywhere else."* These principles can be applied in any situation or business opportunity.

Daniel Del Olmo sees his position to be more a "servant leader" than president in the traditional definition of that role at Sage Hotel Management. As a servant leader, he believes that inverting the typical hierarchical corporate pyramid enables the inclusion of the ideas and emotions of employees and customers to influence the culture and keep it real. "What that means is we are basically flipping; we're turning the organization on its head and empowering the people on the front line to make that connection, to make that impact that is so meaningful."

When we interviewed **Sloan Dean**, CEO Remington Hotels, it became apparent that he worked to shape his career with deliberation! As a trained engineering graduate, he had developed the "process" muscle but recognized that the "people" muscle in his

genetic makeup might not be as strong. He sought out mentors such as Jeremy Welter (Remington). Dean interviewed ten executive coaches and hired one that he paid for personally for six years. His goal was to grow his career, and he decided that he needed to learn how to communicate effectively to teams.

"The differentiation that happens from a VP to CEO is all leadership and communication," Dean commented. He took a hard look at himself and determined that "probably my biggest mistake is just being overly ambitious to the point that people considered me arrogant."

Clearly, he worked on what he considered a personal obstacle to his desired success; Remington has a 4.0 Glassdoor score—equal to that of Hilton.

Dean's self-awareness is impressive. It is tough to realize we need personal improvement. It's even braver to say so out loud, and uniquely impressive to seek out and commit to the mechanisms to make those improvements. This key learning is valid for many of us who possess high technical abilities but less than stellar interpersonal communication skills. There are lots of examples of business and academic leaders that are brilliant *and* arrogant; not as many who have figured out that EI and BI are mutually inclusive to success.

So why is Emotional Intelligence awareness growing so rapidly?

According to the World Economic Forum's Future of Jobs Report,[53] https://www.youtube.com/watch?v=eH1fFdjzJAw) EI will be one of the top ten job skills in 2020 and beyond. More and more employers are aware that the workplace has become more complex than ever, with a generationally mixed workforce, the increasing demand for tech applications[54] and differentiators, and other factors. C-19 has just accelerated all that. The complexity of the stress and anxiety associated with the pandemic can't be ignored. It must become part of the discussion, just as much as frequent debriefings

"Get the Culture Right to Get the People Right and To Build and evolve your Machine" into something great, big, or small.

Ray Dalio, Chairman & CEO Bridgewater

"TalentSmart tested emotional intelligence alongside thirty-three other important workplace skills and found that EQ was the strongest predictor of performance, explaining 58 percent of success in all types of jobs."

Source talentsmart

Source About Emotional Intelligence - TalentSmart https://www.talentsmart.com/about/emotional-intelligence.php

on business conditions and staff meetings to keep the mission on target. Add in the WFH factor, and as a supervisor of teams, your role has become even tougher.

For the Travel, Tourism, and Hospitality industry, it may become even more complex. Most roles are on-site at a hotel, on a plane, on a boat, at theme park attractions, or as part of other leisure-related businesses. Yet a portion of the administration and sales staff may be working from home or working rotationally at a central office: accounting, sales, marketing. Not all managers have high EI/EQ. In fact, many will have to adapt and learn to motivate a team much differently than before COVID. Simply bringing donuts to the office to rally the troops may not have the impact that it previously had - - especially if those troops are no longer all conveniently located at HQ or at supervised "outposts."

Managers, listen up!

 "The pandemic provides the opportunity to express ideas that were considered crazy pre-C-19, like 'Why do we need an office?' Start asking 'why?' about a lot more procedures or ways that you have been conducting your business. ***Crazy Bob in the corner, questioning everything, sounds pretty smart right about now.***"

Alexi Khajavi
President, Hospitality & Travel
Questex Events

The need for an office to house every employee will most likely go the same way as the Boeing 747, on the way to retirement. WFH, whether part-time or full time, is most likely to become the *New Reality and demand new EI skills along with other logistical modifications.*

In a report published by the United States National Bureau of Economic Research, July 2020, they found that the average workday span increased by *+48.5 minutes* (+8.2 percent pre-COVID) partly due to increases in emails sent after business hours, with an increase of +8.3 percent per person per day.

Not surprisingly, the number of external emails and distinct emails (unique emails counted only once) sent, regardless of the number of internal or external recipients, did not significantly change in the post-lockdown period.

The effect of the lockdown on workday span was more consistent; the average workday span of an

> *"In UK's Whitbread group, restaurants with high EQ managers had higher guest satisfaction, lower turnover, and 34 percent greater profit growth."*
>
> **(Bar-On and Orme)**

Impact of COVID-19 Lockdown on Meetings

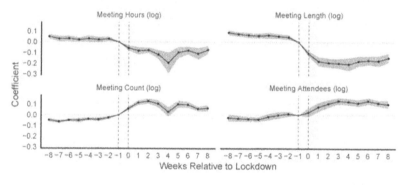

BOX 7

Meetings behaved differently, and we all know how we love meetings, right? Sure! More and longer meetings then? The truth is that during the C-19 period, meetings behaved in an odd sort of way. Meetings were both shortened in terms of length and expanded to include more coworkers. The cumulative effect of these changes has been to consistently decrease the total amount of hours employees spent in meetings each week after the lockdown date.

[53]*Note: The World Economic Forum (TWEF) authors studied 3.1 million workers from more than 21,000 firms in more than a dozen cities in North America, Europe, and the Middle East. They analyzed digital data on meetings and emails from eight weeks before government-backed lockdowns to up to eight weeks after.*

employee was higher every week following the lockdown than any week in the eight weeks prior to the lockdown.

Check out The Work Zone, 7.0 P157 at the back for more data and information on Work from Home.

 Manager's Tip

Donuts do matter, as does cake. Find creative ways to have donuts on Zoom to acknowledge a job well done during particularly stressful times. Maybe Deliveroo or Uber Eats can help!

Managers, what EI key learning is revealing itself?

It's safe to project that the growth in **WFH** versus **Work from the "Physical Business" (WFPB)** will directly impact today's New Reality management style. With two different workforces, with different privileges and rules working in the same company, one thing is certain: a board of directors will be convened to ensure proper governance and that the desired, largely financial, objectives are met. Regardless of where or how the *workforce* is delivering the product or service, the *management team* is charged with delivering the agreed-upon business outcomes. Our New Reality will require highly adaptable and innovative leaders to balance a traditional demand (from Boards) with a New Reality demanded by everyone else.

Could it be that employees contribute more when they do not have to commute and be directly managed? Are employees more engaged, productive, and dedicated because their time and capacity are theirs to allocate? Is it time to use technology and find new ways to connect with your team? Maybe it's not a catastrophe if employees go for a workout, walk the dog, or finish binge-watching *Stranger Things* somewhere in the workday?

C-19 has kicked us in the management gut to stop managing *time*-based performance and *adapt* our management systems to develop a *task*-oriented style. Maybe the key to success might be for the employee to hear: "This is when I need the work completed and the quality I expect," rather than being asked to "Give me a list of what you did today." ***Managers of Sales Forces***, *take note, outcomes are in and micro management of sales activities is out.*

I recently had a call with SKY Ireland (a TV/broadband provider in Europe) for some support issues. The technician was working from home, and we chatted about his experience. Despite having to put up with my stupid questions, he was relaxed and really helpful. He and his wife were both working from their "two WFH spaces," and they loved it. No commute time: they eat at home more, are healthier, and have found two and a half hours a day in their lives to do other things with less cost. When was the last time you had anything positive to say about your broadband service! Things do change.

Here are a few tips on how to develop your EI and be ready to adapt to an evolving work environment:

BOX 8:

1. *Be available*: Let your team know you are available to chat about the adjustment to working at home and the anxiety that may be in the air.

2. *Team meetings:* Zoom is tough, so work with your team and ask them what's working and what's not. Be sure they really know how to use the app! Don't just assume they do. What is the best time for your *team* to hold virtual "stand-ups" versus when it works for *you*? Talk about stress and challenges; these issues are very real, and the employee community can help.

3. *Clear Key Performance Indicators (KPIs):* Be clear as to what performance success metrics look like and how they will be tracked. ***This should be an open-book test.*** There are lots of project tools, such as Tableau, Slack, and others out there to take advantage of. Your team expects you to plug them into the company's vision and strategy to understand where they fit into the company; people want to contribute—make it easy for them to do so.

4. ***Deliver emotional and tech support***: This is an opportunity to adapt, evolve, and reimagine your management style. Be creative and find time windows to hold virtual, or occasionally in-person, one-on-ones. Take time to genuinely check in on how the WFH or CoWorking space is going. Be sensitive that many of us are still social animals and may miss the office gossip (although gossip always finds a way to travel). Listen and work through the issues that are particular to your team.

5. ***Be present on Zoom.*** **No reading emails or sending texts on your phone during the call or engaging in other activities not related to the event.** Equally, employees will need technical, accounting, human resources, and other support services as they and those resources adjust to this new WFH reality.

6. ***Be a manager:*** There will be problems, and they must be handled. The locations may change, but you have an obligation to coach your team to success regardless of where they "sit." Deal with the people problems fairly, as well as the obstacles to delivering your KPIs as a leader.

Sloan Dean gave us a true example of utilizing EI and the tips we've just discussed:

I have a webcast every week for the associates that are working and then a separate one for the furloughed associates. I had my furloughed webcast on Tuesday, and we ended up going two hours. It was an hour webcast, and then we stayed, me, the COO, and the head of HR. We answered over a hundred questions for an hour. It didn't solve a lot of people's problems, but it showed a willingness to continue to communicate...so I think it just comes down to transparency and constant communication...communicate [the tough decisions that had to be made].

Even the USA Air Force missed the target

In one year, the U.S. Air Force invested less than $10,000 for emotional competence testing and saved $2,760,000 in recruitment. (Fastcompany "How Do You Feel")

EQ skills translate to employee-business connection

Since the 1990s, when Prof. Peter Solovey, now President of Yale University, and John Mayer, then a postdoctoral scholar at Stanford University and now a professor at the University of New Hampshire, first set out their concept and joint model of EI, study after study, articles, books, and other research forums have shown that a high IQ or ability to utilize BI is not a guarantee of personal or business success; in fact, many of those studies indicate that those with "average" scores on standard intelligence tests generally outperform those with higher IQ scores about 70 percent of the time! While continued studies and much academic debate has ensued, the findings still lean toward the importance of EI for professional success and personal fulfillment, as well.

For instance, a Texas-based Fortune 500 company had utilized personality assessments for candidate selection for years with few results in reducing turnover in its high turnover salesforce. After turning to an EI-based selection assessment and an EQ training and development program, the company increased retention by 67 percent in the first year, which was calculated to add $32 million to the bottom line in reduced turnover costs and increased sales revenue.

Another example is Sanofi. The French pharmaceutical company focused on the EI skills of its salesforce, which boosted annual performance by 12 percent (see the research by S. Jennings and B.R. Palmer in "Sales Performance Through Emotional Intelligence Development," Organizations and People, 2007). Even though the travel space is our main focus, health care and hospitals can also be a source of inspiration as they, too, are in the people service business. A large metropolitan hospital reduced its critical care nursing turnover from 65 percent to 15 percent within 18 months of implementing an EI screening assessment, according to HR.com.

Approximately 82 percent of global companies now utilize EQ tests for executive positions; 72 percent of these companies give the tests to middle management, and only 59 percent of companies give the tests to entry-level positions (mitrefinch). This is not unusual or new, but moving forward, expect closer attention to be paid to this skill set. When it's focused on, there can be incredible results.

The COVID effect may be putting even more pressure on your management skills these days, but with thirty years of study, thought, and deployment in organizational settings, it's safe to say that the concept of EI/EQ is probably not a fad! If you haven't already, you might want to check out a few EQ tests, readily available online, to get a baseline record of your own EI.

The EI scholars all seem to agree that while a major component of basic human nature, EI is not directly connected to our IQ or our BI. Our ability to learn (IQ) stays stable throughout much of our lifetimes. EI, however, can be acquired at any age and can be continually improved upon with practice and attention. You or I may never achieve the genius status of an Einstein, but with work, we can become wizards of EI and reap its rewards at work and at home.

These EI skills were becoming more and more valued even pre-COVID, and as we have identified, higher EI abilities may well become the requirement to obtain—or retain!—a leadership or customer service role in the New Reality we now inhabit. Fortunately, these EI skills can be learned and nurtured—just ask Sloan Dean. Now may be a great time to seek out a coach or other professional services to boost your EI fitness so that you are the obvious choice to lead as our economies find their new footing.

> "Everything you do, just do it 1% better, every time."
>
> **Guy Lean**

How not to write a business memoir

EI and BI are meaty topics, and we strongly suggest engaging additional professional assistance in assessing your needs in order to build an appropriate program to fit you and your business.

Many books are written by well-known CEOs toward the ends of their careers, chronicling their versions of the "how-to" process of EI and BI management. Many of these are interesting reads. Had these individuals shared their stories much earlier, as they were growing their businesses and developing their leadership styles, it may well have been even more impactful. By the time these CEOs write the books, they're more memoirs than guides. The real "how-tos" have been diminished by time, or in some cases, simply omitted from the book in favor of more "interesting" anecdotes and recollections.

A current book that is particularly relevant is *No Rules, Netflix and the Culture of Reinvention* by Reed Hastings (Netflix cofounder) and Erin Meyer. The authors speak to a culture that is catering to a largely artistic hub. Commercial creativity is valued. But as Hastings highlights, this high-performance, highly measured environment is not for everyone. Netflix is a company that reinvented itself again and again, from delivering videos by mail to becoming a streaming content provider and a studio in its own right.

Hastings set new standards, valuing people over process, emphasizing innovation over efficiency, and giving employees context, not controls. There are no vacation or expense policies. However, at Netflix, "adequate performance gets a 'generous severance,' and hard work with expected results is irrelevant."

This form of EI is clear in its construct of providing freedom to the individual to create winning content. BI then drives the system of producing screenplays, preparing filming schedules, and working out location logistics to distribution, all in a complex choreography to deliver financial targets.

 "It's the Virgin culture," agrees Virgin Hotels and GGT **Raul Leal**. "It's pretty independent. People in the office really set their own schedule, work from home if they want to. Tirelessly responsible and hardworking. People just come and go, and they do what they need to do. It's a pretty free-flowing office, and that's the Virgin brand, for the most part."

Marriott over the years reinvented itself, from being a root-beer stand[55] https://www.youtube.com/watch?v=FRRBDaNxLLQ) to a family-owned hotel company and ultimately a major multi-branded franchisor and management company (Asset-light Model – [56]. ***Arne Sorenson***, CEO Marriott International, has gone through hell recently after being diagnosed with stage two pancreatic cancer in November 2019. Despite his own personal challenges, on March 21, 2020, Sorenson spoke to his team about the impact of COVID on the company, and more importantly, on the people. His communication has been viewed as one of the most genuine messages from any CEO during this crisis. It was personal, contextual, informative, and relatable. Please watch this video on YouTube to see a true professional tell it the way it is with perfect pitch and tone—a classic example of EI at work. **https://www.youtube.com/watch?v=X6af2lVfDDk**

BOX 9: Key Indicators that Emotional Intelligence is Present (Alive?) in the Workplace

- It's expected and accepted that almost all employees will get upset, have bad moods, argue, and just have bad days.
- People listen to each other in meetings.
- People express themselves openly.
- Most change initiatives work.
- Flexibility.
- People have the freedom to be creative.
- People meet outside of work hours.

Sep 14, 2017 blog.retail.org.au › news and insights ›

EI is complex, and there are various ways to connect. Many of the leaders we interviewed spoke about mentoring, one-on-ones, and other forms of coaching. This form of genuine caring and listening is a critical step to being a leader by example.

"Mentoring is one of the most important things we can do in the hospitality industry."

Raul Leal (CEO Virgin Hotels)

You can be the smartest business leader in the room, but unless you can connect your strategic vision to those who will make it a viable, profitable reality and execute the outcome on a daily basis, you will be talking to yourself in an empty room—and chances are the rent will soon come due on that room and you won't have the wherewithal to finance the lease!

> *"To unlock your power as an Adapter and an Innovator, it is imperative to understand what influences and drives you. Have the confidence to secure a professional business coach to enhance your skills."*
>
> **Sean Worker**

Scribble Zone:

a. List four ways that you feel you can adapt your communication to the New Reality.

b. List two people that are going to offer encouragement.

c. Highlight one person on your team that requires a helping hand to up his or her game.

Gutsy Genius Thinker
Daniel del Olmo
President, Sage Hotel Management
Denver, Colorado, USA

Daniel has operated or engaged in business in over seventy countries over the span of a twenty-plus-year career. Talk about adapting on a major scale! He exhibits the qualities of many of the featured GGTs in that he has high EI, BI, and Community drive. He views himself as a servant leader and believes in returning more to the community than he receives. Outside of work, he volunteers at Liberty Children's Home and Pandemonium Productions for children.

We interviewed Daniel early in the C-19 crisis and a couple of weeks after he joined Sage Hotel Management as its president. Like most hotel companies, Sage was reeling from the drop in demand, and Daniel was as concerned about ensuring that his team and customers were at the top of the list of priorities as he was about managing cash flow—a true servant leader.

At Sage, they view themselves as a "collective of relationship-driven individuals and hoteliers that define experiential hospitality and believe in the power of developed relationships." In *The Adapters*, we have focused extensively on having strong EI skills, balanced with Business Process and Business Intelligence to Get Stuff Done. Daniel is quoted a number of times in both segments and is worth rereading. We feel the evolving style of leadership has to balance the expectation of capital returns with the investment in people—with employees and customers. The blend of on-site and a distributed workforce is leaning toward trend rather than fad. Leaders will have to manage both.

Daniel is currently responsible for leading a team of six thousand associates across a portfolio of over fifty branded, lifestyle, and luxury hotels, with nearly twelve thousand guest rooms in twelve states across the United States. The post-C-19 era and the 4th Age of Change will demand a different set of skills, as we noted. Please take time to dig into Daniel's verbatim interview in the book. Be a servant leader—really care about the individuals in your team and empower them to make a difference.

"Now more than ever, leaders have to instill confidence and manage their teams, so they feel properly supported to not only survive, but thrive."
                                        Daniel Del Olmo

Adaption Tips:

- In unprecedented times, you have to think and act nimble, agile, and scrappy.
- Differentiate yourself within your market by caring in a general sense and by recognizing people. Technology can help achieve that.
- Bring art and science together to amplify your experience.
- Don't let the common and conventional norms in your industry define you—what can you do differently than some of the others out there?
- You can only activate experiential hotels if you involve the community around you in a meaningful way.

LinkedIn profile @ www.linkedin.com/in/danieldelolmo/

Company @ https://www.sagehospitalitygroup.com/

Take the time to learn more

Click or use SmartPhone

Gutsy Genius Thinker
Vanessa de Souza Lage
Cofounder & CMO Rentals United
& Founder VRTech Events
Barcelona, Spain

Rentals United *(RU)* has been a major influencer in the world of hospitality tech since it was founded in 2015. It is an advanced distribution platform for professional short-term rental property managers with ten-plus rentals looking to advertise on worldwide booking channels.

When Vanessa, James Burrows, and Emil Majkowski cofounded the business, channel management was available but relatively new to the hospitality sector. Airbnb triggered a revolution in the alternative accommodation space, and owners needed a way to efficiently distribute and market their apartment, beach house, yurt, and more on everything from Booking.com to Vacasa. In stepped this scrappy start-up. According to Vanessa, "The first few months of Rentals United were spent in a dark cellar (literally!) and with a hoard of interns, cold-calling property managers around the world." When a semblance of traction was detected, the first angel investor was found, who funded a new, slightly less-dark office. Fast-forward a few years, and they secured $ 4.2m in venture capital investment and took off.

Like every business in the travel space, C-19 has influenced Rentals United's business volume. C-19 has not stopped Rentals United from driving maximum volume even in a lower-demand marketplace. For those of you who have followed Rentals United's digital pushes, they have become a leading voice (with Data) in speaking to the strength of the comeback of the alternative accommodation and boutique hotels.

Vanessa is a GGT on every level. Her focused energy has invigorated and motivated an entire category, and she is also the founder of VRTech Events, which recently hosted its VRTech Start-up Competition. Adapters are community leaders, "give before they get," and in this case, Revyoos (an all-in-one review aggregator for short-term rentals) was the beneficiary.

"Build partnerships; you get there faster."
Vanessa de Souza Lage

Adaption Tips:

- If you can't win separately, come together.
- Build partnerships; you get there faster.
- Be a force of change; lead the way in professional property management. Travelers will reward you.
- Digital nomads are here to stay; it's a fact, not a fad! Market to them.
- Organizers of events need to widen the attendance at conferences and dig-events to include diversity as a primary goal.

Follow #tieonstage

LinkedIn profile @ www.linkedin.com/in/vanessadesouzalage/

Company @ https://rentalsunited.com/

Take the time to learn more

HOW: Click and Open your Smartphone Camera App, image on the QR code, and it will do the rest! Enjoy!

Click or use SmartPhone

Gutsy Genius Thinker
Sloan Dean
CEO, Remington Hotels
Dallas, Texas, USA

As an industrial engineer and math guy, Sloan Dean learned over the years to be adaptable. As a driven GGT and leader, Sloan realized early that simply being smart was table stakes—developing as a leader required building people skills. We refer frequently in *The Adapters* to the requirement as a leader to have the capability to connect EI with BI. The balanced approach to nurturing an adaptive and successful culture is critical mutual-value creation. During our interview, it was abundantly clear that Sloan is a focused and determined leader.

We do not believe that Sloan has ever hidden his ambition to run a company. But here's the difference: Sloan actively engaged an executive coach to build up his management skill over six years ago, and it has clearly paid off. As he said during our interview, "Once you get to become VP or SVP for institutional companies, those are all table stakes [Education and training]. And so, the differentiation that happens from a VP to CEO is all leadership and communication."

So why should you QR Code through to the Adapters' recorded session? Because Sloan is so up front about the challenges he is working on. He did not hide the fact that he wanted to grow, and came across as slightly "arrogant" as he went on to comment,

> It's a delicate balance between being aggressive and, at the same time, realizing that you can only get to a CEO-type position, particularly at a young age, by motivating and empowering people. And so, somewhere in my early thirties, I pivoted from

being a high-output individual where I was always just striving to be better than my peers, but where I was trying to motivate, empower, and inspire my peers. And I think that's a big pivot for a lot of folks, because most people are just, 'Wow, I want to be better than the other manager.'

Most people would never be this honest and forthright. Based on our interviews, the post-C-19 era is demanding this level of transparency and genuine drive to evolve by including your family and teams in the process. No BS—just do!

Adaption Tips:

- Network like hell.
- Ask the real and tough questions in meetings and interviews.
- Curiosity is a differentiator.
- Sometimes you must step down one level to gain the experience to be who you want to be.
- Be a storyteller, not a waffler.

LinkedIn profile @ www.linkedin.com/in/sloandean/

Company @ https://www.remingtonhotels.com/

Take the time to learn more

HOW: Click and Open your Smartphone Camera App, image on the QR code, and it will do the rest! Enjoy!

Click or use SmartPhone

Gutsy Genius Thinker
James Foice
Chief Executive
Association of Serviced Apartment
Providers
ASAP
Gloucester, United Kingdom

James Foice has made a difference. Not that long ago, the *Serviced Apartment* accommodation category was hiding in the basement of the *Branding* hierarchy. In fact, there were very few defined brands in this space. The last 10 years have seen a transformation and velocity of quality inventory entering the category and expanding beyond a "relocation niche product." It's now a core accommodation category and growth product for all the distribution channels from Expedia to Airbnb. James Foice played a major part in driving a key differentiation, that of "accreditation standards," and energetically formed *The Association of Serviced Apartment Providers* (ASAP). He's a *GGT!*

ASAP is a *not-for-profit* trade association representing over 100,000 apartment owners in 25 countries who offer 3 million bed nights per year. Accreditation was paramount to establish trust in the marketplace. Outside of niche business-to-business travel managers, general retail travelers never understood or trusted the space. Thanks to the hard work of ASAP, other trade bodies around the world, and new conferences, awareness is now universal.

It's comparatively easy to start any business; it's hard to grow, sustain and adapt over time. ASAP under James' leadership have done just that, including forming international alliances to leverage awareness. You will hear in the interview his views on "differentiation, stakeholders, agreement, professionalism, common objectives," all of which are key terms in how "EI" + "BI" is incorporated into your business. As an advocacy group, ASAP's voice is paramount in driving governmental awareness in the UK and beyond during C-19.

Today nearly all major hotel brands have an *Extended Stay* brand of some description. This has driven awareness, and more importantly, trust in accommodation that is "not a hotel room" This lens widening has enabled pure-play "Serviced Apartment" brands to attract conventional institutional investors such as Brookfield to the space. James' leadership at ASAP shone a light on a niche industry that got credit for being "accredited."

> *"I think trying to find a common ground. I talk about it right at the beginning of our discussion with trying to find some common ground that we can all agree in."*
> *James Foice (on running an association)*

Adaption Tips:

- A clear vision of helping the industry to be understood was incredibly hard; there again, this applies to any business—be clear as to why a consumer needs your product/experience.
- Find your point of differentiation and work hard to build consensus/
- Be very aware that you're not influenced by more vocal members.

LinkedIn profile @ https://www.linkedin.com/in/james-foice-7525ab21/

Company @ https://theasap.org.uk/

Take the time to learn more

HOW: Click and Open your Smartphone Camera App, image on the QR code, and it will do the rest! Enjoy!

Click or use SmartPhone

CHAPTER 7

Adaption & Innovation Cycle

"Every process should be run through the *P O'C filter: No thinking, please!*"

Peter O'Connor

PART 3: Business Intelligence

B) Business Intelligence: BI

$$(EI + BI + C) + A \times I = S$$

If EI is about managing your teams and yourself intelligently, *BI is about **being** intelligent about running and optimizing your business.* Businesses are entirely about people (employees and customers), and employees need an efficient way to know how to create for, and deliver a product or experience to their customers.

For instance, you can't just show up and hope that a plane is at an airport and expect to walk onto UA FL118 from Chicago to Edinburgh (well, I guess you could, but it probably would not go too well). However, assuming United has built a solid business process design, enabled by highly capable BI systems that deliver a seamless customer experience, you can probably expect to have a reasonably comfortable flight to Edinburgh on UA118 and four nights at the Balmoral Hotel (a J.K. Rowling favorite writing spot for the *Harry Potter* series, btw). There has to be a pretty solid "backstory" to the product, service, or experience in order for it to be consistently, efficiently, safely, and profitably delivered.

Business Process and Business Intelligence: the 35,000-feet cruising altitude view

There are *two* primary concepts to delivering a business intelligent experience or product:

1) *Business Process* and
2) *Business Intelligence* systems.

What is Business Process?

Definition 1: Business Process (BP) is a series of steps performed by a group of stakeholders to achieve a concrete goal. Each step in a business process denotes a task that is assigned to a participant. It is the fundamental building block for several related ideas such as *business process management*, **then** *process automation*, etc.[58] (KISSFLOW https://kissflow.com/)

Definition 2: Business Process *(a bit more granular)* is a collection of related, structured activities or tasks by people or equipment in which a specific sequence produces a service or product (serves a particular business goal) for a particular customer or customers. BP occurs at all organizational levels and may or may not be visible to the customers. A BP may often be visualized as a flowchart of a sequence of activities with decision points or as a process matrix of a sequence of activities with relevant rules based on data in the process.

The **benefits** of using Business Process include improved customer satisfaction and improved agility for responding to rapid market change. And btw, established BP means people know what to do and how to do it! Process-oriented organizations break down the barriers of structural departments and try to *avoid* functional *silos*. Source: Wikipedia

Here's a timely observation on functional silos by GGT **Cindy Estis Green**, CEO and cofounder of Kalibri Labs, a hotel revenue strategy and benchmarking firm. Within the traditional hotel/ hospitality structure, Green says:

> They're looking at reorganizing because they have to…**can't afford to silo** and have five complete teams with a leader of each. So, the shift is moving. The only solution, which I have professed for a while and I think will be reality, because everyone's forced into it, is to have a *commercial leader*. So, I think there'll be a commercial leader under whom there will be maybe a commercial analyst. We're not going to necessarily have a revenue manager who only looks at pricing. Those are analytical people with analytical expertise, and they might have to apply that expertise to digital and to sales and to pricing. Because we can't afford to have specialists because we are going to have to have one team.

As Estis Green highlights, "we can't afford to silo" in our thinking. Our structures *demand a change* in how we truly address business and its processes, and C-19 will probably require such compression in administrative teams.

BP's Architectural Plan

Think of BP as the architectural plan you hand over to the general contractor to build an efficient hotel or manufacturing plant that is powered with BI automation.

Business Process and its management oftentimes require a technology-enabled strategy to automate the process. The goal is to accomplish the end result properly, with minimum cost and in the shortest time. It is ideal for both simple and complex business problems. Some areas where BP automation is helpful are:

- Achieving greater business efficiency across the enterprise
- Reducing human tasks that can be automated, thereby reducing errors
- Adapting to changing business conditions *(Resilience and Flexibility!)*
- Clarifying roles and responsibilities and maximizing technology to deliver a frictionless experience wherever possible.

Examples of BP and BI are in everything we engage in, from reserving any hospitality product on Expedia, Booking, or Airbnb to booking your spa day at a Six Senses resort. This also applies to how your HR manager posts and tracks a job on Indeed.

BP deserves a book unto itself. (Hmm, is that a future *Adapters* volume?) However, here are a few tips to encourage you to be curious and improve your ability to develop and utilize processes and tools to adapt and innovate.

BP has **4 defining traits** through which you should try to filter decisions. The benefit of this filter is that any manager can apply it from the simplest of tasks to the most complex, from a marketing strategy to redesigning the office post-C-19.[59] – **Business process**: https://www.youtube.com/watch?v=sHhTxeLMyPI)

4 Traits of a Business Process

1. **Finite** – A good business process has a well-defined starting point and ending point. It also has a finite number of steps. This is important to maintain order and avoid "project creep."
2. **Repeatable** – A good business process can be run an indefinite number of times. This allows testing, learning, and more importantly, the ability to *adapt* to changing conditions—like a pandemic!

3. **Creates value** – It ultimately aims at translating creation of value into executable tasks and does not include any step in the process just for its own sake. In other words, if any step in the process isn't adding value, it should not exist. This applies to most events in business, including examining the efficiency of departments and work groups. (Sounds like a good time to check in with the people who are tasked with executing the process. Ask them if each step is essential or just an unnecessary "extra." Conversely, ask them if there's a step missing that might keep them from getting easily—or ever!—from A to B.)

4. **Flexibility** – It has an in-built nature to be flexible to change. When any scope for improvement is identified, the process allows that change to be absorbed within itself with less operational disruption for its stakeholders.

Source: kissflow, T5 strategies

Flexibility and adaption are being tested at unprecedented levels. Many companies are currently revisiting their strategic plans and the processes they support. For some, it is vital as they look for survival trails in the current pandemic landscape.

Sloan Dean tells us that when he moved to Remington Hotels, two of the things he focused on were "process and efficiency." The company had a handbook and other procedural records, but Dean found they didn't focus enough on measurable actions, actions that drive customer satisfaction, or they were simply those that set up a "hero culture" around individuals.

"When you start to scale a business," Dean said, "If all your emphasis is on the individual knowledge of an individual and not a process, you can't replicate it...and I looked at that and said, 'Hey, we're going to be growing a lot. We need to have a more streamlined process, training efficiency.'"

BOX 10. Business Process' Blueprint for Success

TIPS & TAKES

Business processes also need to be revered. If they need to adapt, so be it. Do so. But remember—changing "on the fly" can be costly. Think "job-change orders."

Physical architecture designs have many parallels with technological digital design; change happens! BP, in both cases, is sketched/flowed first, then translated to a design program and handed to a builder/coder to make it come to life. Both disciplines anticipate that there *will be changes*. There is a protocol for this: complete a Change Work Order request.[60] This helps all the parties, who are invigorated by an idea, to slow down and assess the proposed change. A change order must be written out and approved by all parties, which can take time, money, and patience to complete. If all parties involved agree that the change is worth it, then the process or plan is changed.

Imagine constantly walking into your dream home that you are building, and each day, one of the other family members wants to add a door here, move the shower there, and another wants different windows. Imagine that the builder simply says "yes" to everything. What a mess! What will your dream house ultimately look like—and cost? However, if the parties agree to the changes and the costs, well, that's an adapted version from your original plan, and everyone's happy and will enjoy the new digs!

But once Business Processes have been put into action, respect them. If everything is an exception to the rule, then the process, and its outcome, become meaningless. Worse, *the process of the BP* becomes suspect to those charged with its execution. This is also a trustbuster. We can't emphasize enough:

Business Process is important, but developing one and then ignoring it is a serious threat to your business.

Embracing a methodology that encourages a disciplined approach to change is what Business Process is designed to facilitate. Here are a few tips to consider,

BOX 11. 10 Tips to Develop a Meaningful Business Process

1. Identify what tasks are important to your larger business goals.
2. Streamline communication between people/ functions/departments.

Focus on amazing Ux™
Silos align to a singular mission - *driving execution of the company's strategy*

Aligning mission with replicable processes leads to market agility and communication clarity

Is the business Responding or Reacting?

The alignment of your team to the company's mission demands that every department/function is focused on delivering the *promise* to the customer. User experience (UX) and the reviews that go along with it determine if you have the ability to adapt to the ever-changing marketplace.

3. Establish a culture that seeks to improve efficiency and the experience of your client by testing, correcting, and improving processes. It is ideal to do this before (potentially) automating them; otherwise all you have done is make the mess run faster (*and* more expensive to remedy!).

4. Establish processes and assign ownership or you risk the work and improvements simply drifting away—and they will, as human nature takes over and the momentum peters out.

5. Set approval protocols to ensure accountability and optimum resource allocation.

6. Standardize processes across the enterprise so they can be more readily understood and managed, errors reduced, and risks mitigated.

7. Enable continuous change so the improvements can be extended and propagated over time.

8. Improve existing processes, rather than building radically new or "perfect" ones, because that can take so long as to erode or negate any gains achieved. (Adapt!)

9. Prevent chaos from creeping into your day-to-day operations.

10. Standardize a set of procedures to complete tasks that really matter to your business.

Source aim[57], kissflow, T5strategies

Let's assume that your company's culture embraces change to accelerate adaption and innovation. The next step is to build out the processes to deliver insight and BI to your teams. Making better and faster informed decisions can help reduce the stress levels of both your employees and customers as they collaborate in solving the business' challenges.

It's time to layer in the concept of Business Intelligence (BI).

What is Business Intelligence?

Business intelligence (systems enabled by tech) or BI plays a *key role* in the ***strategic*** *planning* and ***execution*** of all organizations. BI has many *tools* for multiple purposes, including *measuring performance* progress toward business goals, *performing* quantitative *analysis,* *reporting* and *data sharing,* and identifying **customer insights.**

Let's expand the definition with a bit more granularity! REALLY? According to *Forrester Research,* BI is "*a set of methodologies, processes, architectures, and technologies that transform raw data* into *meaningful and useful information* used to enable *more effective strategic, tactical, and operational insights and decision-making.*" Under this definition, BI encompasses information management (data integration, data quality, data warehousing, master data management, text- and content-analytics, etc.). Therefore, Forrester refers to data preparation and data usage as two separate but intricately linked segments of the BI architectural stack.

They may not have memorialized their business approach into a formula, as we have, but every single GGT featured in this book has embraced and understands that **(EI+BI + C) + A x I = S** is central to delivering a trusted product or experience. I, as an author and a manager, have made numerous mistakes in my career in the development of my own EI and BI capabilities. Each and every time, you pick yourself up, learn, and move on to try to improve. Data and feedback loops are super important to sourcing the truth. Data is crucial to driving insight.

Bad Data In, Crap Data Out,
whether it's a 360-employee survey or product performance stats!

In essence, the objective for all of us that run businesses is to develop BPs and BI tools that unite and integrate complex systems to synthesize usable data for your business intelligently. (Phew! That's a mouthful!) It is not unusual for really smart people to present data in an unnecessarily complex way. (*Go ahead, say it. We do know what you're thinking.*) The trick is hiring the right people and experts such as a program manager or interpreters to facilitate and manage behaviors to make sense of your BI systems and keep the jargon at a minimum. If the data cannot drive and enhance your business vision, why bother? It's easy to find the good news and difficult to openly present negative trending data to drive adaption and even innovation.

GGT Vanessa de Souza Lage makes sure she has the right team partners at Rentals United to properly interpret the analytics required to successfully run the company. A marketer extraordinaire, Lage says analytics are not her strong point. "The way I deal with it, because at the end of it, I know as an entrepreneur it's something I lack, what I found out with analytical people, and with my team, is that I attempt to overcomplicate the stats…[They then also speak in plain English] Then I know I have the right partners. I think maybe the advice I offer is to find out what you're really good at and find the right partners to do the other side."

> "Marketing without data is like driving with your eyes closed."
>
> **Dan Zerella**

Business Process and Business Intelligence are all around us, from booking an airline flight (UA118 to Edinburgh!) on Booking.com to ordering an Uber. Every keystroke that you tap on your phone has BP and BI systems embedded for you to connect to the service you requested. This includes meeting your Uber driver at your pick-up location to be delivered to your Serviced Apartment, hotel, CoLiving, or CoWorking destination.

The P O'C filter

As **Peter O'Connor**, GGT, Chaired Professor of Digital Disruption, ESSEC Business School, Paris, pointed out, technology should be frictionless and require *NO THINKING* by the end user. Smart technology should enable *an established or agreed-upon* BP to produce a seamless transaction right before your very eyes—or better yet, invisibly! A successful UA118 flight requires a lot of defined processes, from connecting passengers via a hub in Chicago for connecting flights to loading bags, servicing and catering the aircraft, to landing it on runway 1L on time in Edinburgh. Every step of the journey involves a dynamic process and intelligent systems (BI). The Peter O'Connor filter (**P O'C filter**) continues to emphasize that Uber stands out as requiring little or no THINKING. Set up your profile, choose the pick-up and drop-off locations, and you're done.

An industry head-scratcher

The Adapters have long questioned why the hotel and alternative accommodations sector has failed (there *are* exceptions) to embrace widespread, *frictionless check-in* and other services. Rooms, in most cases, make up the majority of the revenue and profit for hotels. Most major hotel brands (franchisors) such as IHG, Marriott, Accor, Hyatt, Radisson, and Hilton *(the brands)* have made every attempt to become asset-light.[61] The brands therefore have to convince owners to invest in any brand change, including such advances as *frictionless/contactless keyless entry* to rooms, which admittedly can be quite expensive. The asset owners largely foot most of the cost to implement such brand changes. Of course, the owners have certain rights to refuse such changes/upgrades. A brand can mandate these upgrades, but that does not necessarily lead to a harmonious relationship, and could actually lead to the ultimate loss of that asset from the brand's inventory.

Interestingly, one of our GGTs is a substantial multi-franchisee, and experienced this particular obstacle to technological adaption from the opposite perspective. He *wanted* to try some interesting new adaptions at the property level but received negative feedback from the brand as his tech-lead changes were not approved by the brand for system-wide rollout. Ultimately, he had to bow to their viewpoint, but he tried the ideas at his own corporate office and was pleased with the results, which were superior to the brand's performance.

Why didn't the brand want to see these advancements made? Could it be the "When You Get So Big, You Are Reluctant/Unwilling to Disrupt Yourself" syndrome? Hmm...

The consumer, on the other hand, demands best in class technology and service. Consumers have spoken loudly that they want a choice between a personal check-in "experience" or choosing the room for themselves and directly heading to that room upon arrival. *Is this an intelligent way to run a business?* The average consumer can choose a seat on a plane, order an Uber, buy anything from Amazon anywhere, but hotels or their equivalents do not generally offer that choice. Wyndham recently announced a rollout "low-contact" stays across six thousand hotels, which was encouraging and will set the bar for other brands. How will the Events and Conference venues and hotels adapt and change due to new preferences and demands? Hopefully, quickly.

> Wyndham Hotel Group announced on Sep 24, 2020, "An app which prioritizes low-contact in-stay features and is slated to be the first to offer mobile check-in and checkout at nearly 6,000 economy and midscale hotels in the U.S.— comes at a critical time as both travelers and hoteliers look for innovative, digital solutions to help navigate the challenges of the coronavirus pandemic."

Many other franchisors in other sectors have embraced BI technology. Restaurant groups such as Taco Bell have already implemented the use of QR codes for their menu selection and to place an order. According to *Restaurant Business*, July 22, 2020, as an addition to the pandemic-induced safety protocols being introduced rapidly in all

Click or use
SmartPhone

industries, many restaurants are now moving to QR only, where waiters use handhelds to order and place food orders and have contactless tableside payment processes. Aha! The ***frictionless P O'C Filter!***

In this instance, the BP + BI story is not over yet. Allocating rooms and making them available is not as easy as picking your seat on a plane or at a concert. UA118 has a specific time when it arrives and delivers its passengers. Equally, it has a set time when passengers board for the next destination, with a lot of important checks and inspections required before the next take-off. (*Known knowns.*)

Hotels, on the other hand, can never really guarantee when guests leave or arrive despite the rules on backs of doors and the fine print. To compound this, not all hotels are operating the same property management system (PMS Notation) that manage billing, room allocation, etc. While it has improved, it is a head-scratcher that a consumer cannot choose a room, or at least be given a time window when a room will be available to check in. Why has this yet to be solved? Let's skip the robotic room service and get people into a room faster—that's where the money is.

This is a high-friction experience that is so contrary to ***Prof. O'Connor's*** *"Frictionless"* digital experience. It brings into question the hotel sector's capability to embrace well-established technology available to drive efficiency and meet the expectations of today's more digitally savvy customers. Siri or Alexa can tell you the weather anywhere and order and arrange delivery of your groceries while you relax in your armchair and binge-watch Netflix, yet I cannot receive a digi-message as to when I can drop my bags at the hotel!

Radisson Hotel Group, CEO of The Americas, **Jim Alderman**, questions why the customers' digital expectations are still largely unmet in many instances. "With the availability of technology, there is no reason a guest should not be able to see the inside of their exact room choice, the view from the window, the situation of the hotel and the precise location on the street as well as exactly where the closest restaurants and attractions all are and what they have to offer. We all do bits and pieces of this now, but there is such a more natural flow that can be integrated to our main landing pages for hotel booking."

> *"The greatest value of a picture is when it forces us to notice what we never expected to see."*
>
> **- pyramid analytics**

> **BOX 12. Early Adapter:** *Radisson is adapting* to the C-19 meeting restrictions by partnering with Zoom
>
> **Radisson International connects live events via Zoom:** Radisson has designed an innovative way to use Zoom to help event organizers rethink large-scale corporate meetings and conferences as hybrid events. Zoom Rooms provides a no-hassle, all-in-one video conference room system at Radisson Hotel Group's meeting venues, allowing attendees to gather in smaller, socially distanced groups and connect by video to other satellite meeting locations with one click.
>
> Zoom blog, September 3, 2020

BP and BI in action

$$(EI + BI + C) + A \times 1 = S$$

> **BOX 13 easy steps to working a problem**
>
> 1. **Identify** the problem that you want to solve.
> 2. **Collect** as much data as possible about the problem.
> 3. **Analyze** the data. Determine if the problem you are trying to solve is either a Fad or a Trend and if it is worth pursuing. Look over the "fence" to see what others may have done faced with similar problems to solve for.
> 4. **Test the data** that you collected, grab a room with a whiteboard, add coffee/beer/wine and snacks, and start the challenging game of BP mapping.
> 5. **Rerun any initial models** such as financials or service flow and test your hypotheses again.

6. **Stop or Go**: If your financials or service flow are negative, then STOP; if they are positive and passed the human element input stage, then GO!

7. **Go**: Now begins the process of defining a scope of work. BP map it or build it out (tech engineers and or physical building) to deliver a product with BI systems.

8. **Test, Learn, Adapt**: Building in flexibility is key as you learn. Our GGTs cautioned that ensuring flexibility as a key element in any Business Process can mean the very survival of the enterprise when faced with major disrupting forces like C-19. Check, and check again. Can the process adapt when faced with adversity?

9. **Open for business**: Ready to go. Now encourage the culture of testing, learning, and collaborating to have an adaptable, innovative, and flexible company.

The teams get in a room and BP map all the actions that must take place to connect all the systems, including how they sell it to solve the problem. They test the data and assumptions rigorously and decide that the business model is worth funding. They engage a BP engineering and BI company to refine the scope of work and modify the existing platform to deliver a BI experience. This will include guest- and employee-facing tools, dashboards, and analytics. Concurrently, the physical buildout is occurring, all elements get connected, and BAM: open for business!

> "Knowledge is the right to answers. Intelligence is asking the right questions."
>
> **unknown**

BOX 14. Case Study: Adapting to Empty Meeting Spaces

We have a problem! Our meeting space is empty. The owner has decided to assess adding meeting tech to expand the virtual meeting capacity utilizing Zoom groups. Along the way they have found that the adjacent CoWorking facility will partner to offer flexible office space, which will add to their product offering.[62] http://www.t5strategies.com/

If only it was that easy, but you get the point.

The *9 Steps of Problem Solving* from the previous page encourage an occasional "touch the brakes" approach to thinking—but not a lapse into institutional inertia! This can help guide participants through a linear framework to a desired outcome. Business Process is a super-important technique to adapting to ever-changing times in an orderly way. BP mapping is an integral part of adaptation and enables us to *think and respond* rather than *react* to change. In the case study above, we are blending the concept of business automation to deliver a product with powerful BI.

Firms such as Appian, Macedon, The Judge Group, and others specialize in BI and automating Business Processes. These implementation firms are process engineers and work to harmonize and interface with existing tools such as accounting systems, sales management, operating systems, and webstores.

Today we are spoiled for choice when it comes to companies that can provide services to address much of our daily business chores. The adapters and innovators that we interviewed spoke little of the detail but a lot about the macro influences of their business. However, *all* use data sources to drive decisions and have applied these best practices in one fashion or another.

> *"The essence of a good start-up is a scalable model, so BP is critical to that. You need processes to be as streamlined, automated, and user-friendly as possible. Every time we encounter a repetitive process, we try to refine and streamline. At the same time, you need BI to understand user behavior so that you can take the right actions. Our best product decisions were driven by a healthy mix of gut instinct and feedback, backed up by BI."*
>
> **Jacob Wedderburn-Day**
> *Cofounder and CEO, Stasher.com*

Business Intelligence is relatively common nowadays and very accessible. We strongly encourage you to be curious and question your process to allow your company to adapt and innovate, becoming better prepared for success in this 4th Age of Change. For an additional level of understanding, turn to page [100] to learn a little more about the ***10 Common Uses of Business Intelligence*** and spend some time thinking about the applied uses of BP and BI in your business.

Scribble Box – Where do you think you apply the principles of BP and BI to your business? More inspiration below!)

Looking beyond travel for inspiration: Business Process and Business Intelligence

Remember a while back we talked about "peeking over the fence" to see what others were doing in industries outside Travel, Tourism, and Hospitality? Well, with C-19, that "fence" may seem to be morphing into a *wall* as we feel more and more enclosed in our own spaces. Grab a mental ladder if need be, but let's keep exploring the "outside" world. Let's keep looking over the wall at a couple of adapters and their use of "insight technology."

Adapt concepts from other industries to enhance your business. It may be faster and cheaper.

> "Perfect prepa-ration doesn't exist. Excellent adaption does."
>
> **Lauren Fleshman**

Netflix is in the news. *Reed Hastings* has recently published his book *No Rules,* acknowledging that Netflix is demanding and not for everybody.

An example of Netflix's thinking is that producers use data models from BI software to recommend decisions around a show. This BI approach is not new; however, Netflix took the method to an entirely new level. Netflix wanted to move out of the third-party content streaming space and into a content production and delivery platform.

How Starbucks uses Business Intelligence – The Seattle-based coffee chain, Starbucks, is also a prominent user of BI technology. Through its popular loyalty card program, Starbucks is able to amass individualized purchase data on millions of customers. Using this information and BI software, the company can then predict purchases, provide offers customized to the individual coffee aficionado, and offer a variety of bespoke payment methods. Via mobile devices, the company informs customers of the offers it believes people will enjoy. This system lets Starbucks draw existing customers into its stores more frequently and increases its volume of sales. In this capacity, BI has a use similar to traditional CRM systems. In fact, many businesses choose to combine BI and CRM systems to get the most out of their data. Source: CCS Technology

Why does this loyalty program work when so many others don't? What can the Travel, Tourism, and Hospitality space learn from this? Several of the GGTs questioned if hotel loyalty programs actually create loyalty, as do I!

Take Amazon, for example. For years they have used your purchasing and browsing history to suggest other products you might be interested in. Better yet, they offer you the option to edit these recommendations to filter out the unwanted items.

Scribble Zone: What can you and your Company do to build true loyalty with your Customer?

How Restaurants and Bars got with QR Codes.

Well done to all for embracing this simple technology due to C-19! This 1994 technology, coupled with a smartphone camera, has revolutionized how we view a menu in seconds. We are challenging all hotels, bars, and restaurants to continue the service long after COVID—and may we also request that you allow us to order on our phones! Speed things up for them and us—and give the time back to the server to tell us more about the great chef specials, drinks, and wine on offer!

 # Go on walkabout!

Just prior to our interview, GGT **Mitch Patel** was in Washington DC for a gathering of the Marriott Advisory Council, of which Patel is the president. As part of the meeting, the group was escorted on an "experiential" walking tour of Georgetown.

Patel reports,

> We didn't know what this tour was going to be about, but we said sure. And then we walked around Georgetown, and we visited about twelve to fourteen different businesses, from coffee shops like Blue Bottle to retailers like Lululemon. It was really just to learn from each one of these businesses. How are they trying? How are they standing out? What are they doing differently to obviously stay relevant in today's world, right? With online retailers, your brick-and-mortar retailers, what are they doing to stand out and get customers in the door? Let's admit it. *The hotel industry is slow to adapt*, right? *We're really slow to adapt.* It's a capital-intensive business, but we're also very slow with embracing *trends* and technology and so forth. And so, it really opened our eyes.

Sounds like a great idea, doesn't it? Have you ever just gone "walkabout" as a consumer, no specific agenda in mind, just to see what's happening in other businesses around you? Give it a try!

The Adapters is teasing you to explore a variety of themes and start your journey to discover more. Business Process, Business Intelligence, and Artificial Intelligence (AI) are omnipresent and will only accelerate during our time in the 4th Age of Change. We're just pointing out the path here. We hope that you engage professionals in each category to further enhance your business.

Scribble Zone: *List four BPs that you will improve either in your department or company. List three BI projects that you would like to change to drive user experience.*

Understanding your employees and customers – it's the intelligent thing to do

Build Emotional Intelligence and Business Intelligence muscle to develop expertise and integrate EI and BI to become a world-class adapter—and maybe even an innovator.

Let's be clear: we recognize that *not all companies utilize this approach* (although all should, to the appropriate degree). Not every enterprise requires a high-level or layered BP inventory. However, nearly *all* Travel, Tourism, and Hospitality companies require some type of a platform to produce and sell cookies, fill beds, run trains, fly planes, or offer walking tours or rental cars to connect a business to customers through distributors such as Rentals United, or Trip Advisor tours.

Today's consumers expect to have a seamless and frictionless in-person and online experience, wrapped in a trusted, secure environment. Not asking much, are they? Your company's BP and BI should be invisible and, therefore, amazing. This "Pavlovian" *now* attitude has placed pressure on all business categories to embrace technology and deliver or fail. The key is to select partners to collaborate with *Respond rather than React* capability to the acceleration of on-demand satisfaction with immediate feedback loops. The irony is that the employees and leaders of Travel, Tourism, and Hospitality and other businesses are also consumers, yet sometimes speak of their customers' requests for a frictionless, *thinking-less* digital experience as being unrealistic and costly. They forget that they probably took the survey, too, and demanded immediate delivery from Amazon and Booking, as well! Do what I say, not what I do?

> "Research conducted with Fortune 500 CEOs by the Stanford Research Institute International and the Carnegie Melon Foundation found that 75 percent of long-term job success depends on people skills, while only 25 percent [depends] on technical knowledge."

Even our GGTs admit that other industries often outpace the TT&H sectors in their embrace of Business Process, automation, and related technologies. The challenge for the Travel, Tourism, and Hospitality community is to look over the wall at what other industries are up to, learn, and incorporate their ideas into their business. Think about how Disney manages lines for its attractions or casinos find a way for you to never know the time of day so that you never leave and just keep spending—it must be the free drinks!

Whether you know it or not, everything we do has a process and a sequence. Imagine for a minute how you leave the house in the morning: you go out, get in your car, and start the engine. That's a repeatable process. Add in the rest of your routine of grabbing a coat, keys, unlocking your car, fastening your seat belt, and turning the key in the ignition pretty much the same way every day, and that is a "business process." Your teams need that predictability as well. They are stressed now, more than ever, and so are you. Having a repeatable, proven plan to follow reduces that stress for both team and leader. Life and business stress have also increased for your customers. They need predictability, too, and to trust that the hotel room is C-19 clean, every time, and that today's service experiences will be as safe and as contactless as possible. Keep the processes running smoothly, and you will build even more trust with your customers—something all business owners and operators will need even more of as we emerge from the pandemic into the New Reality.

EI and BI have been front and center for so many GGTs that lead successful product and experience revolutions, including:

- Kemmons Wilson, one of the first franchisors, Holiday Inn
- Vanessa de Souza Lage and James Burrows, Rentals United
- Piers Brown, IHN Media
- Alexi Khajavi, Questex
- James Blick, Devour Tours and Spain Revealed

All of these individuals have passion. They are constantly adjusting the volume of EI and/or BI to achieve their missions and live the equation of success.

There is still time for TT&H to take advantage of the speed of change occurring during C-19; from QR codes to redefining virtual meetings and even aiming higher for frictionless tasks to become outsourced to technology. Guests get the attention they are expecting and paying for. Travel, Tourism, and Hospitality are the ultimate people-to-people interaction businesses that we all crave. Another beer, anyone?

> "By action and reaction do we become strong or weak, according to the character of our thoughts and mental states. Fear is the deadly nightshade of the mind."
>
> **Edward S. Walker, Jr.**

$$(EI + BI + C) + A \times I = S$$

(Emotional and Business Intelligence + Community)
Adaption x Innovation = Success

Gutsy Genius Thinker
Cindy Estis Green
Cofounder and CEO Kalibri Labs, LLC
Author
Rockville, Maryland, USA

Hey, you, it's all about *data* and the story that it reveals. Solid, professionally interpreted data can help mere mortals make sense of the industry that they compete in. Cindy, through the multiple companies she has founded, has certainly contributed to the "truth" that eventually catches up to us all: thrive, adapt, innovate, or disappear. The genius is in framing the truth. She is also CEO and founder (a title that Anthony Melchiorri, GGT, also prefers, rather than the pedantic "entrepreneur") of Driving Revenue, a data mining and automated marketing company that was acquired by Pegasus. She stayed on for a while before she founded two more companies, with the most recent being Kalibri Labs.

Cindy has advised hotel owners on how to work through the rise of channel distribution that accelerated over the last twelve years since the Great Recession of 2008 and the skyrocketing cost of customer acquisitions, and she continues to do so today. For her current company to be relevant, she needed a source of pure data. She faced the battle to convince hotel brands and hotel owners to share transaction and performance data—that is a gutsy hill to climb. It took over five years to convince them to trust her and then sell it back to them. Smart business model, right? It was so obvious during our interview that she is passionate about the granularity of the detail and wants to drag the industry at least close to modernity. Every other industry has cost-of-sales data (think retail and the tracking of inventory and store sales), but not the broader hospitality space.

Currently, Kalibri Labs is trying to help owners predict the future of C-19 on their businesses. No small feat, considering no one really knows. This form of dynamic interpretation, hunting for the new trends, is gutsy, considering the dark hole that we are staring into, for now. Historical data tells us that this shall pass; there's comfort and opportunity there for sure!

"If Airbnb decides to pivot to being more a week-minimum stays or focus on longer stays, well, that's going to change the degree to which they compete with hotels in urban markets."

Cindy Estis Green

Adaption Tips:

- Data sets you free if you know where it was sourced and who interpreted it.
- Everyone is competing to fill every room. "So now everyone's going to be competing for this middle-range kind of business...you know, local and regional, corporate travel, leisure, transient, then small groups, when groups can begin."
- *Know your market,* and find a way to bridge from here to the *New Reality.* Who knows? Your new customers may become your forever clients
- For a while, the drive market will be meaningful. Actively market to connect to consumers within your drive radius.
- "I think that the hoteliers, in order to thrive going forward, have to understand completely the nature of their demand and the cost of acquisition. And they have to partner with the brands in order to more efficiently and effectively bring business in."

LinkedIn profile @ www.linkedin.com/in/cindy-estis-green-4554a1/

Company@ https://www.kalibrilabs.com/

Take the time to learn more

Click or use SmartPhone

CHAPTER 8

Adaption & Innovation Cycle

PART 4: Community Engagement

$$(EI + BI + C) + A \, x \, I = S$$

(Emotional and Business Intelligence + Community)
Adaption x Innovation = Success

(c) Community Engagement

$$(EI + BI + C) + A \, x \, I = S$$

Our GGTs are a generation of leaders who understand that being *emotionally* aware, as well as *business intelligent are key elements of the powerful formula for success.* So far, we've examined

a. Emotional Intelligence
b. Business Intelligence, to include Business Process and technology

Now it's time to look at the "C" in the Success Formula—**Community Engagement**.

Most of the GGTs we spoke with seem aligned in their firm belief in "community engagement." Actually, that's a term that has been overused for quite some time. In some companies, it's become little more than another bullet point in the strategic plan, trotted out for company rallies, and in some cases, it's just there to add to an organization's PR arsenal.

> "...I think 'community' is spoken of very frequently, but very rarely do companies really have a meaningful experience with communities."
>
> **Daniel Del Olmo,**
> President, COO
> Sage Hotel
> Management

But for the GGTs, "community engagement and relationship" is way more than that. It's a connecting thread that has been woven into their organizations' foundational fabric. It's something that unites many of their companies' players, and frequently inhabits pole position with resources to back the ethos. Just a few examples of how GGTs are getting in touch with their own business backyards:

• Before joining Sage, GGT **Daniel Del Olmo** was a cofounder of another company that assisted emerging brands to get to the next level, oftentimes in difficult emerging markets. They partnered with several on-the-ground organizations that set up free "pop-up" hospitality training classes for locals. Del Olmo told us,

In this particular case we were helping them open up a property in Namibia, in Africa. It was for people in the community that otherwise would have never had a chance to have a shot at a hotel job. We train, and then we hire these folks. We hired about sixty people to join us in that luxury hotel, which is open now in Namibia. So that's one way of really bringing in the community. And when I talk about the communities, [I mean] people in the market that actually live and work there.

Now that he is president of Sage Hotel Management, **Del Olmo** continues to consider community.

It's built into how we do business. You can only activate experiential hotels if you involve the community...in a meaningful way. To me, the experiential side is one that I think requires much more in-depth involvement in the community, giving your locals really a reason to make your hotels, to make your restaurants, to make your bars their local hangout.

Additionally, the company sponsors several charitable efforts that benefit the greater community, as well as the community of its own associates.

> *"Small acts, when multiplied by millions of people, can transform the world."*
>
> **Howard Zinn**

Here Comes the Omni RV

Peter Strebel, CEO of Omni Hotels and Resorts, has a keen sense of community with his Omni Hotel team and the surrounding neighbors where his hotels are located. The "**Here Comes Omni RV Trip**" kicked off in October 2020. The team visited fifteen cities in ten days and donated ten meals for every mile they drove—fifty-one thousand meals in total to Feeding America. Peter stood out among the crowd as an EI communicator with totally passionate and sincere communication to his team in the first weeks of COVID. More of that, please! https://www.facebook.com/omnihotels/videos/122278772902616

Greg Juceam speaks with passion about the plight of the homeless in the United States. Operators of the affordable Motel 6 brand, Juceam and his team are often in a position to see housing instability up close in some of their guests. They have been known to help guests who lose their jobs and become financially strapped by offering accommodation until they can get back on their feet and return to their home, rather than sink further into homelessness.

Their commitment to community extends further into their policies regarding payment for rooms. Juceam said,

It's truly, truly how I feel…We had a discussion about should we only allow a reservation if somebody has a credit card or debit card. Most brands today will only take a reservation if you have some form of credit, but a huge portion of the US population, and in fact the traveling public in the economy space, doesn't have it. And you're shutting them out if you're only going to take credit cards or a debit card or even Venmo…so it was a decision I made to continue to take cash, even though it makes life more complex for us to own and operate hotels. Because it's important to do that…we're providing a service to the traveling public. Yes, you're making tax dollars off of it, but we are doing as a brand something that we need to do because the world needs it…something the US needs.

And if you really want to talk about getting a whole community engaged, *a whole city*, then just look at what **Cait Noone**, *Vice President International Engagement and Head of the College of Tourism and Arts*, Galway, Ireland, was part of. Galway was selected Europe's Capital of Culture for 2020—a really big deal in the European Union. Cait represented the school on the steering committee that began meeting in 2015 to prepare their application for the honor. Noone explained,

Team, team, team effort. None of this would have ever happened without our teams. We proceeded with a parallel application to become a European Region of Gastronomy and won that designation! And it took a number of public bodies and a lot of private support as well from stakeholders…it was all about the people. There was a lot of people working behind the scenes, but it was really driven by the people of Galway.

Of course, most of the celebratory plans went out the window when COVID-19 came through the door. A do-over might be in order, all things considered, but Noone continues to focus on the positives that came from such a massive collaborative effort.

"Those who are happiest are those who do the most for others."

Booker T. Washington

BOX 15. Super 8 China - Built on Community and Trust

Community and cultural understanding matter everywhere. **Mitch Presnick's** journey from Reston, Virginia, to New York to Beijing, China, was long, and he had to read the cultural heartbeat around him to claw his way to success. Fluent in Mandarin, 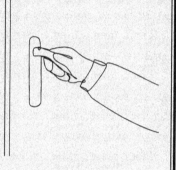 Mitch navigated the Xiaoping era to become a successful hotel owner and master franchisor in a place and time where many other investors feared to tread. According to Presnick, it's hard to win in China as a Westerner. *"The Westerner will win if the Chinese local wins twice as much."*

Mitch had already developed some strong business muscles by the time he ventured into the Chinese market as an entrepreneur, as he was previously head of government relations for Anheuser Busch in China. Using and continuing to develop his EI and community involvement skills helped him understand the foreign business landscape that he was pioneering. Combining those abilities enabled

Mitch to adapt to the social norms in China and grow a business to close to eleven hundred hotels. All of us face these nonlinear decisions: adapt or likely fail. In Presnick's case, this was adapting to a cultural expectation.

Community involvement and your employees

It's heartening to hear so many stories of community concern from our GGTs and others—just because it's the right thing to do. It's also important for today's leaders to understand that such involvement and, in fact, a company's **Corporate Social Responsibility Status** (CSRS) is increasingly important to today's fastest-growing workforce segments—millennials and the generation coming up behind them.

These groups are growing rapidly both as workers (employees, gigs, entrepreneurs) and as consumers, and they are making their interest in ethical business practices clear. Because they are at the apex of the tech-savvy tree, they are easily able to research a company's labor practices, employee satisfaction ratings, and their level of community participation.

In an article published by the University of Ohio titled "Why Corporate Social Responsibility Matters in Today's Society," the authors cited a survey by Deloitte that found that 70 percent of millennials reported that their decision to accept an employment offer was partially influenced by the company's CSR reputation. Boycotting certain products and services that don't meet socially responsible criteria is not enough; many in this generation want to take part in making these changes as well, and look for employers who share their values.

> "Sometimes you gotta create what you want to be part of."
>
> **Geri Weitzman**

Employees want to know the mission of the company and how "we" are making a difference. What business book author hasn't advised that one of the ingredients to corporate success is a relatively happy and stable workforce, understanding of, and committed to the company's objectives? And which of those books hasn't made clear that it takes at least some elements of EI (or however they label it) to build and maintain that environment?

However, these are for-profit businesses and delivering returns to investors is expected, be they private, public, or government-funded. The old thinking has been that "soft" objectives like community engagement are a drain on resources and a distraction from the company's objectives. Our GGTs know that caring for your community—*and that means the company's backyard, the larger global community, the community of your workforce, and even the community of your customers*—and practicing a healthy dose of EI are *not in conflict with the organization's financial goals* when implemented in conjunction with complementary business intelligence and acumen. Emotional connection, community concern, and capital *can* be aligned. The days where shareholder value and reward were central (Jack Welch) have evolved greatly. Businesses realize that reputations are built on acting and being local, no matter how global they are.

Leaders are expected to be more balanced than ever to ensure that their constituent employees, customers, suppliers, and investors are being well served and heard—and all expect results. Sponsoring the local girls' soccer team is probably more important than supporting NASCAR in these very tough days. Reputations will be built and lost depending on how communities perceive business interests and actions in their markets.

To become a world-class adapter, and maybe even an innovator, requires continually strengthening your EI and BI muscles (as Sloan Dean describes them) and consistently seeking to balance them. Not an easy task, but worth the effort.

The adapters and innovators that we interviewed shared their personal experiences with the perpetual struggle to find that balance. Just when you think you nailed it, things change, and we are off to the *adaption races* once again! The previous crises list in our immediate memory bank is long: World Wars, the Spanish Flu in

1918, the 9/11 terrorist attacks, the 2007 financial crisis, SARS, natural disasters, and more. History is a chronicler of what happened and should inspire us to understand that we will emerge from this crisis ultimately with a fresh vision of the future. Odds are that we will rise above the current adversity and adapt to the New Reality, and even innovate beyond it.

Blending EI and BI to become a force multiplier[64] is in our business DNA. There are so many examples, from taming fire and capturing stories to learning to write and transfer knowledge by printing and distribution, using iPhones to connect to most things. Why do we keep adapting and innovating? Survival is a primary driver, but design, exploration, and advancement seem to be homo sapien traits. Possibly having a sense of destiny to change the world (Mars by Tesla), paint like no one else ever has (Picasso), and/or be the best parent you can be, or become an amazing General Manager of a hotel. Each to their own.

> "Perpetual optimism is a force multiplier."
>
> **General Colin Powell (Ret.)**
> USA Military

Through our own experiences, joined with what we have learned from our GGTs, we at *The Adapters* have concluded that appropriate levels of ***EI + BI + Community*** concern, blended with the instinctive need to survive, places us in the best position to succeed in a time that is ripe for accelerated adaption and innovation. Altogether, these elements form:

The Core Business Equation

(Emotional Intelligence + Business Intelligence + Community) + Adaption x Innovation = Success.

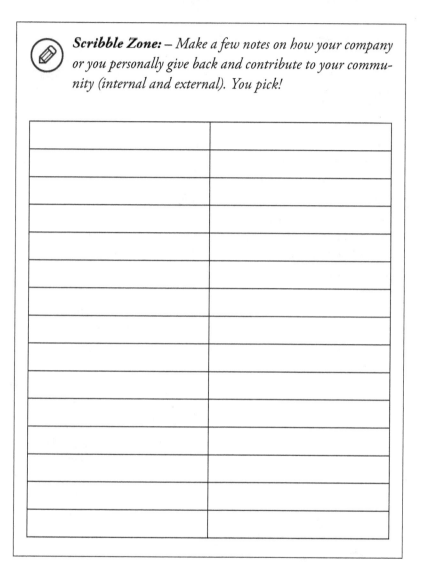

Scribble Zone: – *Make a few notes on how your company or you personally give back and contribute to your community (internal and external). You pick!*

In the 4th Age of Change, leaders are expected to be more balanced than ever to ensure that their constituents—employees, customers, suppliers, and investors—are being well served and heard. Remember, all expect results.

Sean Worker – The Adapters

Gutsy Genius Thinker
Guy Lean
Managing Director, Madison Mayfair
London, United Kingdom

Like all leaders in business, it is all about building knowledge and figuring out what your business will excel at, what market problems you are solving. Guy, a **GGT,** focuses his considerable tenacity on solving Talent gaps and sourcing *"impact players"* for his clients. His foundation was in training and talent development, and it shows in his practice.

Today's executive search firms should be an integral part of a business's support system to build culture to deliver on the mission and financial outcomes of the business. *"It's about making a difference."* It's striking that Guy and his team seek *"impact players."* This narrows the field considerably because the onus is on the candidate to prove this to a potential employer. However, as Guy shared in his interview, the company must *"have a [clear] mission and goals or a vision really know what is needed in a team member. Do you know what you actually do?"* In order to convince an *"Impact Player"* to join, regardless of C-19 or not, mission content and clarity are paramount.

He is also straight up; another common trait of our GGTs. He promotes that his client will engage and get an advisor, guidance counselor, and a business partner. His commitment is that they will find the truth about a candidate to ensure that they will be positively impactful.

C-19 has certainly impacted his business. He has had to adapt and scale his office to match current demand. There is a pivot to mandates seeking Asset Managers and agile leaders that are capable of handling crises. Not all leaders are wartime thinkers. Brexit has also had an impact, with several middle-level managers returning to their home countries to secure a job there. He believes that there will be a *"shortage of qualified staff at a certain level"* post-BREXIT and C-19

Guy is as passionate about his Company as he is about cycling down a mountain on his Mountain Bike. GGTs take risks—calculated ones, of course.

> *"The thing is that we are calling people that are happily employed, doing a great job, and being well paid for it. So, it's all about an opportunity, not a job. It's never about a job."*
>
> *Guy Lean*

Adaption Tips

- As a candidate, be prepared. Be clear on what you are good at and what you are not.
- Be prepared to be tested; don't be shocked. Clients ask good questions; you need solid scenario-based examples.
- Build credibility; trust will follow.
- Everything you do, just do it 1 percent better every time.
- Employers, focus your attention on keeping the "impactful players" you have; it's well worth your efforts.

LinkedIn profile @ www.linkedin.com/in/guylean/

Company @ www.madisonmayfair.com/

Take the time to learn more

Click or use SmartPhone

Gutsy Genius Thinker
Mitch Presnick
Founder – Super 8 Hotels China
and Investor
Raleigh, North Carolina, USA

Mitch's Facebook page is titled "Mind-Energy-Focus," which reflects the essence of EI + BI in three words. As a GGT and an intentional lifelong learner, he brought a freedom of thought and insight to our Interviews that can benefit us all. His energy is infectious. As you engage with his interview, *The Adapters* will provide a seat belt for you to strap in as you go along for the ride.

Mitch is Director and Partner with Marco Polo Pure China Fund and holds an MBA from the Rutgers Graduate School of Business in Newark, New Jersey, a graduate diploma in Chinese language from Peking University in Beijing, and a BBA from James Madison University in Harrisonburg, Virginia. He is fluent and literate in Mandarin Chinese. He's a prominent American business commentator in Asia and a permanent resident of Hong Kong and Raleigh, North Carolina, in the USA. He has spent over 28 continuous years operating in Chinese business circles. Mitch realized that China had immense opportunity and brought the concept of branded franchised economy hotels to that country. As Founder and former Chairman and CEO of Super 8 Hotels (China) Co., Ltd, he launched Super 8 in China in 2004, which grew to over 1,100 hotels. Prior to Super 8, Mitch served as China's country manager for Edelman PR agency. He played an important role in bridging business relations between the USA and China as the former Vice Chairman American Chamber of Commerce in China. I think you get the gist. Mitch has adapted and innovated in some of the most competitive markets in the world.

"If you believe something to be true about the world, then act on it. Don't let anyone tell you otherwise because you know, because oftentimes, the mob is wrong."

Mitch Presnick

Adaption Tips

- Start thinking about what it is you offer that AI or machine learning can't deliver.
- Best-mover advantage is when the timing is right—when everybody else has taken their shot and either succeeded or failed.
- Making sure you take 20 minutes to meditate every single day to separate yourself from your emotions and reconnect to yourself.
- One thing that we know about the sharing economy, it's that getting customers to use something better is easy.
- Once an organization gets to a certain size, it's not in their interest to innovate, because to innovate, they're disrupting themselves.

LinkedIn profile @ https://www.linkedin.com/in/mitchpresnick/

Take the time to learn more

Click or use SmartPhone

CHAPTER 9

The Wrap

If you want to be an adapter, you've got to be willing to take a risk and put yourself out there.

Cait Noone

$$(EI + BI + C) + A \; x \; I = S$$

Adapters and innovators are everywhere in our lives, whatever the industry, whatever the size of the organization: from small to large, business owners running a campsite, a river cruise operator, restaurateurs, travel guides, boutique hotel owners. Travel, Tourism, and Hospitality have evolved as technology has become widely accessible, and travelers began gushing over "experiences." The 4th Age of Change has certainly modernized and legitimized the sector as an investable business model, although most of our GGTs insist that there's some "catching up" to be done in terms of the best uses of BI and cutting-edge technology to deliver the most efficient and user-friendly products, services, and experiences. *(Remember the P O'C filter?)*

These adapters and innovators have promoted or improved many long-needed changes. Examples include:

- Self-check-in and room selection
- Superior conference experiences, largely driven by event-tech platforms like Everbrite moving to entirely mobile app-based experiences
- Apps that provide up-to-the-minute critical data for hotel owners, etc.

Case in point. Here is how **Greg Juceam** of G6 Hospitality is meeting that technological challenge.

Our property management system is just a few years old now. It's a leader in its segment. It is not one of these systems that is old architecture. It's only been invented in the last few years. It was incubated in our offices by a group out of India. They were with us two and a half years working alongside us, building this for us…and it's an app. They can update it in one click, like you can update an iPhone. So the guest checks in on essentially a tablet. It's fully EMV compliant, a hundred percent cloud-based. The guests sign the keypad with their hand just like you would perhaps in retail outlets nowadays. And it's a fraction of the cost to not just maintain, but to update, relative to the rest of the hotel technology.

…with that app we have the ability for owners and managers to run their hotels remotely. I can go in on my iPhone app right now…and see any hotel, how many rooms have been cleaned. I can see how many maintenance work orders have been put in today, how many folks have checked in. I can literally run this app remotely. And a lot of our owners are multi-unit owners and they can manage from not being on site. They can see exactly what's happening in real time. These kinds of things are wonderful because we started from scratch, whereas others are bolting on technology to what they already have.

It is highly likely that COVID will force the reshaping of the industry and its ecosystem quite dramatically. Like all destructive events, there will be a period of adjustment, but opportunities will present themselves for the adapters and innovators that choose to energetically seek them out and embrace them. People *will* travel, *host* weddings, *meet, eat, cruise, fly, and rent cars again.*

But if we do not make our own adaptions and drive our own innovation in the space, be assured, says **Prof. O'Connor**, someone from the outside probably will. The professor adds:

> So, what I would say, we're so far behind, and as a result, there's the potential for people from outside our industry to come in and grab our business…what do travel suppliers think about the potential for, let's say, the Amazons or the Alibabas or the Facebooks of this world to come into the travel sector? Do suppliers think this is going to be good, or do suppliers see that as a threat? *This is a threat,* and the honest answer is most suppliers have not even considered this. This is something that should be on their horizon. It's something that is a major strategic threat for most of the large travel companies. But it isn't even getting on their horizon at this present moment.

Lest we forget, in less than fifteen years, a meaningful travel tech industry has sprouted! The financial crisis occurred in 2007/2008, and in less than twelve years, the velocity of change and peak travel volumes occurred.  Back-office interfaces have certainly adapted and scaled with companies like Amadeus/Travel Click, CRM (Customer Relationship Management), and platforms like Guesty and Salesforce, with HR performance management systems such as SABA rounding things out. Channel managers like SiteMinder and Rentals United have made it easier for both hoteliers and non-hotel accommodation providers to connect efficiently to distribution networks.

> "Your life does not get better by chance; it gets better by change."
>
> **Jim Rohn**

There are some hidden traps—many of our own making. With the avalanche of apps that now flood the market, guests can be spoiled for choice and possibly overwhelmed. Travelers are managing their trips on multiple apps, from ordering an Uber to airline seat selection to hotel room temperature settings. There are apps such as TripIt that can consolidate the itineraries and bookings, and which add yet another step on the pathway to personal travel management. The core issue is that each "service" has its own app, and the burden is on the travel user to download and coordinate this maze. According to 9to5mac.com, the average smartphone has about thirty apps, and the user interfaces with the bundle about 2.15 hours per day while launching nine apps per day. You know what you use the most! Maybe C-19 will encourage further innovation and consolidation to bring "frictionless" clarity to the offering.

> "The great growling engine of change. TECHNOLOGY."
>
> **Alvin Toffler**

It's a reasonably safe bet to predict that during the 4th Age of Change, we will continue to see ever-more dramatic tech-enabled advancements in experiences and general efficiency. However, most of our GGTs were highly customer- and employee-centric and see tech as the enabler of the experience—***not the experience itself.*** Their view is that the space will be forced to embrace more and more technology and efficiency tools to stay competitive in the mind's-eye of their users (guests). Sure, they use tech as a *tool* to deliver a service. A few are pure play-tech companies, but all understand that customers have to love *their* brand and service to avoid defecting to other providers. Finding that balance of being profitable and friendly and easy to do business with in a "frictionless" way is critical and fragile.

Although we skimmed the surface of EI and BI and community engagement, we are suggesting that we, as leaders, take stock from some of the data developing about the effect of COVID-19 on us as people. Change is hard, especially when you do not want it. According to UHH Hospitals,[65] https://www.uhhospitals.org/ the five major stresses in life are: **Death of a loved one, Divorce, Moving, Major**

illness, and **Job loss.** A single one of these events is bad enough, but there are families that have experienced all five concurrently because of COVID.

Value your strong points, but hunt and find a coach, an online course, or a mentor to develop the skill set that is not your current strength—a skill set that may serve you well both at home and work (even WFH-ing). Being a balanced leader reaps dividends.

Our GGTs have shared with you their experiences. You have gotten a sense of who they are and their passion for what they do. They differ widely in career paths, experiences, and how they have developed and utilize their traits and talents. All have determined their own path to *(EI + BI + C) + A x I = S.*

Our formula for success, and many of the takeaways and tips we've shared are valid in all moments in time, but let's face it: *C-19 has changed everything.*

People are stressed. Supply chains are stressed. Institutions are stressed. And we have many unknowns that lie ahead. We do not know when stabilized unemployment rates will be established, what each city and country's funding gaps will be, or what will be the consequences of the new US presidential administration or Brexit. It is equally frustrating being unclear as to when our sector will return to fully functioning and

> *"Business models change. As technology processes, business models change."*
>
> **Marsha Blackburn**

staffed bars, restaurants, hotels, convention centers, cruises, casinos, air travel, and when gatherings of more than five hundred will return anywhere. Yes, this is tough to internalize.

One portal that we must pass through is vaccinating a significant portion of the global population. Speaking on Fox Business in August 2020, Bill Gates said that he thinks that by the end of 2021 or early 2022, with the Food and Drug Administration approved vaccines, "It will bring the pandemic to an end." He added that even if only 30 to 60 percent of the population willingly receive a vaccine, that could be enough to slow and eventually stop the spread. The challenge then for Travel, Tourism and Hospitality and their supporting ecosystem is to adapt to survive and innovate to be relevant after the *New Reality* is established.

For additional context, the Adapters Team surveyed a number of the interviewees, who highlighted threats that they see in the short- to medium-term. Their responses were influenced by where they live and work.

 ## Macro Short-Term Outlook Q4 2020 – Q4 2021

1. **Travel health passport:** Due to the unlikeliness of deploying an effective vaccine at scale in the next 12 months, countries must find efficient ways to allow people to travel while under the current health conditions. Ireland and Spain, for example, are trying to achieve efficient pre-departure quick testing to allow entry—effectively a rudimentary form of "health stamp"—by January 2021. With 3 major pharmaceutical companies with very promising vaccines already in limited distribution, we expect this to partially impact the 2021 summer travel season. 2022 should see a change in the velocity of travel to the upside.

2. **Real unemployment rate:** Most Western and some Asian countries implemented some form of subsidized unemployment schemes that will begin tapering off, and we will see the effects of this in the unemployment rolls. Truth is freeing, although often painful, which will impact the sector negatively.

3. **US election: A turbulent beginning:** As previously noted, Bidens first year may be buffeted by the storm started by Donald Trump's actions in January. 2021 will test the largest democracy and economy in the world. However, Warren Buffet's famous quote that he is "Long on America" is a perspective we should all take. Except to see Congress inject considerably more stimulous into the US economy as

a defensive move. C-19 is still raging in the USA, with little or no co-ordination. If chaos continues in the distribution of the vaccines, this will definitely impact the US's ability to fight the pandemic, to stabilize the economy and government institutions. The latter half of 2021 may well see inflation trends (yes. inflation) and heavy investment in infrastructure. We still believe that the RAVING 20's will pop with enthusiasm in 2023 into 2024 when USA's mojo comes back.

4. **BREXIT:** What will be the impact on Europe and the UK, even though a trade deal has been negotiated at the last minute? The recent border closures at the ports between the UK and France, ostensibly because of the discovery of the surge in cases of the "variant" virus throughout southeast England, provided an uncomfortable preview of what life – and trade – can become when thousands of truck drivers were left stranded at ferry depots, overflowing onto major motorways and into makeshift lots converted from airstrips, taking days to clear the backstop after conditions were agreed upon to re-open the borders.

    Trade agreements between the EU and the UK may have been agreed, but there are still a lot of loopholes to be examined and many new stumbling blocks to be addressed.

5. **Bankruptcy, administration, and restructuring:** As we **Pretend and Extend** that the day to day financial obligations are being met while Extending loans and other obligations, we are simply deferring the envitable defaults and carnage. Expect to see impacts on the multifamily and residential housing market as rent payments continue to be late and widespread evictions start to occur. As of September 2020, 14 percent of apartment rents were late, compared to 11 percent for the same period last year. This is significant, as this could lead to thousands of evictions. Hotels, malls, and event companies' loans that are past due (because of

low revenue) will increase, leading to possible foreclosures. The author of this book has seen mandates to advise on distressed businesses have accelerated; sadly, it is expected to gain velocity.

Note: According to FitchRating, CMBS loans are[66] https://www.fitchratings.com/) stretched, with close to 30 percent of loans in the USA past due over sixty days and likely to default. This may cause a house-of-cards collapse in CMBS loans and send a ripple effect through the institutions holding the loans. However, institutions such as Brookfield, Goldman Sachs, Blackstone, and Sortis Holdings have all raised funds to take advantage of this distress—*and so the cycle begins once again.*

6. **Realization phase:** Humanity is beginning to push back on lockdowns even as vaccine therapies are rolled out. The societal effect and impact are yet to be felt. Will more protests erupt, or will there be other bouts of civil disobedience? Who knows?

> *"This is a fantastic time to be entering the business world, because business is going to change more in the next 10 years than in the last 50."*
>
> **Bill Gates**

 # Macro Medium-Term Outlook Q3/Q4 2021 – Q1 2023

1. **Vaccines:** Phase 1+ wide release of effective vaccines must be delivered in 2021. According to the Gates Foundation, at least 30 percent of the population must be vaccinated rapidly. Furthermore, we should expect no more than 50 percent of the world's population to be vaccinated.

2. **Travel and meetings:** Travel and meetings must be achieved with a higher volume of safe corridors and vaccine safe zones. Some form of health passport will be needed to eliminate quarantines. Business connectivity for goods and services must be built to survive until Q4 2021. With the rapid acceleration of logistics, health, and contactless technology being deployed, we hope that governments and regulators'

activities align for the seamless exchange of traveler data to ensure that we rebound as quickly and safely as possible.

3. **Tariffs:** Some form of rational agreement between the US and China will be necessary to enable supply chains to function with some fluidity. This is paramount to returning confidence to the economies. It is difficult to see any movement until Q2, and most likely Q3 2021.

4. **BREXIT effect:** Although we believe that BREXIT will have many unknown consequences, including possible future fracturing of the "Union," the country still has just under 10 percent of Europe's population of 747m people (Worldmeter) and the second- or third-largest economy in Europe, according to Full Fact. Regardless of the bantering and bluster, if Britain stumbles, many other European countries will most likely break an ankle.

5. **Reopening problems:** With so many businesses mothballed or shuttered for good, opening and restoring service jobs may be much harder and more expensive than originally thought. This reshaping of the high and main street may be a benefit, as we noted previously ("The Hole in the Candy" (pXX)). Although holes are appearing where business and people are moving out, the high street may see Amazon's Pick-Up and contactless Amazon Go grocery stores moving in. We will share in the hopes of James Blick and Yoly Martín that the cities will see that "Regeneration is a thing" and be revitalized with a new and reasonable cost basis.

6. **Buying opportunity:** Fund managers have raised cash and have already started purchasing distressed assets. Now the task will be to determine how they should be repurposed. Have Amazon distribution centers become the new anchor mall tenant? Actually, yes, they have already start leasing up. As an example in the Hotel space, the emergence of Sonesta as one of the largest hotel companies in the world with 1200 hotels within 10 Months is phenomenal. SPT, owner of

Sonesta International Hotel Corporation also acquired RLH and its Franchise system. Expect a lot more convergence and acquisition to reshape TTH.

7. **Jobs being reshaped:** This period may give us some indication of the jobs of the future, and retraining programs are initiated as hiring starts to occur again. Expect a lag between the loss of the *"old"* jobs and the creation of the *"new."*

This may sound grim, and in the micro, it may well be. But history has shown that in times of crisis, innovation has occurred. Let us reflect that on January 9, 2007, Steve Jobs presented the iPhone at MacWorld, which spawned the personal tech interface revolution, followed by the 2008 global financial crisis year. Facebook (2004), Amazon Web Services (2006), Uber (2009), Lyft (2012), Airbnb (2008), WeWork (2010), and Marriott/Starwood acquisition (2016) all began or flourished during tumultuous times.

What might lie ahead

The Adapters and GGTs are looking forward and creating growth opportunities possibilities:

1. **Unusual relationships:** Hotels partnering with CoWorking businesses to offer safe meeting environments for small groups and individuals.

2. **Meeting like we have never seen:** Expect to see half and half, with in-person and avatar-like settings. As of December 2020, we are aware of numerous technologies from virtual experiential streaming interactive church services (even hosted by our own HunterGatherer) to live virtual avatar auctions with immediate pay capability to Car launches

where you are able to sit in the car and look around and ask questions of the salesperson, all from the comfort of your living room. Meeting organizers will be heavily impacted and face pressure to invest to stay relevant.

3. **Zoom looks dated, and Skype is a neanderthal:** It's amazing that Zoom, a company that may have saved the fabric of society for us social creatures, has begun to look dated to The Adapters team. But not for long. There will be a rush to upgrade the experience to enable far more sophisticated breakout rooms with whiteboards and real-time private chats, "written" with voice recognition. We expect to see AI and sensory translation to be added. Imagine being able to "shake hands" via your 'digital glove!

4. **Package what?** Hotels, CoLiving spaces, rental cars, and airlines lure users with subscription or package purchases. Rental Car Companies might broaden their marketing to offer "buy a 2-week car rental package and get a week free," or a Hotel Brand might offer a "spend three nights at a Hampton Inn teaser and get eight hours of CoWorking space next door."

5. **Health-check:** Consolidated travel data to cross borders. Companies such as CommonPass and Clear join forces to integrate passport and vaccination tracking for "safe traveler status." Probably more valuable than "Premier Status" on most airlines! The Airlines are just starting to offer the testing service for free. Hey, Governments, get with it; pay for free testing to open up your economies. The faster we move again, the less stimulus cash to the airlines!

6. **Hotels and other accommodation types** adapting to being workplaces and stayplaces. Expect to see many hotels returned or converted to "homes." Why? If airlines are not going to be at capacity (pre-COVID), less volume into the major cities, excess rooms lead to capacity for locals to repopulate the "Hole in the Candy."

7. **Food delivery:** This industry has a real opportunity to kick it up a notch with WFH and Work From Work snacks and meals. And how about alcohol for the Friday night Happy Hour at home? Managers need to deliver Wednesday donuts to create a "coffee" morning; let the App do the work to build a sense of community again.

8. **Glamping:** Finally goes mainstream—so pack your yurt! According to NPD analytics, Cycling, Paddling, Golf, Camping, Nature sighting, and Bird-watching surged in activity and sales during COVID (not new news). The experiential side of the business has fallen off a cliff, as one would expect. Much like the WFH phenomenon, where if 50 percent of the WFH trend sticks, which will be major structural change, much the same may apply as we predict that families and individuals have a whole new appreciation for the outdoors. As a long-term cyclist, once you get hooked, then you have to buy an upgrade; we have already crossed that threshold. Upgrade sales are up as well. Who would have thought that it would take a pandemic to revive Golf? Entrepreneurs, get at it.

9. **Helipad anyone?** Luxury gets more privileges, and destination resorts are even more desirable. The resorts that can convince travelers to work from their properties for a month could be big winners. Comes with helipad privileges, of course.

10. **Y2K. Well, kinda:** System and process upgrades. Many have already started, but this is your Y2K moment. Upgrade process, product, and promotion. Yes, it's difficult and cash draining, but if you have the resources to take advantage of this time to be ready when your spaces are full again, you will win! Business owners, take note, you have no choice but to upgrade your technology to simply to stay current, you are never finished upgrading to stay relevant.

11. **Gamble on:** Online gambling has certainly seen a boost. Let's talk bricks. How about a Casino Bubble? Guests get to

roam around the facility as they please and are tested daily for free. They cannot leave for the duration of their stay. They don't leave anyway, but now they'll get rewarded! Bring on the buffet!

12. **Airline Business class is Dead, and RyanAir will be the winner:** According to the Airlines, planes are being reconfigured to add Economy and reduce Business class seating. Companies' CFOs have seen what can be achieved using Zoom, and other platforms and budgets have been cut. Let's face it; the exuberance and silliness of sending 3 employees for a 1-2 day meeting in $8–10k business class seats are finished. Spend on one and let the others Zoom in to chat with that so-important client. Another prediction is that Business class pricing will be unbundled to cut the cost of tickets. If what you need is a bed and carrying on, why pay for luggage and food? We may see sub-$1,000 tickets on business seats yet. Expect leisure travel to "take-off" to satisfy pent-up demand. Ryanair, easyJet, Southwest Airlines, and other cohorts may be the big winners, smaller aircraft and no frills to fly you to paradise. NOTE: Cruises may experience a similar boom in 2022 and beyond.

13. **Airbnb IPO freaks out the major brands:** Airbnb IPO will set the tone of low-RISK distribution for the next decade. According to their filing documents, they view OTAs as more of a threat than the hotel brands. The major Hotel brands will load their extended stay products on Airbnb, maybe even a branded storefront like the old days of eBay. Hotel rooms will be next. Airbnb may well become the Amazon of hospitality, then who knows? Amazon buys Airbnb even with a $100bn valuation, their *data* alone may be worth it!

14. **PropTech, TravelTech, and FinTech converge:** Adaption and innovation finally enable PropTech, TravelTech, and FinTech industries to collaborate. Property and Finance

Technology make it easier to list, rent, buy, and sell any type of property in real-time. Investors from all sectors will be motivated to streamline operations, background checks, and financial vetting. With the world awash with investable cash, these become the new Unicorn IPOs of the future!

15. **Roaring 1920s hits the Raving 2020s:** 2023–2028 becomes a mad boom time. COVID has passed; pent-up demand to travel to see friends, family, and rediscover the world grabs hold. Short breaks will be in favor. RyanAir has unlimited flights to Cabo and Ibiza to party hearty. Berlin and Barcelona will have come off major uncertainty; innovation will have accelerated; technology will have finally become ubiquitous; and we will finally be able to check-in for every leg of the journey on ONE SUPER APP. New business will solve new problems. Be prepared; it could be another crazy time. (**Steve Lowry**, Anglo Educational Services, and I had a great chat about this.)

This period will see a lot of change, adaption, and innovation. (We know, you've got it; you've got it!) We are swirling around in the mud of the estuary where that freshwater river meets the deep blue ocean. Will you find your energy to struggle through the mud to reach the vastness of those seas or swim back upstream to the relative safety from where you came?

The adapters and innovators that you have met here are a resilient, hardy, and optimistic bunch. You should be, too. Being forced out of your comfort zone to learn new skills is a plus. It may not feel like it now, but times like these are the times when you will kick some ass. This is where reputations are crafted and built. This C-19 event will end, and the 4th of Age of Change will continue to drive even more adaption and innovation than before.

Remember—the Adapters Hub is designed to deliver updates on the progress of our GGTs in their journey to balance EI, BI, and Community Engagement while delivering to their constituents and adapting to the changing circumstances imposed by a novel coronavirus. You can visit www.theadapters.net and our YouTube channel—Adapters. The Adapters team is committed to sourcing information, being completely authentic, and discovering what leaders do, why they make the decisions they do, and how they pivot when things don't work out as planned. We round them up and get them talking, deciphering their stories of adapting and innovating in a world where business is reshaping and reinventing itself at a rate never seen before. What's in it for you? INSIGHT, and a chance to learn from some of the best.

This is the 4th Age of Change, and we will prosper in this age as we have in the previous three. Welcome to the 4th Age of GGTs—adapting and innovating. The Adapters are thrilled to document their future and hope to see you included in the chronicles of the GGTs soon!

> *"If you want to be an adapter, you've got to be willing to take a risk and put yourself out there."*
>
> **Cait Noone,
> Head Galway
> International
> Hotel School
> Vice President
> International
> Engagement,
> GMIT, Ireland**

Scribble Zone: – *TAKE 20 Minutes*

Take twenty minutes or so and review your Scribble boxes. As an adapter and innovator, you have the inner energy to GET STUFF DONE (GSD). This is your chance to take your SCRIBBLES and do something about them!

ACTION ZONE

IDEA	ACTIONS	ACTION DATE

$$(EI + BI + C) + A \, x \, I = S$$

Gutsy Genius Thinker
Keith Kefgen
Managing Director & CEO
AETHOS Consulting Group
New York, New York, USA

Experts abound in the Travel, Tourism and Hospitality industry, and Aethos have placed many "Experts" in their roles. The Adapters believe that EI + BI (see PXX), when used in combination, is a powerful culture energizer. Like many of the Adapters in this book, Keith is not at all bashful to share what he believes is the best fit for your Company or the state of the industry. As a _strategic partner_ to many firms, he noted that the Companies that he works with have slowed searches "because people just don't have line of sight" into how C-19 will influence the market." It's hard to solve a people problem when you have no idea what you are trying to solve for!

Depending on the source of the mandate, Aethos notes that most mandates start with a similar demand as he commented, "We always say when Clients are telling us about what they're looking for in an individual, it's someone that tends to have a Cape and an S on their chest" Calling all Super Women and Men—give Keith a call; he may have a home for you

Pre-C-19, the Tech Start-up world "pressured the other public companies and the other more traditional companies to think more like fast-moving growth organizations, and they don't have time to be thinking about 10 and 20 years out," which may have impacted their natural growth cycles. This has led to some unrealistic demands on non-starts to monetize. Post C-19, no one knows; the deck chairs have been blown overboard. Keith and the Aethos Team have weathered many storms and have a clear and rigorous process to select the right talent for the right time.

"A great business plan without talent doesn't work. Talent without a business plan might work once in a while, but tends to fail often."

Keith Kefgen

Adaption Tips:

- Take time to talk with clients, and make sure that you understand where they are going and what they're trying to do.
- Be who you are in Interviews.
- Expect Executive Search Technology to enable placements to occur within days, not months in the future. Be clear; your social profile matters.
- Be a Start-up of YOU – Reid Hoffman

LinkedIn profile @ www.linkedin.com/in/keith-kefgen-8091b08/

Company @ www.aethoscg.com/

Take the time to learn more

Click or use SmartPhone

Gutsy Genius Thinker
Jacob Wedderburn-Day
CEO & Cofounder, Stasher.com
London, England

It's all about looking for and at the GAP in the market. Jacob and his cofounder, Anthony, built a travel tech start-up that connects travelers looking to store luggage with shops and hotels providing storage space. Jacob and Anthony, friends from their time studying economics at Oxford together, cofounded the business in 2015. None of this was easy. It is somewhat like the Airbnb model, except for bags. The market was there, and they went about gathering "hosts"—hotels, retail shops, etc.— to join their platform and then started marketing it to travelers. In fact, they are now a partner with Airbnb.

It takes a GGT to figure out how to raise money. Believe it or not, "cold-call emails" work. They sent a cold email to the CEO of Big Yellow Storage, James Gibson—he loved the vision and joined as their first investor. They turned their prototype into a fully functioning business. The Venture Capital world took notice and added Howzat Partners and others as investors. Stasher now has a presence in 250 cities. Jacob is yet another GGT that shares the truth and is super transparent. This is one of those chats where you learn a ton about how a business was formed. Sure, there are some potholes that twist an ankle, but you recover. People, Culture, Hosts (Suppliers), Community, Investors all matter. Above all, Trust and Transparency become the currency.

> _"I kind of thought, oh cool, we'll build this thing, you know; in a few years we'll sell it and fly off to an Island or whatever. [The reality is], obviously, it's a long process, and at the same time is very much true of investment. Rule number one is keeping your cash flow healthy."_

There are a lot of bigger Companies that could learn from the cultural foundation that Jacob and Anthony have cultivated. To quote Jacob, "People are quite happy and motivated, and I think a lot of that comes from the sort of autonomy that we strive to create, which is just that your thing is your thing. You have full responsibility for it, and we're not going to tell you how to run it, but we're going to sort of work together."

Click through and listen to a savvy leader that has built a Company that has staying power.

Adaption Tips:

- Side hustles turn into start-ups, and it's never too late to start.
- Get used to rejection, especially when raising money.
- Make sure you've got a standard, sensible vesting[67] https://www.youtube.com/watch?v=afl25nlf9q0 agreement in place.
- Ideally, source people you can turn to within your [expanding] network—mentors, advisors that are able to guide you through this.
- Recognize that we're not really experts in anything; be humble and learn from others.

LinkedIn profile @ https://www.linkedin.com/in/jacob-wedderburn-day-499258111/

Company@ https://stasher.com/

*Disclosure: The Author is an Advisory Board member of Stasher. Any statements are extracts from the interview and offer no insight of future performance of the Company.

Take the time to learn more

Click or use SmartPhone

CHAPTER 10

GGT UPDATES – December 2020

So, did you cheat to take a peek? If you did and started with the GGT updates, so what? *The Adapters* encourages curiosity and breaking the rules. The GGTs have offered us all insight into how they reacted and responded to the events of the last year. The "Updates" are "unedited" so that you can get a sense of tone. Their honesty is humbling and inspirational as to how they all dealt with the issues facing so many. We are all appreciative of the GGTs being so candid.

Insights and Updates

 Gutsy Genius Thinker
Piers Brown
Founder & CEO International
Hospitality Media
London, United Kingdom

1. **Stepping back to March 2020. When did you think C-19 would end and we would be back to normal?**
   - End of 3rd quarter 2020

2. **What are the 3 biggest issues you have had to face so far because of C-19? What happened?**
   - Seeking out where the future client business is, maximizing engagement with transparency/advice, and identifying fresh solutions for them
   - Upping team members' skillset to extend the business' 'reach' and to highlight our media channels as 'the place to go'—e.g., Editorial now has a multi-faceted 'multimedia' skillset, e.g., hosting webinars, doing thought leadership video pieces to camera. 5,000+ registered for our webinar series, which is ongoing
   - Predicting how media and people do business will change

3. **What have you changed in your business/role/ university to get through this crisis? Tell us how you Adapted/Innovated and scaled - (up or down) - your business/role/university.**
   - Increased the responsibility and autonomy of team members
   - Kept morale high by promoting 2 individuals within the team
   - Recruited talent made redundant by other business to position IHM better for the future (hopefully)

4. **What worked and what failed. Why for both?**
   - FAILED: Offering broad discounted advertising when the hospitality / real estate world was in paralysis
   - WORKED: Giving team members lots of autonomy to make decisions, knowing that the wrong decision is ok, provided they learn by it

5. **How did you personally deal with the stress? Tips for others?**
   - Spent more quality time with my family and appreciated it more.
   - Look to the long term

6. **What surprised you the most about your Family or business response/reaction to this difficult time?**
   - How business leaders react when faced with adversity—head-on, or head in the sand.

7. **How would you describe your outlook for the next 12 months? Expand as much as possible. What is influencing your views?**
   - Optimistic, particularly with the 'cut-through' the business has achieved staying close to market during crisis
   - Looking forward to working with some new businesses started during crisis. e.g., Low-touch, tech-enabled companies
   - Hopeful events and flights will resume shortly.

Gutsy Genius Thinker
Daniel del Olmo
President, Sage Hotel Management
Denver, Colorado, USA

1. **Stepping back to March 2020. When did you think C-19 would end and we would be back to normal?**
   - We knew that it would take a widely available vaccine before the world would be able to return to some semblance of normalcy. However, we believe our 'next normal' reality will be much different from what we were used to before, not dissimilar to how flying changed quite significantly after 9/11.

2. **What are the 3 biggest issues you have had to face so far because of C-19? What happened?**
   - Cash preservation and management has been our top priority, reducing the amount of capital calls for our owners to get through the next 18-24 months. We took a very conservative approach to forecasting the remainder of 2020 and budgeting 2021, with topline demand strengthening only in the latter two quarters. We do not foresee RevPAR to return to pre-COVID levels until 2024 in most of our markets.
   - Focus on health and safety: Early April, we implemented Sage Forward, a company-wide initiative that provides tools, training, and resources for all property teams to ensure the health and safety of our associates and guests, while also providing guidelines to adapt the guest experience based on the ever-evolving local and national restrictions. This initiative, along with various innovative sales and marketing programs and promotions, has ensured that our October RPI has increased to 110.3 percent. (vs. 98 percent in April)

- Focus on wellbeing of our associates to minimize burn-out: We had to permanently lay off 4,000 of our original 6,132 associates, with the remaining team members forced to wear multiple hats and work multiple shifts to adjust to intermittent levels of occupancy. We launched 'You Belong' that provides a wide range of resources and support to stimulate physical wellbeing, mental health, and professional growth. Each property team has complete autonomy to implement programs for the team, and every associate can access the tools at any time.

3. **What have you changed in your business/role/ university to get through this crisis? Tell us how you Adapted/Innovated and scaled (up or down) your business/role/university.**
   - An acute focus on the immediate need, and a higher sense of urgency than ever before, resulting in swift decision making
   - Over-communication as a standard both internally and externally with partners, investors, and communities
   - Greater emphasis on nurturing relationships with existing partners/investors and prospects, which to date has resulted in 6 new management agreements and the retention of 4 agreements related to asset dispositions, representing approx. $5M in stabilized annual fee revenue.

4. **What worked and what failed? Why for both?**
   - What worked: As a result of deeply rooted culture created by the founders, the team has been able to not only persevere but thrive and deliver strong results for our current partners/investors and attract multiple new owners and investors

- What did not: Diversifying our demand or re-inventing our business. We explored pursuing alternative residential leasing but were unsuccessful in attracting this segment given that our non-extended stay product does not meet the requirements of residential dwellers.

5. **How did you personally deal with the stress? Tips for others?**
   - Tap into your community/ies: I am a member of YPO, and both my chapters (Hollywood and Rocky Mountain) and my forum provided significant support at every level by having the ability to share learnings and discuss challenges in a confidential setting with others who are leading organizations in different industries.

6. **What surprised you the most about your Family or business response/reaction to this difficult time?**
   - Resiliency: While undoubtedly the greatest challenge we have ever faced collectively, everyone has been remarkably resilient and has been coping and adapting much better than I would have ever imagined. I do believe strongly in the power of positive energy, and if you can both freely share and receive, it allows you to conquer any adversity you will face.

7. **How would you describe your outlook for the next 12 months? Expand as much as possible. What is influencing your views?**
   - Next year will be a tale of two worlds. The distribution of the vaccine sometime mid-next year will undoubtedly mark the highlight for everyone that will have access but will prove elusive for a large swath of the population who will continue to feel paralyzed until

the vaccine arrives. As a result, the first half of the year will continue to be incredibly tough for the hospitality industry, with no real growth in business or group travel. The second half of the year, however, will feel like a resurgence and a breath of fresh air for most in our industry, with travelers finally starting to feel more secure in picking up where they left off.

Gutsy Genius Thinker
James Foice
Chief Executive
Association of Serviced Apartment
Providers
ASAP
Gloucester, United Kingdom

1. Stepping back to March 2020. When did you think C-19 would end and we would be back to normal?
   - Feb 2021

2. What are the 3 biggest issues you have had to face so far because of C-19? What happened?
   - Not knowing how long it would last and how to plan, with little or no points of reference to assist
   - Guidance, leadership, and direction for member organisations who have been profoundly impacted
   - Balancing and delivering the support network of a trade association with the intrinsic challenges we face to continue to exist
   - We dug deep, embraced the challenge with a newfound energy, and have asked for help when needed. We have found a real appetite for collaboration and cooperation.

3. What have you changed in your business/role/ university to get through this crisis? Tell us how you Adapted/Innovated and scaled (up or down) your business/role/university.

Came together as a group, membership, and remained super positive and optimistic. Tough times require strong leaders, and we have attempted to be that organization.

4. What worked and what failed? Why for both?

Support and recognition for our efforts have been at an all-time high. This is because we were clear in how we could step up to the mark and help. Keeping focused on that objective and communicating it externally has been very rewarding and delivered significant results.

5. **How did you personally deal with the stress? Tips for others?**

Tough!!!! I have encouraged my team to take time out for themselves and have done the same. The importance of rewarding efforts has never been more important. So, recognizing individuals, encouraging team engagement, and trying to introduce some fun has been my priority.

I have found the need to allocate "time away" and have disciplined myself to see it through.

6. **What surprised you the most about your Family or business response/reaction to this difficult time?**

Humility is one of my personal values, and I believe when exhibited, it has enormous impact. I have seen significant support for what we are doing. If you can pull a positive out of this, it's how human beings behave during tough times. The important thing is to reference these times when we are on the other side.

7. **How would you describe your outlook for the next 12 months? Expand as much as possible. What is influencing your views?**

I am incredibly positive about the outlook for our industry. We have made safety, honesty, and transparency our core objectives for our industry, and never has it been so important.

Travelers will start travelling again, and this is our time!!!

Gutsy Genius Thinker
Cindy Estis Green
Cofounder and CEO Kalibri Labs, LLC
Author
Rockville, Maryland, USA

1. **Stepping back to March 2020. When did you think C-19 would end and we would be back to normal?**
   - I thought we would have 12-18 months of disruption. I figured there would be more severe impact in some markets, but didn't expect a 3-5 year recovery.

2. **What are the 3 biggest issues you have had to face so far because of C-19? What happened?**
   - Re-organizing my own business and staff to operate effectively and plan for a new way of looking at the business.
   - Recognizing that our clients have had to largely alter their teams and that the new organizational structures are substantially different and that has altered their priorities. I am spending more time with clients in consultative discussions about how these changes can be implemented.
   - Accepting that the changes to day-to-day living have a meaningful effect on how people interact. The persistence of limited in-person visits in some ways makes many actually more accessible—Zoom calls are easier to arrange than on-site meetings—but it removes the option for the ways we build deeper relationships by having meals/drinks together at conferences or in other more "natural" settings.

3. **What have you changed in your business/role/ university to get through this crisis? Tell us how you Adapted/Innovated and scaled (up or down) your business/role/university.**

- We reduced staffing and are now building it back up. This crisis laser-focused me and the team on what matters as we consider every role we hire with great scrutiny. We have many discussions about each product, service, or communication we share with the industry to make sure it's tightly aligned with the needs of our clients. We have much shorter planning and evaluation cycles than we did before. We focus on the areas of greatest interest to the hotel community, which is around predictive models and forecasts, and that was underway before COVID but is now the centerpiece of our work.

4. **What worked and what failed? Why for both?**
   - We started with a quick solution for forecasting performance through 2023 for a select group of markets but realized we needed a more robust solution that could be updated monthly and provide detailed insight by rate category and channel to support continual forecast updates. Many clients realized they couldn't budget in the usual way for 2021, so instead are doing rolling forecasts. We focused on getting the predictive data in production by hotel so we can roll it up by submarket or market as needed. The longer-term solution is the one that is working and has resulted in a product that was in our roadmap but is much more prominent and will be sustainable for many years.

5. **How did you personally deal with the stress? Tips for others?**
   - I run every day, and that is an important time for me to reflect and also burn off stress/anxiety. I work long hours but have blocked time for reading and entertainment every night, unrelated to any industry work I do. I always have a book in process and have

a steady flow of Netflix and Amazon series in play. I also speak to old friends on weekends.

6. **What surprised you the most about your Family or business response/reaction to this difficult time?**

   - I have found everyone seems generally more supportive. Given that every person I deal with globally is going through the same issues, both personally and professionally, I find that others take time to be more thoughtful and helpful. This was a welcome surprise.

7. **How would you describe your outlook for the next 12 months? Expand as much as possible. What is influencing your views?**

   - I am optimistic that the hotel industry will see the beginning of steady improvement in business by mid-2021. Business volume will be muted until then, making the first half of 2021 difficult given that it will be over a year of operating at reduced business levels. But once the recovery is more visible, with steadier gains, I anticipate the mood to become more positive.

   - I think a more aggressive approach to the pandemic by the new US administration, with a more coordinated federal emphasis on testing and other preventative measures, along with vaccines and therapeutics, will restore the confidence for businesses to hit the road again. There will be a ramp-up for corporate travel and meetings, with some industries maintaining tight spending for some time, making it more gradual through the end of 2021.

   - There is so much pent-up demand for travel, but this will vary quite a lot by market. The result of this protracted lean period will have some good outcomes. For example, hotels are learning to become more skilled at attracting the leisure traveler, where before they focused largely on business segments. I think the hotel teams will be more resilient, more versatile, and more streamlined about where and how resources are deployed, and ultimately more efficient and better in generating revenue and managing the business.

Gutsy Genius Thinker
Greg Juceam
President, G6 Hospitality
Chicago, Illinois, U.S.A

1. **Stepping back to March 2020. When did you think C-19 would end and we would be back to normal?**

    - I knew it wasn't going to be a 90-day blip—but I can't say that I would have predicted well over a year. As fast as the world moves nowadays, and as motivated as the entire globe was for an effective vaccine, medical research takes time to safely conduct. Even if a vaccine was identified immediately, the questions about how to manufacture and distribute millions of doses equitably were going to be complicated and controversial to answer. I recall thinking (back in March) that it would take roughly 8-12 months. It seems we will all need to be slightly more patient.

2. **What are the 3 biggest issues you have had to face so far because of C-19? What happened?**

    - The first issue clearly was ensuring the safety of guests and team members working in the properties. We literally had to decide whether to keep the hotels open…and, if so, whether we would offer our full suite of products and services or some curtailed offering. A small team of us spent a lot of time speaking with medical professionals, researching ever-changing CDC guidelines, and collaborating with our suppliers to ensure we were using materials proven to be safe and effective. In the end, I was comfortable staying open in most of our hotels, with carefully constructed Pandemic Protocols in place (it was nice that we were later recognized by *Forbes* as one of the "Safest Hotel Chains to stay at" during Coronavirus).

- The second issue was ensuring ongoing liquidity of the company; we needed to feel comfortable that we could weather the financial storm, and we had to find prudent ways to reduce our burn rate. Because we are a privately held company, this entailed running sensitivity analysis scenarios to try and project our cash needs for our Board. Fortunately, we were able to secure some internal bridge funding to ride us through 2020 and the anticipated recovery in 2021.

- The third issue we had to face was supporting our franchisees through the worst year in the history of the hotel industry. With more than 1,100 franchised hotels, each of which is a small business unto itself, many of our Owners were struggling to achieve positive cash flow due to the overnight reduction in demand. With so many fixed costs in the hotel industry, franchisees needed temporary flexibility from us on brand fees, extensions on renovation deadlines, and leeway regarding certain brand standards.

- Because our brand typically outperforms during economic downturns, I was confident that our brands would ultimately shine...but we needed our franchisees to keep their doors open in this time of unprecedented need; in the end, the concessions we offered were more than a goodwill—they enabled our franchisees to preserve cash flow and make it until brighter days. Fast forward to now; our franchise owners were able to stay open and grow considerable market share against their respective competitors. There is a lot of momentum around new deals today because of our willingness to be supportive partners that stood alongside our franchise community during COVID-19.

3. What have you changed in your business/role/ university to get through this crisis? Tell us how you Adapted/Innovated and scaled (up or down) your business/role/university.

Despite the many headaches it caused, COVID-19 brought about opportunities to adapt and to improve our business.

Accentuating Our Simplicity/Safety:
- Notably, COVID-19 gave us an opportunity to "flip the script" on those that had been professing the "death" of the Motel business. Some believe that Motels are a passé concept from days gone by... that customers want more and more amenities, and that simplicity is a bad thing.

But think about what COVID-19 brought about in terms of consumer preference:
- Guests didn't want to be in big lobbies or meeting rooms or restaurants; most Motels don't have these.
- Guests didn't want to get in elevators or walk through a maze of interior hallways to get to their rooms; many Motels still offer drive-up room access and exterior corridors.
- Guests did not want to "share air" in the heating/ cooling system with other neighboring rooms; most Motels have air that is specific to each guestroom.
- Guests didn't want to pay higher room rates for amenities or services that they weren't going to use; Motels offer low rates and don't make all pay for extras that are used only by some.

In fact, many in the medical community began touting the simplicity of Motels as a safer option than larger, fancier hotels and resorts. My company has been able to notably outperform the industry during COVID-19 because the remaining traveling public recognized the beauty, the value, and the safety of simplicity. Our marketing messages were tweaked to promote these items, once viewed by some as a liability, as a strength instead.

Appealing to New Capital Sources:
- Another key adaptation has been that developers and institutional investors began to realize that Economy segment hotels/motels and extended stay (apartment-like) properties provide a more stable return on investment. As Bankrate reminds us in their annual survey—roughly 60 percent of Americans cannot afford to pay for a $1,000 emergency out of their liquid savings.
- Sadly, the Economic divide in our country is only worsening in this downturn—and our citizens struggle to pay rent or save a buck in times like these. People need a place to live, even if just for a period of time until they can get back on their feet. Small business Owners, especially those in "Essential businesses," need to travel to earn a living. Economy Hotels/Motels and Extended Stay properties provide affordable rates, flexibility to check in/out as needed without any commitments, and hassle-free access to utilities, cable TV, and internet. So, while convention hotels are closed these days, and white-collar business hotels are running less than half full, the Economy segment continues to roll along. At G6, the essential service that we provide to local communities (in good times and bad) is both recognized and celebrated; this is what our decades-long mantra of "Leaving the Light On" truly means.
- In one example, we worked with the State of California to turn nearly a dozen of our hotels into temporary housing for vulnerable populations. What

started as a series of projects to assist our local communities turned into a bigger opportunity when the State ended up purchasing 6 of our hotels to help solve homelessness issues.

- Meanwhile, institutional investors who typically favor the Upscale hotel segment are inquiring in droves about investing in our Motel 6 and Studio 6 brands. The appeal of the Economy segment as more "recession proof" has been magnified by COVID-19. It is hard to deny that Economy hotels are less expensive to buy, build, or renovate—and that the lower cost to operate for supplies and labor equates to higher margins and steadier cash flow.

4. What worked and what failed? Why for both?

Above, I addressed a couple of things that worked. I certainly can offer more of these, if needed.

- While I cannot think of any epic failures from this Pandemic, I would say there are two areas I wish we could have done better, in hindsight.
- One of these areas was doing a more consistent job training our staff to be more instinctive in serving our guests under such extraordinary circumstances. No doubt, our teams served with their heart and were empathetic to our guests. But there were instances where standard operating procedures just needed to be shelved—perhaps when guests were quarantining locally and needed an extra hand beyond our typical services. It took us a few weeks to recognize we were going to need to think more outside of the box for requests that were beyond our typical suite of services.
- Another opportunity was our inability to secure more "on-call" staffing to supplement our core

team member base. We were especially particular about requiring team members to stay home if they weren't feeling 100 percent, even if just as a precaution. If someone was suspected as COVID positive, we were aggressive in contact tracing as well. Since our hotels are smaller and have lean employee counts, this made it difficult to fully operate if there were labor absences. In those circumstances, hiring more temporary labor as a backup plan was the right idea. But, even with higher unemployment rates, people were cautious about working in hotels during the Pandemic. In the end, our execution was not as crisp as it could have been; this caused us to shut down certain rooms in some markets until our staffing was able to get back to full health and attendance.

8. **How did you personally deal with the stress? Tips for others?**

- No doubt, there were times of significant stress for everyone during 2020. As a true competitor, I never want to see numbers in the red for my company—or any others, for that matter. The Hospitality Industry is stronger when we are winning together.

- But all experienced leaders know there is a trough for every peak. For me, I used the opportunity to spend more time with my nuclear family, connecting every day on teleconferences with our various teams, and exercising a bit more than I had in recent years.

- While I am a strong advocate for travel and in-person relationship building, we all learned that there are certain benefits to a world that is slightly more virtual.

9. What surprised you the most about your Family or business response/reaction to this difficult time?

For me, what was most impressive was the resilience that individuals displayed when adversity was at its peak. *Some that stood out include:*

- The tireless hotel workers that showed up to serve their guests and communities, even though there may have been personal health risks from being around the traveling public. The Pandemic was one thing—but we were also dealing with Hurricanes in the East, Fires in the West, and elections and civil unrest just about everywhere. Some industries folded up their tents—but the Economy segment of the hotel industry stayed open as an essential business that kept truckers on the road, traveling medical professionals in the game, and local residents in shelters when fleeing from natural disasters and when safely quarantining from their families and neighbors.
- At G6, our regional and corporate teams really stepped up and were laser focused on providing servant leadership to the property employees and franchisees.
- At home, my children were just so understanding that everything was going to be different. They, like so many others their age, rose to the occasion by adapting to the twists and turns and not sitting home complaining about the many burdens caused by COVID-19.

Like most of us experienced on the heels of 9-11, teams have been strengthened, and focus has been sharpened as a result of this COVID-19 experience. When we look back on this entire chapter in our lives, we will long remember the stories of how individuals and companies rose to the occasion during this unprecedented time.

10. How would you describe your outlook for the next 12 months? Expand as much as possible. What is influencing your views?

- I am optimistic for a full recovery in the next 4-5 years. All of our historical experience in the hotel industry points to every downturn being eventually followed by recovery past the prior peak. We will learn to combat COVID-19, and we will be smarter for having gone through this Pandemic—because it won't be the last.

- Specific to a 12-month time horizon, recovery is already well underway: we are past the elections, we have begun to address some of the root causes of the civil unrest of 2020, and vaccines will likely be distributed and dispensed to at least half of the U.S. population. Those businesses that have liquidity and relevance will recover gradually over the next 12 months.

- The hotel industry will face difficult times until conventions return fully; it will not likely return to 2019 levels until 2024 because of the lead times needed for citywide special events. That said, individual business travel will resume, and leisure travel will outperform, based on pent-up demand. This should prop up the entire travel ecosystem, both domestically and internationally, until we can return to historical levels.

- One thing is for sure…leaders who continue to adapt to demand trends and market opportunities will own the future.

Gutsy Genius Thinker
Keith Kefgen
Managing Director & CEO
AETHOS Consulting Group
New York, New York, U.S.A

1. **Stepping back to March 2020. When did you think C-19 would end and we would be back to normal?**

   I looked closely at the 1918 Spanish Flu pandemic and thought there would be parallels. I figure that 2022 is the recovery year. 2021 is going to be a lag year, and it will take time for a vaccine to take hold.

2. **What are the 3 biggest issues you have had to face so far because of C-19? What happened?**

   Keeping teammates positive. Cashflow. Keeping myself busy and motivated. It has not been easy, but letting people know this will pass and we are supporting them has been important. I have kept in closer contact with those around me. I have been doing more outreach. I have taken on other projects like a board seat, starting a Podcast, and writing my second book. On the cashflow front, I have been frugal without being short-sighted.

3. **What have you changed in your business/role/university to get through this crisis? Tell us how you Adapted/Innovated and scaled (up or down)your business/role/university.**

   We let only two people go and kept the remainder on payroll. We have been focused on relationship building and our other services (compensation consulting and performance management), which have been less susceptible to recession. Our search process has been modified to be quicker, without losing quality.

4.   What worked and what failed? Why for both?

Probably too early to tell. We have stayed true to our "way" of doing business but have focused on other areas.

5.   How did you personally deal with the stress? Tips for others?

Planned more activities with my family. Drove around a lot just to get out of the house. Reading is a detox for me. Always helps to clear my head. Cooked at home a lot more. Got a grill and a bunch of recipe books. Play cards (Euchre) with my extended family online.

6.   What surprised you the most about your Family or business response/reaction to this difficult time?

On the upside, how resilient people are and how quickly we can bounce back. On the downside, how people can crawl up into a shell and retreat. I guess I am a push-forward kind of person.

7.   How would you describe your outlook for the next 12 months? Expand as much as possible. What is influencing your views?

I think it will be a tough 2021. I am in a lag business, so it is going to take some time for us and hospitality to rebound significantly enough to call it a recovery. But it will happen. This is a case of perseverance and being able to stay afloat. Many in hospitality will not make it, but those that do will benefit greatly. I have seen this rodeo before, and you have to stay strong and survive.

Gutsy Genius Thinker
Alexi Khajavi
President, Hospitality & Travel
Questex
London, United Kingdom

1. Stepping back to March 2020. When did you think C-19 would end and we would be back to normal?

I honestly thought it would be back to normal within 3 months.

2. What are the 3 biggest issues you have had to face so far because of C-19? What happened?

As President of the Hospitality & Travel Group we've seen our customers—lodging, bars, restaurants, and travel operators—face huge challenges to survive and keep their businesses open and their employees on payroll. We're fortunate in that our business is diversified, with digital and research complementing our events portfolio, but we're also active in the Life Sciences, Healthcare, and Technology sectors, which are performing much better than hospitality and travel.

That said—it's been the most difficult period in my career. The 3 biggest issues we've faced are:

- Uncertainty in nearly every facet of business and decision making—the sands are consistently shifting, and there is very little visibility. Business and people like certainty, and the reality is that many decisions are never binary, but you at least had the benefit of a baseline. COVID has removed the baseline.
- Our people are our most important asset, and yet it's a challenge on how we care for them across five offices on three continents with everyone working from home.

- Many of our customers, many of whom we consider friends, in hospitality and travel, are struggling to survive. There have been insolvencies, redundancies, furloughs, and many, many difficult conversations with lenders, landlords, and employees the past 9 months. We have an obligation to inform and connect, and we've tried to do that with integrity as we've been forced to cancel over 200 events worldwide. We have upheld all our obligations to vendors, venues, and contractors across the portfolio while giving our clients a full credit to future events and marketing campaigns—it's put us in an incredibly challenging position, but it's the right thing to do.

3. **What have you changed in your business/role/ university to get through this crisis? Tell us how you Adapted/Innovated and scaled (up or down) your business/role/university.**
   - We've simplified the organizational structure by eliminating layers and creating a relatively flat structure of three tiers from the Executive Committee to the Senior Leadership and the rest of the company. The goal is to empower everyone, at all levels, to make quick decisions and avoid the bureaucracy. Ironically, we're probably communicating more than we did before with everyone on video-conferencing calls, but communication isn't the same as collaboration, and more importantly, decision-making. We have to make Go/No Go decisions all the time, and our people closest to our customers are being empowered to make those decisions quickly and with authority to do the right thing for our customers and our business.

4. **What worked and what failed? Why for both?**
   - We've moved quickly to integrate digital acumen into our live events teams and accelerated to an

integrated model where digital content, access, and connections are layered into our live events. We were going in that direction anyway, but we've probably advanced that by 2 to 3 years because of the pandemic. That's something we've done well.

- One thing I wish we would have done better is anticipate the enormity and longevity of this pandemic and done a better job of making decisions sooner and on our own terms for our customers and our employees. We've been at the mercy of government, venues, transportation, public health, and many other stakeholders—all doing their best effort to understand and mitigate the risks, but in hindsight, we could have been more decisive.

5. **How did you personally deal with the stress? Tips for others?**
   - If you've ever skied in trees, you know you don't look at the trees; you look through the trees to where you're going. Once you look at a tree—you're going to crash right into it. I try to look through all this and at the path that leads us out of it. That keeps me focused on solutions and not the problem. We've all been living in crisis mode since March, and that's not a good place to be mentally or physically.
   - Also, do what you love and go outside. Movement is life, and pre-COVID that meant a lot of air travel for many of us. Now, I try to walk the dog or hop on the bike for a few miles every day—it's simple but works.

6. **What surprised you the most about your Family or business response/reaction to this difficult time?**
   - How important human connection is. I knew it, but I never experienced something like this to reinforce it. We are social animals, and there are 7 billion examples of family, friends, and colleagues who haven't

been able to see each other, hug each other, have a drink with one another. I sincerely miss people, and I can't wait to get back out there and see them all. So, when I hear all the talk about how people will prefer to video call from now on, I don't even pay attention to it because a pandemic is not going to wipe out 10,000 years of human behavior.

7. **How would you describe your outlook for the next 12 months? Expand as much as possible. What is influencing your views?**

- 1H 2021 is going to be difficult, and I expect us to still be dealing with the health crisis quite severely for the next few months, particularly with how things are now in November across Europe and the US. The news on the vaccine is extremely positive, and I look forward to seeing it deployed to global citizens very soon. I'm much more optimistic around 2H 2021, and I think it will be quite an exciting time to see advanced economies like the UK, Spain, France, and the US experience high single-digit GDP growth. I'm extremely impressed with how Asia has managed the crisis, and I believe they will continue to lead the economic recovery out of this health crisis.

- The longer-lasting impact will be the employment, the environment, and geopolitics. We had big challenges before COVID, issues like climate change, populism, youth unemployment, and social justice, and those issues haven't gone away. I hope that this crisis will be a catalyst for governments, private sector, and global citizens to align around addressing and resolving those global challenges.

I'm encouraged by the creativity and ingenuity of what we can do when we collaborate towards a common goal, and I am hopeful we'll all be kinder and more thoughtful moving forward.

Gutsy Genius Thinker
Guy Lean
Managing Director, Madison Mayfair
London, United Kingdom

1. **Stepping back to March 2020. When did you think C-19 would end and we would be back to normal?**

   - March 2021 does seem a long time ago, and looking back, we felt the onset of C-19 was going to be a big disrupter in the market. As time evolved into April and May, I became increasingly aware the arrival of a Vaccine would be the turning point for the world, and it was difficult to see a light at the end of the tunnel. The sense was it was going to take 12 months to get some confidence back in the market, with a return to some normality Q3 2021.

   - It became clear that the objective would be to work our way back to 2019 figures but to be realistic.

2. **What are the 3 biggest issues you have had to face so far because of C-19? What happened?**

   - The first significant change was the pipeline of business and forecasting went out of the window. Cash preservation became key, and all the larger organizations started to consult with their employees in great numbers.

   - The hospitality industry faced huge unrest and uncertainty. Therefore, there was great need to check in on everyone and listen to how they were feeling, lending support and advice wherever, and being a true partner.

   - The need to ensure our people and their mental health were ok, the wider impact on their families, and ensuring them all would be ok. It became clear that our model of R3 (Revenue, Results, and

Relationships) was still relevant and important, but relationships were at the top of the list.

3. **What have you changed in your business/role/ university to get through this crisis? Tell us how you Adapted/Innovated and scaled (up or down) your business/role/university**
   - Firstly we embraced the technology of Zoom and MS teams, connecting with the team remotely (we suggested, where necessary, they return home, some in different countries). We made the decision to not let anyone go and keep the teams together. We held some virtual team fun sessions and took the time to revisit our vision and goals.
   - We wanted to stay positive and take time to rest and focus on the mental health of our market.
   - Revenue has dropped by 50 percent, but we have still delivered on 100 percent of the roles we worked on. We have broadened our offering and, in some cases, passed on a more cost-effective solution if needed.

4. **What worked and what failed? Why for both?**
   - What has worked well is taking the time to speak with people, especially people who needed to discuss their situation, listening to everyone. Often, we have not had a solution but just taken the time to be there.
   - We failed to maintain our activity and sales levels, but we realized there is no need to bang our head against a brick wall; this wasn't going to be like a classic recession where you just need to work harder, make more calls, and keep selling. As they say, "Don't try to teach pigs to fly; it's frustrating and just annoys the pigs."

5. **How did you personally deal with the stress? Tips for others?**
   - Re-organize your day. Some periods of activity and some downtime. Go cut the lawn. Walk your dog.

Paint a room. Just sitting, staring at your laptop does not help.

- Do an activity that requires your total attention. i.e., mountain bike, etc.
- Learn something new. I baked cakes!
- Reach out to the community and talk to people.
- Write some letters the old-fashioned way.
- Sell some stuff on eBay and treat the family to a local takeaway.
- Do not feel you have to change. Be yourself,
- Clive Woodward (England rugby coach) is a proponent of doing 100 things 1 percent better.
- Paul O'Connell (Rugby Captain) – Let's be the best at the things that require no talent.

6. **What surprised you the most about your Family or business response/reaction to this difficult time?**
   - Simply everyone pulling together; the realization that we were all in this together. We might be on different ships, sailing in different directions, but we are all in the same storm.

7. **How would you describe your outlook for the next 12 months? Expand as much as possible. What is influencing your views?**
   - We are buoyant about the future; we believe everyone has a built-in desire to travel and see the world. The market will return stronger. We believe the staycation market will be a boom and that the industry will naturally evolve. Our customers will still be with us, but their wants and desires will change, and we need to adapt. There will be a new norm, which will include how we work and rest. The pandemic has exposed our strengths and weaknesses, and we must work on both for the next 12 months

Gutsy Genius Thinker
Cait Noone
Head Galway International Hotel School
Vice President International
Engagement, GMIT, Ireland

1. **Stepping back to March 2020. When did you think C-19 would end and we would be back to normal?**
   - Having lived in China during the SARS epidemic, I never anticipated a 'return to normal' date, but like many, I had hoped we would be in a better place by December 2020. The reality is we need to learn how to live with diseases, and I wonder if the concept of lockdowns has been fully considered in light of what the public perceive it to be and the realities. Any close-down of society has significant impacts across the globe, not only on economies, but most importantly, on human behaviour and interactions.

2. **What are the 3 biggest issues you have had to face so far because of C-19? What happened?**
   - I work in Higher Education in Ireland, and undoubtedly, the sharp pivot to online delivery with so little advance preparation was an important adjustment. Like many higher education institutes, our organisation was delivering some courses via online learning. However, the entire organisation had to embrace this new world, and it has presented challenges and opportunities.
   - Parallel to embracing new working modes, our organisation began the process of business continuity planning almost immediately in March 2020. This has been challenging on many fronts, not least facing the unknown. We also welcomed a new President to the organisation on March 18th, so one

can only imagine how her first 100 days evolved. The management team had to plan for multiple possibilities, and this planning takes time, expertise, and reflective processes. On occasion, the former left little room for the latter.

- Supporting the workforce—your colleagues—during such a difficult time comes with challenges. People fear the unknown; it is completely understandable and acceptable, and when you don't have immediate answers, people become frustrated. Eventually, matters are resolved. However, that does not take away from the difficult days and weeks when you are trying to keep everyone in the communication loop and are dependent on human behaviours to engage with you.

On a personal level, concern for family, when I don't live too close to them, can be difficult to manage, especially when you have no control of outcomes.

3. **What have you changed in your business/role/ university to get through this crisis? Tell us how you Adapted/Innovated and scaled (up or down) your business/role/university.**
- Change is constant in any business, and over the last decade, higher education in Ireland has faced continuous change, mainly due to new policy developments and diminishing financial resources. As a higher education provider on the west coast of Ireland, we had to review our business model and adapt. During this pandemic, financial resources have been reallocated, where necessary, to support other immediate business needs, including purchasing hardware and software for online delivery. Additional resources have been sought to support the student learning experience beyond the

classroom. e.g., additional counselling, academic online supports, laptop loan schemes, and financial supports are now available. The college has been incredibly supportive of the environment we find ourselves in and has certainly not been found wanting.

- As a public sector organisation we had to rely on all staff to engage with this new approach to our world. This meant faculty upskilling and retraining while also delivering classes. Administration and technical staff had to adapt to working from home where possible, and many of these colleagues remained on site to ensure those working from home were enabled and supported. In my opinion, people are an organisation's best resource, and colleagues across GMIT certainly rose to the challenges we faced. I would suggest one of the greatest pressures was on Heads of Department who manage multiple resources. These colleagues are often the unsung heroes in higher education, and for what it is worth, I am very much in awe of their dedication and brilliance.

- As an organisation, we set up BOLT—a Blended online teaching initiative to provide supports for all to move to online engagement. The process was nimble and agile, key characteristics that are essential when changing business engagement. BOLT was supported by the Executive Board, Management Group and the Business Continuity Team, and this, coupled with talented administrators and faculty, led by a highly innovative and creative Computing Services team, ensured the project could succeed.

- As a school we felt a huge responsibility to support Tourism industry colleagues across the globe. Closer to home, we worked with colleagues to co-author a paper which was presented to the national Tourism Taskforce, established by the Irish government in

May 2020. The paper outlined a proposal to develop a resource that could support the CPD needs for tourism employees, with a specific focus on upskilling, reskilling, and retaining talent. At the time of writing, the proposal has featured in the recommendations to government, and we are hopeful this will be actioned in the coming months.

- In June 2020, the organisation signed the final stage of a memorandum of understanding with St. Lawrence College in Canada. Colleagues from both organisations have worked collaboratively to develop an International Hospitality Management course that will allow for faculty and student exchange, accredited work placement in reciprocal locations, in addition to degree completion opportunities for Canadian students in Galway.

- Finally, we are actively involved in dialogue with higher education partners in South Africa, led by THENSA— The Technological Higher Education Network South Africa. We are co-developing a proposal to create a Tourism Education, Research, and Training Cluster which will support Irish and South African stakeholders across industry and education platforms.

- The final activity approved during lockdown that will enable further internationalisation happened on March 17th, our national holiday in Ireland. On this date, the Chinese Ministry of Education approved an application for our school to work with Lingnan Normal University on a cooperative education programme for culinary students. The five-year project will provide opportunities for shared learning, student and faculty exchange. In addition, our culinary team will be invited to teach in China in Year 2 and 3 of the degree, and our school will provide degree completion opportunities for Chinese students in Culinary and Gastronomic Sciences.

4. **What worked and what failed? Why for both?**

   - To date, all of the above are actions in progress, so too early to report any failures. One action I had hoped to address was to provide additional supports for industry partners as they emerged from lockdown in June 2020; however, that was not to be. Sometimes ambitions can overtake the realization of what we can get done, and occasional failure is a position I can live with.

5. **How did you personally deal with the stress? Tips for others?**

   - In the interest of honesty and fairness, I did ok and learnt from mistakes made in the first lockdown to ensure they were not repeated in the Autumn/Winter lockdown. I had no freak-outs or major dramas, but I guess I failed to recognise that even during a global pandemic, not everyone will work at the same pace.
   - Being a manager in higher education can be an incredibly lonely job. You are a point of contact for many or expected to fix problems. Some might even suggest that is my job, but of course, it's not. Very often we were finding solutions hours before meetings, and I sensed staff were often annoyed we did not have all the answers, but that is the reality of the situation we were all living in.
   - I am an early riser. It's not unusual for me to be up at 5 a.m., and I enjoy the early morning calm and solitude. I really enjoy walking alone in the morning. I live on the west coast of Ireland, so the Atlantic Ocean is always in my view. I find the sea incredibly calming in the early hours of the day; winter mornings, however, can be a different matter. I do some gentle mindfulness in the early morning and meditation in the evening, which helps me unwind. And I have

been known to use the occasional app to help with easing myself into sleep. I need at least six hours to function. And I am not against the occasional great Irish gin and tonic to help me relax.

Finally, turn off the devices at the same time every evening, no exceptions. If it's urgent, somebody will phone.

6. **What surprised you the most about your Family or business response/reaction to this difficult time?**
   - My family are incredibly resilient, so not even a global pandemic shook them despite some of them losing their jobs due to the pandemic. My husband is a chef, so he, too, was furloughed and is still working three days per week, but he is happy to do his job and support me.
   - I really missed not seeing my parents for five months; that was incredibly difficult as my dad was ill last year, and I saw lots of him, so this was a significant contrast.
   - My workplace really surprised me. With the sudden move to online delivery, academic digital heroes emerged all over the college. No question was deemed silly; it was a true team effort across all campuses, enabling 7,000 students and hundreds of staff. As a nation, the Irish are particularly resourceful and dynamic when our back is to the wall. Colleagues across the organisation were phenomenal, truly incredible educators, administrators, and professionals who went above and beyond.

7. **How would you describe your outlook for the next 12 months? Expand as much as possible. What is influencing your views?**
   - Well, it would be great to say it's all coming to an end, but it is not. However, in my opinion, the next twelve months will present so many opportunities.

Yes, there will be challenges, but we already know that, so let's focus on the opportunities. Now is the time to adapt your business model. Now is the time for the Tourism industry to truly invest in your talent team because if you do not, they will be hired by other industries.

- Now is the time for enterprise and educators to come together and demonstrate what collaborative partnerships can look like. My views are informed by twenty-five years of experience networking with the industry across the globe. I value my professional relationships with alumni, industry partners, and all education partners as much as I value personal relationships. You should never underestimate the importance of authentic working partnerships.

- Whether we like it or not, the world is always changing. The Tourism industry is at a global crossroads, and where we go next will inform future strategic ambitions and will certainly impact on local and national economies. We may never have an opportunity such as now to change how we do our business and lay the foundations for the next generation of tourism leaders.

As we say in Irish—**Is féidir linn!** (Yes, we can).

Gutsy Genius Thinker
Peter O'Connor PhD.
Chaired Professor of Digital Disruption
at ESSEC Business School,
Paris, France

1. **Stepping back to March 2020. When did you think C-19 would end and we would be back to normal?**

   I've been skeptical that we would get out of this crisis quickly since the very beginning. Already trapped in a (what turned out to be seven-week) lockdown in France and looking at the complacency in many different parts of the world, my fear was that this challenge would drag on and on.

   - And, unfortunately, I was right, and we still continue to try to muddle through rather than take the (often hard but necessary) steps to stop this virus in its tracks. Even now, with multiple potential vaccines appearing, it will take a long time to organize ourselves logistically to deploy and administer this solution, assuming, that is, that we can convince people to take them.

   - More visionary people than me have talked about returning to normal by end-2024. While others are optimists and predict a quicker recovery, I'm a realist and hope, for everyone's sake, that we can achieve that 2024 goal.

2. **What are the 3 biggest issues you have had to face so far because of C-19? What happened?**

   A recent Harvard Medical School study claims that flying on an airplane is safer than going shopping in a supermarket. Well then, I am the unluckiest person in the world, as I, along with over 20 percent of my fellow passengers, were infected on a flight to Australia.

Luckily, neither my wife (also infected) nor I got very sick, and our three kids, cooped up in close contact with us in a Perth quarantine hotel, became infected. And spending 36 days in quarantine together really helps to connect you as a family.

- Working in education, I've been luckier than many people in the hospitality business who have been furloughed or laid off. Schools and Universities have been forced to move to digital to survive, requiring teachers to develop and use new skill sets and competencies so as to connect with students through digital media. As a self-acknowledged geek, this transition was probably easier for me than for many, but I dearly miss the interaction, comradery, and fun that comes from being in a physical classroom. Digital channels do have their advantages, but face-to-face interactions are, for me, simply richer and more fulfilling.

- Travel, previously a major part of my life for both work and leisure, has altogether disappeared, to be replaced by a drove of Zoom, FaceTime, and Teams calls, which I'm not sure is necessarily a good thing. One worry I have is that I will never now be able to add to my tally of countries that I have visited—currently standing at 72.

3. **What have you changed in your business/role/university to get through this crisis? Tell us how you Adapted/Innovated and scaled (up or down) your business/role/university**

- At Essec Business School we moved to 100 percent online teaching very rapidly, demonstrating the adaptability and flexibility of both our professors and students. We were both lucky and relatively prepared as we were already ahead of the curve in terms of technology adoption with the development of our Digital Campus. As the situation calmed, we moved back to a blended approach, with some students on campus and others at a distance, allowing us to combine the advantages of both approaches and increase our reach to students who, for one reason or another, had to remain at a distance.

4. **What worked and what failed? Why for both?**
   - My biggest regret is that many students finished their college experience sitting isolated in their dorm room or parents' spare bedroom. For me, University education is all about connections and relationships, something almost impossible to replicate and develop in the online environment.
   - In my orientation speech to incoming students, I often tell them that the person sitting on their right or left may develop into their best friend or their bitterest enemy. I explain the importance of networking and how that person that you meet after an event may be the contact that helps you get a job or even your future boss or business partner. Despite virtual get-togethers and cocktail parties, developing these kinds of casual relationships on online channels is (to date) impossible.

   Now there's an interesting business idea for someone.

5. **How did you personally deal with the stress? Tips for others?**

   Many, many, many deep breaths.......

   And a fair number of cold beers!

   - In particular, working from home is challenging for everyone. In addition to trying to work full time, parents are transformed into full-time teachers, babysitters, nurses, confidants, playmates, and in my case, for some reason, goal keeper. And yet most of us get through it, all the while doom scrolling social media, trying to find any evidence of light at the end of the tunnel.

- I read recently something about the challenges that our grandparents and parents endured. In Europe, this included WWI, the Spanish Flu, the Great Depression, WWII, and the Cold War, amongst many others. And I take solace in the thought that, despite our short-term frustrations, "this too shall pass."

6. **What surprised you the most about your Family or business response/reaction to this difficult time?**

- I have been amazed by the reaction of certain hotels and hotel companies in terms of how they have opened their doors to their communities during the COVID-19 crisis. Despite the risks, many have remained open, providing accommodation for free to essential workers or those needing to self-isolate away from their families. Several have set up solidarity funds to support employees, in some cases cancelling dividends so as to better support their stakeholders. Overall, we as an industry have been exemplary in terms of our response, putting people before profits and focusing on getting back to normal as quickly as possible.

7. **How would you describe your outlook for the next 12 months? Expand as much as possible. What is influencing your views?**

- With what seem to be effective vaccines on the way, the future looks a bit rosier than before. However, it's clear that everything has changed and that nothing will go back to how it was pre-COVID. The crisis has accelerated the move to digital at a rate unimaginable previously, and everything from retail to travel to medicine has been drastically transformed. This demands entirely new skill sets from everyone, as well as an upheaval in how we work, shop, interact, and play. The digital revolution has truly arrived, and it has been enabled not by tech companies and platforms, but by an invisible virus.

Gutsy Genius Thinker
Vanessa de Souza Lage
Cofounder & CMO Rentals United
& Founder VRTech Events
Barcelona, Spain

1. **Stepping back to March 2020. When did you think C-19 would end and we would be back to normal?**
   - We gave it until the end of 2020 and made a budget accordingly. A month after the crisis started, we were already presenting the 3 plans to the board—good, not-so-good, bad.

2. **What are the 3 biggest issues you have had to face so far because of C-19? What happened?**
   - Cash-flow management, people motivation, forecasting. What happened? We got a forced crash course in all three aspects! I think we've learned a lot from it, though, and if being cashflow positive was always a goal, it is now more than ever. Forecasting is now a multiple of "IF, THEN," and people's motivation; well, we thought that would be an issue, but in fact, productivity is at an all-time high.

3. **What have you changed in your business/role/ university to get through this crisis? Tell us how you Adapted/Innovated and scaled (up or down) your business/role/university.**
   - We have adopted a flexible, remote-working policy. We restructured internally so that customer-facing employees have more time to focus on customers. We set up a contingency scheme to help out clients in financial difficulty.

4. **What worked and what failed? Why for both?**
   - It's all been for the better.

5. How did you personally deal with the stress? Tips for others?

- One day at a time. The importance of a good night's sleep to deal with the stress and be able to cope with what a start-up throws at you every day! Taking at least 1 day off a week.

6. What surprised you the most about your Family or business response/reaction to this difficult time?

- The team was so incredibly supportive of how we decided to handle the situation. It brought us together even more than before.

7. How would you describe your outlook for the next 12 months? Expand as much as possible. What is influencing your views?

- Outlook is positive! We're putting an extra focus on collaboration with partners...We really believe that now more than ever, we need to help each other grow! So, we created a white label for them, and we're also opening our code to allow others to write to it.

- We also see a lot of convergence happening between the real estate and hospitality sector, so we're planning for that. This year has given our strategy meetings a whole new level of creativity as we're determined to get this company to grow today and beyond the pandemic!

Gutsy Genius Thinker
Paul Slattery
Cofounder & Director, Otus & Co.
Advisory
London, United Kingdom

1. **Stepping back to March 2020. When did you think C-19 would end and we would be back to normal?**

   Did not know. No knowledge when a vaccine would be available or the plans for mass vaccination.

2. **What are the 3 biggest issues you have had to face so far because of C-19? What happened?**

   Conducting business only digitally. Extreme creativity is required.

3. **What have you changed in your business/role/university to get through this crisis? Tell us how you Adapted/Innovated and scaled (up or down) your business/role/university.**

   Adhere to mask, wash hands, retain space.

4. **What worked and what failed? Why for both?**

   Adhering to mitigation has worked so far because that is all we have. Nothing failed; it just took longer and was harder.

5. **How did you personally deal with the stress? Tips for others?**

   Hard work, Pilates, and the belief that "a day without wine is like a day without sunshine."

6. **What surprised you the most about your Family or business response/reaction to this difficult time?**

   Their commitment to mitigation. Hotels that do not refund deposits when they are locked down.

7. How would you describe your outlook for the next 12 months? Expand as much as possible. What is influencing your views?

Hopeful for vaccination, tracking, and improved treatments. Excited about persuading governments and corporates about the changes needed in sector policies to get the economies and their hospitality businesses recovering and growing.

Gutsy Genius Thinker
Jacob Wedderburn-Day
CEO & Co-Founder, Stasher.com
London, England

1. **Stepping back to March 2020. When did you think C-19 would end and we would be back to normal?**
   - Back in March 2020, I remember speaking to Sean about the pandemic before things had really kicked off in the UK. Sequoia had recently published an open letter to their founders, calling C-19 the Black Swan of 2020 and urging financial prudence above all else. Being the founder of a travel business and seeing the early spread of lockdowns across Asia, I was mindful that if things spread to Europe, we'd be in trouble.
   - What's amazing, looking back, is how even right up until the weekend before lockdowns were announced in the UK, people had no concept of how serious this would be. I went to a conference at the Excel centre in London on the last day it was open! Now it's a Nightingale Hospital.
   - I hoped the impact would only be felt for a month, back in March. My first forecast was of a 3-month impact, and we'd be back on track in the summer, just in time for peak tourism.
   - But for prudence's sake, I also made a forecast in which revenues were depressed to 0 for the entire of 2020. Sadly, this is the one that's proven most accurate!

2. **What are the 3 biggest issues you have had to face so far because of C-19? What happened?**
   - **Cashflow management** – the pandemic was a disaster for Stasher's revenues. Fortunately, we run a lean organisation, and we're asset light. I'm proud of how quickly we went into crisis mode, slashing all

surplus expenditure. Our burn rate has never been this low since we took on VC funding back in 2018. The stressful thing has been keeping one eye on the runway—if this goes on too long, it will eventually pose an existential threat to Stasher.

- **People and redundancies** – we've been very fortunate, in the UK, that the furlough schemes have allowed us to keep staff on our books at minimal extra cost. Initially, we let go of a small number of employees, but we wanted to keep a strong core. Partly this is practical—we have people with good relationships and some domain expertise, and we don't want to re-hire them. Partly it's sentimental, though, and I acknowledge that. We like our team; as a start-up, many of them have been with us since the early days—and we want to do good by them in bad times. Keeping morale up this year has been challenging, but we've at least had our own small sense of community to tide us through.

- **Delayed goals** – as a founder, my one clear objective has always been to keep Stasher growing. Whether there's an exit or not, the important thing is Stasher keeps scaling and reaching its potential. This year is the first in its history that Stasher hasn't grown (we've never done less than 2x in the past). That's been tough. From talking to our competitors, many of whom are in a similar position, it's a mental challenge to face the fact that it might take years just to build back to a level we had previously achieved. That's hard to take.

3. **What have you changed in your business/role/ university to get through this crisis? Tell us how you Adapted/Innovated and scaled (up or down) your business/role/university.**

- As alluded to above, the key thing was to recognise this pandemic was a disaster and go into crisis mode accordingly.
- Once costs were reduced, we spent a month experimenting with viable alternative uses of the platform. We've dedicated much of the year to building out two new revenue streams.
- First, we've looked at licensing our software to hotels for use with their own guests, and we have some trials ongoing. Second, we've integrated with a delivery partner to handle luggage shipping as well as storage.
- Both these avenues give us new strings to our bow for the future—although neither are likely to generate much revenue while tourism is depressed, they've given us something to focus on and cause for future optimism.

4. **What worked and what failed? Why for both?**
   - The jury is still out on the new products because it's taken time to launch and integrate them. I view this as a positive, because if times had been good, we would never have committed as much time and effort to these new product lines, but they could both prove to be very impactful. However, in terms of success, delivery is launching next month, and the software trials had only just started when new lockdowns were imposed. So, time will tell!
   - The cost management was unequivocally a success. I should also thank Sean for his advice, back in March, to raise the cadence of communication with investors and pre-emptively send them new forecast plans. I feel like we've won a lot of credit for proactively handling the financial impact of this, and I was very proud when one of our board members said,

"Out of 70 companies I invest in, your communications have been the best."

5. **How did you personally deal with the stress? Tips for others?**
   - I like to be active, and I've had to plug the gap that full focus on Stasher normally occupies. I love sports and do a lot to keep fit anyway, but lockdowns allowed me more opportunity to focus on my running, cycling, and gym. (I was way ahead of the home-gym curve. I've had gym equipment in my lounge since 2017!)
   - But sports can only fill so much time, and I don't like to spend too much time relaxing, so in addition to Stasher, Ant (my cofounder) and I have kept busy with two other projects.
   - The first is an everyday philosophy podcast called the Morality of Everyday Things. Eight episodes in, we're ranked in the Top 5 percent of podcasts for downloads (we had some viral success with a few episodes, such as "Are you a bad person if you work at Facebook?"). This has been a fun new challenge and helped keep us sane when things were incredibly quiet in the summer.
   - The second is a new start-up called *Treepoints.com*. Treepoints is a platform to manage your carbon footprint—we make it very easy to offset your emissions and manage your green life. Climate change is the defining issue of our time, notwithstanding this pandemic, and building this platform from scratch and now marketing it has been another rewarding challenge.
   - In the meantime, we're keeping on top of Stasher as much as can be done. I've found, with everything on, I'm as busy now as I was back in January, but with

lots of variety! It's fun to keep feeling productive in spite of the prevailing circumstances.

6. **What surprised you the most about your Family or business response/reaction to this difficult time?**
   - In some ways, I'm grateful for my responsibilities at Stasher. It's because of them that I was aware of the pandemic and its risks early on. Talking to friends and family back in March, I felt like a doomsayer from having done more research. I remember warning my parents not to go to Spain the weekend of the 16th—and they ended up enduring a horrible journey back to Britain to escape the Spanish lockdown!
   - So, in the early days, I felt like many people were surprisingly complacent or in denial about the impact this would have. I feel like the same holds true, but in a different way as the pandemic has continued. I've taken pains to be as well informed as possible about the impact of the pandemic. Frankly, I don't blame the UK government at all for their handling of the "first wave," as they were up against the unknown. I am, however, hugely disappointed in their handling of the eminently predictable "second wave," which has still found our test and trace systems lacking and the same cry as before that hospitals risk being overrun—which is something that risks happening every year just in bad flu seasons!
   - As a result, I feel more politically engaged than ever before, which I suppose is no bad thing. In the past, I've had enough on my plate just worrying about Stasher—but this year, I feel much more responsible as a business owner and citizen. Although being politically engaged can be deeply frustrating at times, I think that's a positive.

7. **How would you describe your outlook for the next 12 months? Expand as much as possible. What is influencing your views?**

- I'm always an optimist. Someone, probably Mark Twain, said, "If you're a pessimist, you experience bad things twice." I try to balance my optimism against what's realistic. So, here's my forecast.

- Even before the recent vaccine news, I predicted that the distribution of a vaccine would break the PR stranglehold C-19 is exerting over the media. A vaccine—symbolically—means victory, or at least a path to victory. And that's what people need to feel safe to move around again.

- So my hope and expectation is that we're still in for a bumpy few months, because respiratory diseases like C-19 are at their worst in winter, but we'll be entering 2021 with a feeling of far greater optimism for the summer. People will begin making plans with more confidence. When measures begin to ease in the Spring, people will have a lot to celebrate and a year of missed experiences to make up for. There will always be some people who are too scared and will continue to sound a note of caution, but the tide will be moving against them—people do not want to live restricted lives unless they absolutely have to.

- 2021 will be the year of experiences. This was a prevailing trend in the last decade, and 2021 will restart that where it left off. People will be so desperate to get out and have fun again. Personally, I can't wait. I want to go on holiday, go to parties, and go to festivals once more.

For Stasher, this brings good news—travel and events are the key to our success.

CHAPTER 11

Work Zone – Tips, Takes, and Stuff to Do

 ## Now *You* Take the Wheel!

You made it! I'm sure there were times you were wishing that the next words you would read were "The End." I get it. Some of these topics get a bit heavy. But you have arrived at the place where you can take the steering wheel and navigate your own path.

So, what can you do?

Well…

- You can skip around through the Tips, Takes, and Summaries of some of the concepts—whatever is most useful for you.
- You can try out the Work Zone exercises to continue your journey and take the tests to gauge your own adaptability. No worries: it's open-book, and there are no grades!
- You can get an introduction to the GGTs of this edition by reading the one-pagers that tell you more about who they are, what they do, and what's on their minds.
- At the end of each profile page, you can "meet" the GGT using the QR code link that will take you to the actual interview.

Learn more by key topic? Listen to the GGTs.

- *Want to know more about BI and data analytics?* Check out the conversation with **Cindy Estis Green** of Kalibri Labs. QR CODE HERE

- *Interested in how academia presents the Travel, Tourism, and Hospitality sectors and their ecosystem?* May we suggest an hour with **Prof. Peter O'Connor, ESSEC Business School** or **Cait Noone** of the International Hotel School in Galway, Ireland? QR CODE HEREx2

- *Want to follow the money trail and learn more about the financial and investment aspects of Hospitality, Travel, and Tourism?* **Mark Greenberg** of Silverstone Capital Advisors and **Paul Slattery, Otus & Co.** are your go-to guys! QR CODE HERE x2

- *Curious how the job market looks, what's hot and what's not, and more?* **Keith Kefgen** of Aethos Consulting Group out of New York, and **Guy Lean** with Madison Mayfair, based in London, can give you insight with a global perspective. QR CODE HERE x 2

- *Want to hear the inspiring stories of some Travel, Tourism, and Hospitality ecosystem adaptors/innovators?* Don't miss spending some interview time with **James and Yoly Blick,** and they will tell you about personal reinvention from Madrid, Spain. Or "visit" with **Anthony Melchiorri** of *Hotel Impossible* TV fame as he tells us about leaving a successful hotel career behind to try something dramatically different at age forty-five! **Jacob Wedderburn-Day** will tell you how Stasher.com, the app-run system for storing your luggage while you wander with ease, came to be. QR CODE HERE x 3

- *Worried you may never get to attend another industry conference? Want to know how their organizers are adapting for the New Reality and beyond?* The interviews with **Piers Brown** of International Hospitality Media, and **Alexi Khajavi** with Hospitality & Travel, Questex, will soon bring you up to speed and alleviate some of those fears. QR **CODE HERE x 2**

- *Are you looking to get hows, whys, and wherefores directly from the top leaders of some of the industries' most prestigious hotels—owners, brands, and management companies?* We've got a few of the best for you to meet, like **Daniel Del Olmo** of Sage Hotel Management; **Greg Juceam** of G6 Hospitality; **Mitch Patel** with Vision Hospitality Group; **Mitch Presnick**, founder of Super 8 Hotels in China and an investor; **Raul Leal**, Virgin Hotels; and **Sloan Dean**, leading Remington Hotels. QR CODE HERE x 6

- *Interested in how the Serviced Apartment sector is faring?* **James Foice**, Chief Executive of the Association of Services Apartments, is on hand to tell you more. QR CODE HERE

- *And what about the channel managers?* Barcelona-based **Vanessa de Souza Lage** has more on that, as well as providing a personal example of how she and her gang used adaption and collaboration to come to their own rescue when faced with the arrival of the "big boys"—as she describes them—on the scene. QR CODE HERE

Remember, these GGTs are certainly experts in their own fields and will focus on that expertise, but over the course of some interesting and remarkable careers, they have compiled an amazing warehouse of experiences and information about all the industry sectors and the ecosystem that supports them and that in turn is fed by them. Don't miss out. Find the time to "meet" with them all. Don't fall into the "wall" trap—take a look over and see what else is happening out there.

Ready?

The Adapters' Tips & Takes – Topics for Meetings and Discussions

1. **"I do not know"**: It takes guts to say, "I do not know." The next step is to source those that *do* know and who can help—even a competitor! Find a person of insight and inspiration.

2. **Leverage your community:** Source and find those that matter in your space. Tim Ferris, author of *Tribe of Mentors*, had to make hundreds of phone calls to secure one hundred interviews of the brightest minds of our time. Imagine the community he has built, the network he has engineered. Now is the time to share and find new information...fast.

3. **Adapt:** When COVID-19 made its impact known, without exception, every single Adapters' interviewee immediately ceased referring to the budget and went to scenario forecasting and cash-flow management. They were trying to face the New Reality that was gripping them. Accumulate information, adapt, and make decisions to *move forward.*

4. **Confusion: *Survival planning and implementation is not innovation***; it is not even adaption. It is simply finding a way to make it until tomorrow. It is okay to be confused as much of the data has no historical merit, and the situation is fluid, at best. Now that you have found tomorrow, what will be your approach? Will you respond or simply react? We saw several companies, particularly in the CoLiving, CoWorking, and Serviced Apartment spaces start to pivot to the lower-risk model of becoming franchisors or leasing/renting to those that needed space. Is this innovation or merely a way to mitigate risk? Either way, adapt, pivot, iterate, and innovate your way through this. ***Take it in small steps to deliver a big plan.*** Remember the principle of climbing a mountain on a bike—three meters at a time.

5. **Consolidation:** Now that COVID has revealed possible outcomes and time frames, it is possible that merging or acquiring may be an outcome. Scale and cost-cutting, although painful, can drive innovation. Oddly, those that were laid off may become entrepreneurs, leading to an avalanche of innovation over the next decade. But we must make it to at least 2022 first. Our GGTs still feel like the crystal ball for seeing options and the time frame for the future is still too cloudy to be of much use.

6. **Lifelong learning:** Daniel Del Olmo, Cait Noone, Raul Neal, Mitch Presnick, Greg Juceam, and others spoke about lifelong learning and the importance of staying relevant. This singular attitude will permeate their organizations as well as their personal lives. You seek learning because "you don't know" something, or you desire to improve and increase your knowledge to achieve a certain outcome. I (Sean) moved to Spain and had to learn Spanish. Andrea, my wife, who speaks the language fluently, was my translator, and that was certainly not fair to her. My choice was to learn, adapt, or not (risking the growing wrath of my wife!). Gracias!

7. **People:** The adapters and innovators featured on The Adapters media hub are different. They have a powerful inner drive to develop people and give back. Daniel Del Olmo funds a charity personally. Greg Juceam is passionate about helping combat homelessness, while Cait Noone gives back by being a leader in her community and helped her city of Galway, Ireland, win the European Capital of Culture for 2020. (She's hoping the officials will give Galway a 2021 "do-over," considering the circumstances of 2020!) Raul Leal has developed businesses across the USA and helped ignite community development with the launch of his hotels. Their traits have also helped them find unique people to make their organizations successful.

8. **Beyond experience:** Curriculum vitaes and résumés are always a starting point to learn about a potential candidate. In the tough times, diverse experience is helpful. Look for external and internal teammates that have moved for the company or have regional/international experience and speak another language or more. They had to adapt when they moved, find a home, love a family, learn a language, and build a new community. They have skills that may not be recognized in a review.
Go beyond: **(EI + BI + C) + A x I = S** (Emotional and Business Intelligence and Community) + Adaption + Innovation = Success.

9. **Communication and 360 feedback loops and tactics: Three simple tips**

   a) **Quarterly Reviews (QRs) with Customers to Build Trust and Find Truth**

      i. Offer to hold a "360" with your customers that can benefit both, to include: your company and customer performance against each other's goals. Service, revenue, and people goals—the good, bad, and ugly, including billing history. Get the truth and build real relationships versus the often empty "partnerships" that businesses and clients tout.

      ii. **Market updates:** Help make your client smarter by adding an adaption and innovation section. Look for those things trending, and above all, broaden the lens on what is happening in your respective and cross-over spaces.

      iii. **Bring the right people:** The account manager is always the lead. Depending on the agenda, bring along the right experts from your company to theirs. It shows depth and confidence. If there's an IT issue, bring in the experts. If it's a collections matter, bring in the CFO (chief financial officer), or better still, the accounts-receivable manager; it's great learning and exposure.

iv. **Take notes and follow up between reviews:** Think of the QRs as customer/client board meetings.

b) **Regular updates to your company's leading indicators:** In his book *The Start-Up Way*, Eric Ries recommends posting key metrics on screens for all staff to see in real time if possible. That's the extreme, but at least post regularly, and it can be done. We at The Adapters have achieved this in companies that we have run. Never be fearful of transparency.

c) **One-to-one:** Each layer of management should hold regular one-to-ones with direct-report teammates. Think thirty-minute chats, half yours and half your teammates'. This can be held anywhere, preferably in a relaxed, casual setting, including breakfast, snack time, or lunch; change it up. Ideally, you should arrange these monthly and agree on a dynamic agenda. This allows for a polite catch-up and active bilateral coaching.

10. **Stand-up huddles:** Find a place and cadence to have an info session. Set an agenda and vary the speakers and leaders. This is a way to develop leadership, public speaking skills, and share information. Hold a huddle in or around a "metric monitor" to refer to company performance. The tech community is generally good at this, and the concept is not new, but the discipline to hold regular meetings is always a challenge. Consistency, transparency, and predictability influence confidence and build trust. Ask your teammates to provide feedback on the topics and speakers to ensure the topics are relevant and helpful.

It is hard work, emotionally and intellectually, to be responsible for anything. (Parents know this!) Business requires more strength and fortitude than ever. Deploying both *EI and BI* can become a force multiplier. Lifelong learners know this. Relevant skills change over time, and much like products can become irrelevant (Kodak). Expertise needs to be built, nurtured, and honed with equal parts EI and BI. It's easy to find a class and certificate for BI—not so much for EI. Do the math.

TIPS & TAKES

The Adapters' Tips on Alignment of Concept to User Experience

Alignment process flow™
Connecting across your business through questions......

5	4	3	2	1
Concept + Capital	Teammates	Product Development	Go to Market	User Experience "Ux"
How aligned is your Concept with Capital to support your vision	Is your Team "fit for purpose" to scale your business	How tuned in is your product to your current and future clients needs	Is yours Sales and Marketing message really speaking to specific needs of your clients / Be priced for profit	Nothing else matters / Does your Company offer the optimum USER experience in your catgeory

$$(EI + BI + C) + A \times I = S$$

To be a successful *Adapter and Innovator,* there are five critical elements to *Getting Stuff Done "GSD"*

1. **The Founder and the Capital source** must be in complete alignment as to what you believe to be the right product for the right time.

2. **Culture:** This is the fuel that drives innovation and adaption. Hire and keep the best people. Refer back to **Ray Dalio** and Reed Hastings for inspiration while viewing **Arne Sorenson** and **Peter Strebel's** videos to their teams. See page 203 for the link.

3. **Product:** Try not to be the company that has a solution looking for a problem; be the company that has identified a problem and has built the solution.

4. **Know how to talk with and learn from your market:** Your hotel, tour company, serviced apartment, CoLiving space, cruise, or airline needs a go-to market strategy that speaks to the problem that your client/guest/ passenger wants solved, not the other way round. The sales and marketing strategy

has to identify and be clear that your company is solving a pain point for them.

5. **User/guest experience:** The other four do not matter if your customer has a terrible experience when buying your product or when using it or asking for help post-purchase.

> "Trust is highly flammable, so try hard to avoid blowing it up."
>
> **Sean Worker**

3.0 The Adapters' Tips on Alignment of Processes and People

Focus on amazing Ux™
Silos align to a singular mission - *driving execution of the company's strategy*

Really HAPPY customers!

Aligning mission with replicable processes leads to market agility and communication clarity

Is the business Responding or Reacting?

1. **Alignment process flow:** "APF" facilitates a macro conversation about how each major departments' actions should align to the business mission. Then the detailed work begins with developing/documenting Business Processes. Leadership should collaborate with each department to define the BP and determine how the departments' interdependent needs will align to deliver an amazing and profitable UX experience.

2. **KPI transparency:** Ideally, leadership should build a transparent Key Performance Indicator matrix (KPI).[68] https://www.youtube.com/watch?v=2tuWjtc2Ifk
KPI frame processes ensure *actions* and desired *outcomes* are aligned to the vision and mission of the company.

3. **Project owner:** It is recommended that where possible, a dedicated project manager is appointed or hired to manage the process and support the department heads to achieve their part of the puzzle.

4. **Employee- and customer-centric:** The desired outcome is to have your customer "LOVE" your brand. This same level of energy is expected to be given to build a culture that is equally as strong as the company's relationship with the customer. This is not easy.

5. **Outcome:** The desired outcome is to have a thriving, adaptable, innovative, and respected business that delivers a trusted promise to employees and customers/users or guests.

Alternatives to KPIs are Objectives and Key Results (OKRs)

OKRs are a collaborative, goal-setting tool used by teams and individuals to set challenging, ambitious goals with measurable results. OKRs are how you track progress, create alignment, and encourage engagement around measurable goals.

 ## 4.0 Adaption and Innovation – How Well are You doing?

This is ideal for leadership teams to connect and assess your Adaption and Innovation truths

(i) ADAPTION – How engaged is your company?

Modification of a task, concept, or object to make it applicable in situations different from originally anticipated.

QUESTION	ANSWER
1. List how your Company measures market changes, awareness of new competitors, and how you share this information with your company.	
2. How do you currently deliver bad news to your team or Company?	
3. How do you encourage your colleagues to deliver good and bad news? List some examples.	
4. What job title makes most of the decisions?	
5. What 3–5 major sources of intelligence do you use to define if your product or service is effective and valued by the customer?	
6. What percentage of employees receive the data?	
7. What method do you use to define success and failure?	
8. How aligned is your research and development team with sales marketing and technology?	
9. What feedback loop exists to test the product/experience/process that you intended to adapt?	
10. What percentage of your company's employees know that you are open both to adapting and to the progress of the action?	
11. List the major Adaptions your company has made to your top 5 products in the last 2 years.	
12. In the same 2-year period, scribble in your market-share trends. What story is developing?	

(i) INNOVATION – How Engaged is Your Company?

The process of translating an idea or invention into a good or service that creates value for which customers will pay.

QUESTION	ANSWER
1. What percentage of managers and supervisors can define the difference between adaptation and innovation?	
2. What innovation metrics are used to define success and failure?	
3. On a scale of 1-10 (1 crap; 10 awesome), how innovative are your top 5 products/brands/experiences?	
4. What came first, the problem or the solution, for your top-selling experience or product?	
5. What percentage of employees believe that your company is innovative? List the products or experiences that your company created in the last 3 years.	
6. List the products or experiences that your company created in the last 3 years.	
7. What competitor that you admire could beat you in the next 24 months?	
8. How do your foster "inside entrepreneurs" programs? (Some may be viewed as agitators; others view them as "innovative sparks.")	

9. On a scale of 1 to 10 (1 did not have a clue; 10 wow), how confident would the CEO/founder/owner be to walk up to any employee and ask them, "Can you tell me what you do and how you make a difference in our company?"	
10. List the date windows when you asked your top 5, middle 5, and bottom clients why they buy from you.	
11. Ask the same group of clients to list the products/experiences that they believe you have adapted or innovated in the last 3 years that made their lives better and made their customers that bit more loyal, as ranked by your board or investors.	

**Not Specific to a Start-Up Versus Existing Business. Size-Agnostic

Scribble Zone 1:

Adaption: List the top three take-aways from the discussion. Assign a sponsor to lead further discussion within 5 days, with recommendations to the same group within 10 business days.

Issue	Assigned project leader

Scribble Zone 2:

Innovation: List the top three take-aways from the discussion. Assign a sponsor to lead further discussion within 5 days, with recommendations to the same group within 10 business days.

Issue	Assigned project leader

5.0 Emotional Intelligence – 10 Qualities People with High EQ Share

1. **They don't strive for perfection:** At the conclusion of the 1998 film *Pleasantville*, Bud (Tobey Maguire) is finally transported home, and when consoling his sobbing mother, he comes to the realization that even the most idealized settings aren't perfect and have their own shortcomings. Likewise, in business, romanticizing perfection can get in the way of achieving goals since it leads us to look for answers that aren't always there.

2. **Balancing work and life is natural:** Constantly obsessing over every workplace task, along with family and social obligations, can make some people go crazy. But those with high EQ know how to balance their work and life appropriately because they don't see everything coming their way as a challenge.

3. **They embrace change:** Fear of change can be paralyzing to those whose behavior style is steadier in nature. But rather than viewing change as a threat to their success and happiness, emotionally intelligent people are flexible and welcome adaptation – or at the very least, they can come to terms with the situation and get on with it!

4. **They don't dwell on the past:** Playing the "what-if" game and feeling sorry for yourself won't allow you to overcome past mistakes and opportunities. Emotionally intelligent people let the past stay in the past, because they would rather contemplate new ideas and possibilities in business rather than dwell on any past mistakes.

5. **They're good judges of character:** When we make the right decisions to set ourselves up for continued success, we undoubtedly make new connections and associate with like-minded people. Over time, emotionally intelligent people become exceptional judges of character and start distancing themselves from those who tend to bring them down.

6. **They neutralize negative self-talk:** The more we continue ruminating on negative ideas and experiences, the more power we give them. In the end, these are simply thoughts, not facts. Emotionally intelligent people can separate these thoughts from facts to make decisions that can positively impact them and their colleagues or loved ones.

7. **Give and expect nothing in return:** Emotionally intelligent people tend to be selfless individuals because they're constantly thinking about others' well-being.

8. **They're self-motivated:** Emotionally intelligent people get down to business quicker and with greater ease than others because they know their strengths. They are true go-getters who initiate conversations to strategize how something should be accomplished.

9. **They are difficult to offend:** Let's be real—certain words and actions can be upsetting. But emotionally intelligent people have built up a certain level of self-confidence that allows them to brush off negativity. Their thick skin might even allow them to poke fun at themselves.

10. **Above all, they're empathetic people:** Being able to relate to others, show compassion, and provide strategies for self-improvement are some of the hallmarks of emotionally intelligent people. Plus, being empathetic shows a level of sincerity and curiosity that often is the starting point of forging new relationships in business, life, and love.

Taking stock of these qualities and seeing how you can nurture them in your life can help strengthen and form new relationships, including the one you have with yourself. Whatever your behavioral style, working on heightening your emotional intelligence helps you fully take control of your own well-being and positively impact others.

Source: www.blog.ttisi.com

6.0 Business Intelligence – 10 Common Uses of Business Intelligence

1. **Reporting:** Flat output documents from number of check-ins/check-outs, to how many cabins were occupied. This is flat information about a task—helpful, but not particularly insightful.

2. **Online analytical processing:** How many views, impressions before conversion to purchase rooms, cabin meals, etc., are on your company's website?

3. **Analytics:** Drilling down on the efficiency of flying from Dublin to London (on-time arrival record, fuel consumption, etc.) against benchmarks, industry, and expected equipment efficiency ratios.

4. **Data mining:** Dig through the hotel database to source, for example, how many guests check in by day, time, spend rate, check out. Also look at timing and capacity by minute to discover patterns. This could influence how you staff and reduce wait time.

5. **Process mining:** Questioning and mapping data from the initial online order to when cash payment is received; for example, when a relocation company places the order for a serviced apartment, process mining can involve arrival-to-departure information, how many cleans during the stay, and when cash was received for the stay, which can rank clients. Yes, indeed, clients need to be rated as well!

6. **Complex event processing:** Many industries demand that inventory is delivered "just in time." Imagine supplying a Norwegian Line cruise ship. This requires complex project BI mapping to order, purchase, manufacture, deliver, and resupply the ship. This process will be repeated within days at another port and might even be made more interesting with a crew change; that's a lot of coordination and collaboration.

7. **Business performance management:** BPM starts to inform the organization of how the previous six points are performing against goal and other metrics inclusive of product and employee performance. There is a reason why there are five key dials on a vehicle's dashboard; it's about all we can digest quickly. *We need to know the big drivers of our business.* Focusing on the data that matters, as an early warning system for your business, is critical. How confident are you about your BPM?

8. **Text mining:** Done right, this process enables a company to use text patterns to assess consumer and employee reactions. More positive key words are clearly better than disgruntled! This is known as Knowledge Discovery Data (KDD). This scraping technology allows your marketing team to hunt across multiple platforms such as Twitter, Instagram, Facebook, and many more to "hear" what is being "said" about your company. Add this to your insight dashboards to discover some possible EI patterns to assist in communicating with employees and customers

9. **Predictive and prescriptive analytics:** These utilize AI and machine learning[70] to mine current and historical facts. Predictive Analysis then takes it to another level and offers complex understanding of patterns and suggests a variety of options to consider. This can be used by large entities like airlines (United), cruise ship operators (Carnival), distribution companies (Booking), and accommodation platforms (Airbnb) to predict, demand, supply, and assess supplier of product patterns, pricing, agile pricing, and usage.

10. **Benchmarking:** Here's your scorecard. All that activity must convert into economic activity and profit. Early-warning systems to indicate the health of your business must be clear and easy to read. Reed Hastings at Netflix set liberal parameters for personal freedoms such as unlimited vacations; however, performance at the highest levels is expected. For EI and BI to act as force multipliers, the two need to be in balance.

Scribble Zone:– TAKE 20 Minutes

Take twenty minutes or so and review your Scribble boxes. As an Adapter and Innovator, you have the inner energy to GET STUFF DONE (GSD). This is your chance to take your SCRIBBLES and do something about them!

ACTION ZONE

IDEA	ACTIONS	ACTION DATE

7.0 Work from Home (WFH) Trend Data

COLLABORATING DURING CORONAVIRUS: THE IMPACT OF COVID-19 ON THE NATURE OF WORK

Evan DeFilippis Stephen Michael Impink Madison Singell Jeffrey T. Polzer Raffaella Sadun Working Paper 27612 http://www.nber.org/papers/w27612 NATIONAL BUREAU OF ECONOMIC RESEARCH 1050 Massachusetts Avenue Cambridge, MA 02138 July 2020 WF[69] https://www.nber.org/people/evan__defilippis?page=1&perPage=50

For daily email activity, we find that several email measures increased in the post-lockdown period. Specifically, we find significant increases in the average number of emails sent and received among people from the same organization, which we refer to as internal emails (+5.2 percent [+3.0–7.6 percent], +1.4 emails per person per day). We also find that there was a significant increase in the average number of recipients included on emails sent in the post-lockdown period (+2.9 percent [+0.3–5.5 percent], +0.25 recipients per email sent).

However, external emails and distinct emails sent (unique emails counted only once, regardless of the number of internal or external recipients) did not significantly change in the post-lockdown period. Using the span of time defined by the first and last email sent or meeting attended in a twenty-four-hour period, we also find the average workday span increased by +48.5 minutes (+8.2 percent [+7.1–9.3 percent]), partly due to increases in emails sent after business hours (+8.3% [+4.0–12.7 percent], +0.63 emails per person per day). The results for these post-lockdown changes of meeting and email variables are further detailed in Appendix, Table S2. Results, except for that of email recipients, are robust to weighting regressions by the total number of users in each MSA, with an additional positive and significant result for emails sent distinctly under this specification. See Appendix Table S3.

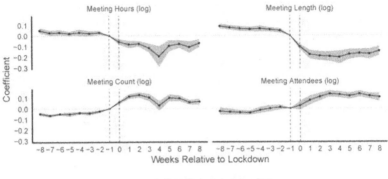

| Base Week | Lockdown Date

For meeting variables, we find consistent increases in the size and count of meetings and consistent decreases in the length of meetings each week after the lockdown date. The cumulative effect of these changes is to consistently decrease the total amount of hours employees spend in meetings each week after the lockdown date. For email variables, we find a more varied pattern of results. The total number of distinct, internal, and external emails sent increased sharply the week of the lockdown and then persistently decreased each week, returning to pre-lockdown levels or below by week four. The average number of recipients per email demonstrated a similar effect, with a small spike the week of the lockdown, followed by a gradual leveling out. Note, however, that by week eight, the average number of recipients per email remained significantly higher than the level eight weeks prior to lockdown (See Appendix, S5). The average workday span of an employee was higher every week following the lockdown than any week in the eight weeks prior to the lockdown.

Careful inspection of these weekly results reveals that some communication patterns began to change even earlier than one week before the lockdown. To account for this variation, in Appendix Figure S4 and Figure S5, we recreate Model 2, but we set the reference category to eight weeks prior to the lockdown date in order to formally test whether meeting and email trends eight weeks

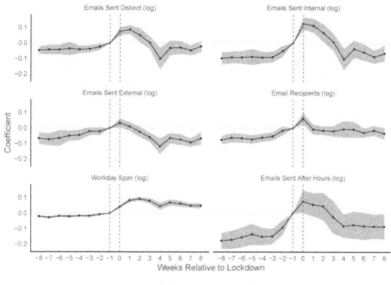

into a lockdown were different from the trends observed eight weeks prior to the lockdown. We find that, for the meeting DeFilippis et al. (2020) variables, the changes that occurred after the lockdown persisted over time. Specifically, compared to meeting activity eight weeks prior to the lockdown, the decreases in average meeting length and meeting hours that we observed were maintained throughout the post-lockdown period. At the same time, the average meeting size and number of meetings remained higher throughout the post-lockdown period.

References, Reads, and Notations

EI Reads

- *Emotional Intelligence*
Book by Daniel Goleman, 1995

- *Primal Leadership*
Book by Daniel Goleman, 2001

- *EQ Applied: The Real-World Guide to Emotional Intelligence*
Book by Justin Bariso, 2018

- *Go Suck a Lemon: Strategies for Improving Your Emotional Intelligence*
Book by Michael Cornwall, 2010

BI Reads

- *Hyper: Changing the Way You Think About, Plan, and Execute Business...*
Book by Gregory P. Steffine, 2015

- *Business Intelligence in Plain Language: A Practical Guide to Data Mining and...*
Book by Jeremy Kolb, 2013

- *Data Strategy: How to Profit from a World of Big Data, Analytics and the Internet of Things*
Book by Bernard Marr, 2017

- *Big Data in Practice: How 45 Successful Companies Used Big Data Analytics to Deliver Extraordinary Results*
Book by Bernard Marr

Other reads

- *The Storm Before the Calm*
Book by George Friedman

- *The Start-up of You*
Book by Reed Hoffman and Ben Casanocha

- *The Soul of America*
Book by Jon Meacham

- *21 Lessons on the 21st Century*
Book by Yuval Noah Harari

- *Click Here to Kill Everybody: Security and Survival in a Hyper-Connected World*
Book by Bruce Schneier

- *Don't Be Evil – The Case Against Big Tech*
Book by Rana Foroohar

- *Tribe of Mentors*
Book by Tim Ferris

- *Turning the Flywheel*
Monograph by Jim Collins

Where the GGTs were mentioned

Jim Alderman	pxxiii, p45, p75, p136, p183, p313
Piers Brown	pxix, p128, p137, p196, p236, p288, p313
Vivi Cahyadi-Himmel	pxxiii, p119, p120, p313
James Blick	pxix, p117, p118, p93 p196 p223, p313
Leonardo Da Vinci	pxix, xxvii, pxxix, p9, p19, p20, p36, p313
Daniel Del Olmo	pxix, p144, p150, p163, p164, p202, p238, p289, p291, p313
Sloan Dean	pxix, p132, p150, p156, p192, p167, p175, p241, p289, p131
James Foice	pxix, p71, p144, p169, p170, p242, p289, p313
Benjamin Franklin	pxx, p16, p23, p24, p158, p313
Mark Greenberg	pxx, p134, p139, p140, p288, p313
Cindy Estis Green	pxx, p172, p198, p199, p244, p287, p313
Greg Juceam	pxx, pxxvii, p96, p97, p132, p203, p216, p282, p289, p29, p313
Bob Hecht	pxxiii, p23, p32, p112, p118, p313
Alexi Huntley Khajavi	pxx, xxiv, p5, p6, p11, p130, p152, pp158, p196, p258, p288, p313
Keith Kefgen	pxx, p231, p232, p256, p288, p313
Raul Leal	pxxi, p28, p60, p124, p160, p161, p289, p291, p313
Guy Lean	pxxi, p159, p210, p211, p262, p313

Karolina Saviona   pxxiii, p119, p120, p313

Vanessa De Souza Lage   pxxi, pxxviii, p34, p144, p165, p166, p180, p196, p277, p289, p313

Tracy Lowy   pxxiii, p76, p313

Yoly Martin - Medieta   pxix, p83, p93, p94, p313

Anthony Melchiorri   pxxi, p15, p21, p22, p100, p232, p288, p313

Cait Noone   pxxi, p28, p58, p59, p92, p109, p132, p144, p204, p215, p229, p265, p288, p291, p313

Dr Peter O'Connor   pxxi, p28, p67, p68, p69, p108, p157, p171, p180, p181, p272, p288, p313

Mitch Patel   pxxi, p42, p62, p63, p226, p313

Mitch Presnick   pxxii, p32, p150, p212, p213, p289, p291, p313

Paul Slattery   pxxii, p43, p80, p134, p141, p141,142, p279, p288, p313

Jacob Wedderburn-Day   pxxii, p40, p101, p187, p233, p234, p281, p288, p313

(") End Notes

Preface

1. **B to B Business to Business (BtoB):** A form of transaction between businesses, such as one involving a manufacturer and wholesaler, or a wholesaler and a retailer. Business-to-business refers to business that is conducted between companies, rather than between a company and individual consumer. Business-to-business stands in contrast to business-to-consumer (B2C) and business-to-government (B2G) transactions. *Investopedia*

2. **Start-up:** The term refers to a company in the first stages of operations. Start-ups are founded by one or more entrepreneurs who want to develop a product or service for which they believe there is demand. These companies generally start with high costs and limited revenue, which is why they look for capital from a variety of sources such as venture capitalists. *Investopedia*

   Start-up founders: A founder is a person who comes up with an idea and then transforms it into a business or start-up. Founders can set up a business on their own, or they can do it with others. For example, Larry Page is a founder of Google. *www.start-ups.com*

   Eric Ries: Eric Ries (born September 22, 1978) is an American entrepreneur, blogger, and author of *The Lean Startup*, a book on the lean start-up movement. He is also the author of *The Startup Way*, a book on modern entrepreneurial management. *Wikipedia http://theleanstartup.com/*

Introduction

3. **BREXIT:** The withdrawal of the United Kingdom from the European Union. *(Oxford Languages)*

4. **Entrepreneur:** A person who undertakes the risk of starting a new business venture is called an entrepreneur. An entrepreneur creates a firm,

which aggregates capital and labor in order to produce goods or services for profit. Entrepreneurship is an important driver of economic growth and innovation. Jul 1, 2020, *Investopedia*.

5. **Business intelligence**: BI plays a key role in the strategic planning of organizations and is used for multiple purposes, including measuring performance progress toward business goals, performing quantitative analysis, reporting and data-sharing, and identifying customer insights. (Forrester)

6. **Robin George Collingwood** FBA (/ˈkɒlɪŋwʊd/; 1889–1943) was an English philosopher, historian and archaeologist. He is best known for his philosophical works, including *The Principles of Art* (1938) and the posthumously published *The Idea of History* (1946). *Wikipedia https://www.goodreads.com/author/quotes/506443.R_G_Collingwood#:~:text=Collingwood%20quotes%20Showing%201%2D30,and%20thus%20what%20man%20is.%E2%80%9D*

Chapter 1

7. **Charles John Huffam Dickens** FRSA (/ˈdɪkɪnz/; 7 February 1812 – 9 June 1870) was an English writer and social critic. He created some of the world's best-known fictional characters and is regarded by many as the greatest novelist of the Victorian era. His works enjoyed unprecedented popularity during his lifetime, and by the 20th century, critics and scholars had recognised him as a literary genius. His novels and short stories are still widely read today. *Wikipedia*

8. **Blue ocean strategy**: The simultaneous pursuit of differentiation and low cost to open up a new market space and create new demand. It is about creating and capturing uncontested market space, thereby making the competition irrelevant. It is based on the view that market boundaries are not a given and can be restructured by the actions and beliefs of industry players. (See also "Blue vs. Red Ocean"). *www.blueoceanstrategy.com*

9. **Important inventions of our time BOX XX:**

10. **Adaption:** Any alteration in the structure or function of an organism or any of its parts that results from natural selection and by which the organism becomes **better** fitted to survive and multiply in its environment. A form or structure modified to fit a changed environment. Dictionary.com

11. **Descent: The Descent Beckons Towards a New Reality**, Sean Worker T5 Strategies May 9, 2020, Serviced Apartment News https://shorttermrentalz.com/features/descent-new-reality-sean-worker/

Chapter 2

12. **Wonderwerk Cave** is an archaeological site, formed originally as an ancient cavity in the dolomite rocks of the Kuruman Hills, situated between Danielskuil and Kuruman in the Northern Cape Province, South Africa. It is a National Heritage Site, managed as a satellite of the McGregor Museum in Kimberley. Geologically, hillside erosion exposed the northern end of the cavity, which extends horizontally for about 140 m (460 ft) into the base of a hill. Accumulated deposits inside the cave, up to 7 m (23 ft) in depth, reflect natural sedimentation processes such as water and wind deposition, as well as the activities of animals, birds, and human ancestors over a period of some 2 million years. The site has been studied and excavated by archaeologists since the 1940s, and research here generates important insights into human history in the subcontinent of Southern Africa.[1][2] Evidence within Wonderwerk cave has been called the oldest-controlled fire. [3] Wonderwerk means "miracle" in the Afrikaans language. *Wikipedia*

13. **Artificial Intelligence**: Refers to the simulation of human intelligence in machines that are programmed to think like humans and mimic their actions. The term may also be applied to any machine that exhibits traits associated with a human mind, such as learning and problem-solving. Mar 13, 2020, *Investopedia*

14. **The Fourth Age of Change:** We are in the 4th age. This period is the most accelerated period of change in human history. It is defined as starting approximately 400–500 years ago, very slowly. Our Age of Change with the most impact started in the 80s, accelerated in the 90s, and burst into full bloom in the last 10 years, but it's barely begun. https://www.youtube.com/watch?v=sQFgzz3xvTY

15. **Byron Reece:** Byron Reece is a serial entrepreneur with a quarter-century of experience building and running successful technology companies, with multiple acquisitions and IPOs along the way. In addition, he is an award-winning author and speaker, as well as a futurist with a strong

conviction that technology will help bring about a new golden age of humanity. His most recent book, *The Fourth Age,* was published in 2018. https://byronreese.com/

16. **George Friedman:** Friedman György, born February 1, 1949, is a Hungarian-born US geopolitical forecaster and strategist on international affairs. He is the founder and chairman of Geopolitical Futures, an online publication that analyzes and forecasts the course of global events. Prior to founding Geopolitical Futures, Friedman was chairman of its predecessor, Stratfor, the private intelligence publishing and consulting firm he founded in 1996. *Wikipedia*

Chapter 3

17. **Multiplier effect:** The multiplier effect refers to the proportional amount of increase or decrease in final income that results from an injection or withdrawal of spending.

    The multiplier effect refers to the proportional amount of increase or decrease in final income that results from an injection or withdrawal of spending.

    The most basic multiplier used in gauging the multiplier effect is calculated as change in income/ change in spending and is used by companies to assess investment efficiency.

    The money supply multiplier is also another variation of a standard multiplier, using a money multiplier to analyze effects on the money supply. *Investopedia*

18. **Channel Manager:** A *Channel Manager* is responsible for improving customer consumption, planning and implementing customer presentations, overseeing account profiles, monitoring competitor activity, helping all communications with resellers, creating plans for growing market share, and communicating **channel** activities.

19. **ICOA Codes:** The *ICAO* airport code or location indicator is a four-letter code designating aerodromes around the world. These codes, as defined by the International Civil Aviation Organization and published in ICAO Document 7910: Location Indicators, are used by air traffic control and airline operations such as flight planning. *Wikipedia*

20. **Worldometer:** Worldometer, formerly Worldometers, is a reference website that provides counters and real-time statistics for diverse topics. It is owned

and operated by data company Dadax, which generates revenue through online advertising. *Wikipedia*

21. **25 Major cities (BOX) + points guy:**

22. **ALHA:** The American Hotel and Lodging Association and Ethiopia Hotel Market Association is an industry trade group with thousands of members including hotel brands, owners, management companies, Real Estate ... Wikipedia

23. **Commercial mortgage-backed securities (CMBS):** Fixed-income investment products that are backed by mortgages on commercial properties rather than residential real estate. CMBS can provide liquidity to real estate investors and commercial lenders alike.

24. **Rent Deferral period:** Although rent deferment agreements vary in their preconditions, terms, and operation, they generally allow the tenant to defer paying certain rent obligations under a lease for a specified period...Rather, they allow for that payment to be made at a later date. *Lexology.com*

25. **STR, Inc.:** A division of CoStar Group that provides market data on the hotel industry worldwide, including supply and demand and market-share data. *Wikipedia*

26. **Anchor Store:** In retail, an "anchor tenant," sometimes called an "anchor store," "draw tenant," or "key tenant," is a considerably larger tenant in a shopping mall, often a department store or retail chain. With their broad appeal, they are intended to attract a significant cross-section of the shopping public to the center. *Wikipedia*

27. **NBRF:** The *National Bureau of Economic Research* (NBER) is a private, nonpartisan organization that facilitates cutting-edge investigation and analysis of major economic issues. It disseminates research findings to academics, public and private-sector decision-makers, and the public by posting more than 1,200 working papers and convening more than 120 scholarly conferences each year. https://www.nber.org/

Chapter 4

28. **José Mário dos Santos Mourinho Félix, GOIH:** A Portuguese professional football manager and former player who is the manager of Premier League club Tottenham Hotspur. He is widely considered to be

one of the greatest managers of all time and is one of the most decorated managers ever. https://en.wikipedia.org/wiki/Jos%C3%A9_Mourinho

29. **Invent TOMORROW by Learning From TODAY**, Sean Worker T5 Strategies July 30, 2020, IHM Media https://www.servicedapartmentnews.com/features/setting-a-new-course-invent-tomorrow-by-learning-from-today/

30. **Y2K:** Y2K is the shorthand term for "the year 2000." Y2K was commonly used to refer to a widespread computer programming shortcut that was expected to cause extensive havoc as the year changed from 1999 to 2000 at the turn of the Millenium.

Instead of allowing four digits for the year, many computer programs only allowed two digits (e.g., 99 instead of 1999). As a result, there was immense panic that computers would be unable to operate when the date descended from "99" to "00." *Investopedia*

31. **Regenerative Tourism:** *The New York Times* defined the term in a recent 2020 article titled: "**Move Over, Sustainable Travel. Regenerative Travel Has Arrived.**" According to that piece's definition, regenerative travel/tourism is "leaving a place better than you found it."
According to the *NYT*, previous iterations of 'doing tourism better' were about doing less harm. According to the article, "sustainable tourism" aims to counterbalance the social and environmental impacts associated with travel." *WTM Global Hub*
https://hub.wtm.com/what-is-regenerative-tourism-and-how-should-we-deliver-it/

32. **Elain Gluanc** *New York Times***:** https://www.nytimes.com/2020/08/27/travel/travel-future-coronavirus-sustainable.html

33. **James Blick:** He is the founder of Devour Tours and passionate about helping local culture thrive through food tours and online experiences that connect curious travelers and teams with local communities, cuisines, and traditions. He is also founder of Spain Revealed, a media brand that helps curious travelers experience Spain like locals. His principal channel is YouTube, which receives 500,000+ monthly views from people planning their trip to Spain, or who are curious about the country. *LinkedIn* https://spainrevealed.com/about-james-blick/

34. **citizenM Hotels:** The citizenM philosophy is "affordable luxury for the people," offering guests all the luxuries they would expect from a

high-end hotel in a prime location, but without sky-high prices. citizenM was founded by Rattan Chadha, the founder and former CEO of the fashion brand Mexx. https://www.citizenm.com/

35. **Blue Ocean: – refer to Notation 8**

Chapter 5

36. **Adaptation Vs Innovation -** The Threat of Short-term Thinking – www. Sangfroidstrategy.com April 2020

    www.insideoutcomes.co.uk Darren, May 27, 2016 Innovation V Adaptation

    https://www.insideoutcomes.co.uk/2016/05/27/innovation-vs-adaptation/

37. **The Circle of Influence** are the things that concern you that you can do something about. For example—you may be worried about climate change (i.e., circle of concern). However, what can you do about it? (i.e., your circle of influence) www.habitsforwellbeing.com

38. **SaaS Model Software** as a service (or *SaaS*) is a way of delivering applications over the Internet—as a service. SaaS applications are sometimes called web-based software, on-demand software, or hosted software. Whatever the name, SaaS applications run on a SaaS provider's servers. www.salesforce.com

39. **Stasher:** Stasher is the world's first luggage storage network. We connect you with hotels and stores that can keep your luggage safe while you enjoy your time in a city. No need for cash—with Stasher, you can book on-demand and leave your luggage in secure storage rooms. https://stasher.com/about

40. **White Label:** A white label is a site that sells your products directly but under a different domain, brand, or company name. This type of site is different to an affiliate or drop-shipping site, although they share some characteristics. They're particularly popular in the retail, travel, and gambling sectors

41. **Great Restaurants** 30 Best Restaurants in London | Condé Nast Traveler (cntraveler.com) https://www.cntraveler.com/gallery/best-restaurants-in-london

42. **Venture capital:** Venture capital is a form of private equity and a type of financing that investors provide to start-up companies and small

businesses that are believed to have long-term growth potential. Venture capital generally comes from well-off investors, investment banks, and any other financial institutions. However, it does not always take a monetary form; it can also be provided in the form of technical or managerial expertise. Venture capital is typically allocated to small companies with exceptional growth potential or to companies that have grown quickly and appear poised to continue to expand. Though it can be risky for investors who put up funds, the potential for above-average returns is an attractive payoff. For new companies or ventures that have a limited operating history (under two years), venture capital funding is increasingly becoming a popular—even essential—source for raising capital, especially if they lack access to capital markets, bank loans, or other debt instruments. The main downside is that the investors usually get equity in the company, and, thus, a say in company decisions. James Chen. *Investopedia.*

43. **DIR Barcelona:** Gyms in Barcelona, Spain, and Sant Cugat, with all the fitness and wellness, pools, solariums, and more. https://www.dir.cat/en

44. **Blackrock:** BlackRock, Inc. is an American global investment management corporation based in New York City. Founded in 1988, initially as a risk management and fixed income fund manager. *Wikipedia* **https://www.blackrock.com/corporate**

45. **Work from Home (WFH):** WFH means an employee is working from a house, apartment, or place of residence, rather than working from the office. Many companies have a WFH policy or remote work policy that allows their employees to work from home either full time or when it's most convenient for them. *Jul 26, 2019, OWL Labs*

46. **Inside entrepreneurs:** An internal entrepreneur is known as an intrapreneur and is defined as "a person within a large corporation who takes direct responsibility for turning an idea into a profitable finished product through assertive risk-taking and innovation." *Wikipedia*

47. **Balance Sheet:** In financial accounting, a balance sheet is a summary of the financial balances of an individual or organization, whether it be a sole proprietorship, a business partnership, a corporation, private limited company, or other organization such as government or not-for-profit entity. *Wikipedia*

48. **Earnings quality:** Also known as quality of earnings (Q of E), in accounting, this refers to the ability of reported earnings (income) to predict a company's future earnings. It is an assessment criterion for how

"repeatable, controllable and bankable a firm's earnings are, amongst other factors, and has variously been defined as the degree to which earnings reflect underlying economic effects, are better estimates of cash flows, are conservative, or are predictable." *Wikipedia*

49. **Corporate governance:** The structures of rules, practices, and processes used to direct and manage a company. *Investopedia*

50. **Business continuity planning (BCP):** The processes involved in creating a system of prevention and recovery from potential threats to a company. The plan ensures that personnel and assets are protected and are able to function quickly in the event of a disaster. *Investopedia*

Chapter 6

51. **Daniel Goleman** (born March 7, 1946) is an author and science journalist. For twelve years, he wrote for the *New York Times*, reporting on the brain and behavioral sciences. His 1995 book *Emotional Intelligence* was on the *New York Times* bestseller list for a year-and-a-half, a best seller in many countries, and is in print worldwide in 40 languages.[1] Apart from his books on emotional intelligence, Goleman has written books on topics including self-deception, creativity, transparency, meditation, social and emotional learning, ecoliteracy and the ecological crisis, and the Dalai Lama's vision for the future. *Wikipedia*

    Emotional intelligence (otherwise known as emotional quotient or EQ): The ability to understand, use, and manage your own emotions in positive ways to relieve stress, communicate effectively, empathize with others, overcome challenges, and defuse conflict. (Goleman)

52. **Ray Dalio, Chairman & CEO Bridgewater**: Raymond Thomas Dalio (born August 8, 1949) is an American billionaire hedge-fund manager and philanthropist who has served as co-chief investment officer of Bridgewater Associates since 1985. He founded Bridgewater in 1975 in New York. Within ten years, it was infused with a US$5 million investment from the World Bank's retirement fund.

    Dalio was born in New York City and attended C.W. Post College of Long Island University before receiving an MBA. from Harvard Business School in 1973. Two years later, in his apartment, Dalio launched Bridgewater. In 2013, it was listed as the largest hedge fund in the world. In 2020, Bloomberg ranked Dalio as the world's seventy-ninth wealthiest person.

Dalio is the author of the 2017 book *Principles: Life & Work*, about corporate management and investment philosophy. It was featured on the *New York Times* bestseller list, where it was called a "gospel of radical transparency." https://www.youtube.com/watch?v=Y1OpbDWp8KY https://www.principles.com/

53. **World Economic Future of Jobs Reports:** The World Economic Forum, based in Cologne, Geneva Canton, Switzerland, is an international NGO, founded in 1971. The WEF's mission is stated as being "committed to improving the state of the world by engaging business, political, academic, and other leaders of society to shape global, regional, and industry agendas." Wikipedia
https://www.weforum.org/reports/the-future-of-jobs-report-2020

54. **Application: An app is a type of software** that allows you to perform specific tasks. Applications for desktop or laptop computers are sometimes called desktop applications, while those for mobile devices are called mobile apps. When you open an application, it runs inside the operating system until you close it. www.edu.gcfglobal.org

55. **Marriott and Root Beer:** Marriott International, Inc. is an American multinational diversified hospitality company that manages and franchises a broad portfolio of hotels and related lodging facilities. Wikipedia
Click the link to listen to how Marriott grew and transformed from a Root Beer store to a global hotel brand.
https://www.youtube.com/watch?v=FRRBDaNxLLQ

56. **Asset-light model**: A business model where a business owns relatively fewer capital assets compared to the value of its operations. It is popularly adopted by a number of start-ups because of its ability to get the company to higher skies when compared to traditional business models. Jul 28, 2018, business-standard.com

57. **Association for Intelligent Information**: Based in Colesville, Silver Spring, Maryland, this association is dedicated to helping its member organizations solve information-driven business challenges. https://www.aiim.org/

Chapter 7

58. **Kissflow**: A USA- and Indian-based workplace process, collaboration, and project management company. https://kissflow.com/

59. **Business Process:** A business process, business method, or business function is a collection of related, structured activities or tasks by people or equipment in which a specific sequence produces a service or product for a particular customer or customers. *Wikipedia*

60. **Change work order:** A change order is work that is added to or deleted from the original scope of work of a contract; however, depending on the magnitude of the change, it may or may not alter the original contract amount and/or completion date. A change order may force a new project to handle significant changes to the current project.

61. **Asset Lite:** See Notation 40

62. **T5 Strategies:** T5 Strategies helps companies in the travel and hospitality sector identify and work through issues efficiently and calmly, especially in challenging times. We help our clients see clearly, giving them the confidence to make the right decisions and deliver optimum solutions. http://www.t5strategies.com/

63. **QR Codes:** A QR code is a type of matrix barcode first designed in 1994 for the automotive industry in Japan. A barcode is a machine-readable optical label that contains information about the item to which it is attached. *Wikipedia* https://www.youtube.com/watch?v=zZXCt1Ud_zE

Chapter 8

64. **Force multiplier:** Force multipliers are tools that help you amplify your effort to produce more output. A hammer is a force multiplier. Investing in force multipliers means that you'll get more done with the same amount of effort. *personalmba.com*

Chapter 9

65. **UHH Hospital systems:** University Hospitals is one of the nation's leading health-care systems, providing patient-centered care that meets the highest standards for quality and patient safety and has received numerous awards and recognitions from some of the most prestigious institutions in the country for leadership and exceptional patient outcomes. As an accountable care organization, we foster long-term patient-provider relationships that help promote preventive care, increase

wellness and healthy behaviors, decrease emergency episodes, and prevent hospitalizations. https://www.uhhospitals.org/about-uh

66. **Fitch ratings:** Fitch Ratings, Inc. is an American credit rating agency and is one of the "Big Three credit rating agencies," the other two being Moody's and Standard & Poor's. It is one of the three nationally recognized statistical rating organizations designated by the U.S. Securities and Exchange Commission in 1975. Wikipedia https://www.fitchratings.com/

67. **Vesting "start-ups":** Vesting is a legal mechanism that guarantees the permanence of founding partners, employees, and shareholders of the company. It gives them an incentive to stay with the company for a certain period of time or until they meet the agreed objectives. In other words, it is the period of time every founder or employee has to work to obtain 100 percent of their share. The general recommendation is a period of four years to release the total value of shares, annually dividing the percentage. This means that holders will receive 25 percent of the total value per year. *Latamlist.com*

68. **Key Performance Indicators "KPIs":** A performance indicator or key performance indicator is a type of performance measurement. KPIs evaluate the success of an organization or of a particular activity in which it engages. *Wikipedia* https://www.youtube.com/watch?v=2tuWjtc2Ifk

69. **WFH see Endnote 45**

70. **Machine Learning:** An application of artificial intelligence that provides systems with the ability to automatically learn and improve from experience without being explicitly programmed. Machine learning focuses on the development of computer programs that can access data and use it to learn for themselves. Aug 26, 2020, *expertsystem.com*

71. **Savills:** The company provides consulting services and advice (such as valuation, building consultancy, project management, environmental consultancy, landlord and tenant, planning, strategic projects, and research) in connection with commercial, residential, and agricultural properties, property-related financial services, and investment management, which includes investment management for institutional or professional investors. Savills operates from over six hundred owned and associate offices, employing more than thirty-nine thousand people in over seventy countries throughout the Americas, Europe, Asia Pacific, Africa, and the Middle East. *Wikipedia. https://www.savills.com/*

T5 Strategies
Business Architects & Advisors

T5 Strategies, the "parent" of The Adapters, assists companies in the Travel, Tourism, Property, and Hospitality sector to identify and work through issues efficiently and calmly, especially in challenging times. As TravelTech and PropTech specialists, we help our clients see clearly and think expansively while giving them the confidence to make the right decisions and deliver optimum solutions. T5 has an experienced team of entrepreneurs, advisors, and hands-on leaders. We have a wealth of insight to bring to your business—to help it run smoother, faster, and more profitably. We look for the "traps" and help you avoid them to effectively adapt and innovate. We listen. We talk openly. We ***Get Stuff Done***.

Seán Worker
Managing Director & Principal
T5 Strategies
Business Architects & Advisors
"Building the future of business"
sean@t5stratgeies.com

LinkedIn @ www.linkedin.com/in/seanworker/
Company @ www.t5strategies.com

** In December 2020, Sean Worker joined HoCoSo, a Zurich-based consulting firm. HoCoSo specializes in offering a variety of services to the Travel, Tourism, and Hospitality sector. Sean will lead the Technology, Adaption, and Innovation solutions group. He will continue to lead T5 Strategies.
https://www.hocoso.com/

CPSIA information can be obtained
at www.ICGtesting.com
Printed in the USA
FSHW011731210122
87842FS

9 781662 905407